BLISS CARMAN

A REAPPRAISAL

LISS *CARMAN*
A REAPPRAISAL

Edited and with an Introduction by Gerald Lynch

Jan. 7, 1990

To David,
with warmest regards
and much gratitude for your
help with the Introduction,

Gerald

University of Ottawa Press
Ottawa • London • Paris

REAPPRAISALS
Canadian Writers

LORRAINE McMULLEN
General Editor

Canadian Cataloguing in Publication Data

Main entry under title:
Bliss Carman: a reappraisal

(Reappraisals, Canadian writers; 16)
Includes bibliographical references.
ISBN 0-7766-0286-1

1. Carman, Bliss, 1861–1929—Criticism and
interpretation. I. Lynch, Gerald, 1953–   .
II. Symposium on Bliss Carman (1989: University
of Ottawa). III. Series.

PS8455.A72Z58 1990   C811'.52   C90-090510-7
PR9199.2.C3Z58 1990

UNIVERSITÉ D'OTTAWA
UNIVERSITY OF OTTAWA

©University of Ottawa Press, 1990
Printed and bound in Canada
ISBN 0-7766-0286-1

Typeset by Nancy Poirier Typesetting Ltd., Ottawa
Cover design by Judith Gregory

Cover and frontispiece photos
courtesy of Queen's University Archives

Introduction

GERALD LYNCH

Bliss Carman (1861–1929) achieved something of an overnight success with the publication of his first volume of poems, *Low Tide on Grand Pré* (1893), a success that seemed to have been secured by the widely popular volumes of vagabondia poems that he co-authored with Richard Hovey (1894–1900), the multi-volumed *Pipes of Pan* (1902–1905), and *Sappho* (1905). Yet Carman, to a greater extent perhaps than his fellow Canadian writers of the nineteenth century, has suffered from the misrepresentation and neglect that can be attributed to the slash-and-burn tactics practiced by many Canadian critics on their own literary heritage since the beginning of Canadian modernism in the 1920s. He lived to experience destitution and obscurity towards the end of the second decade of this century and a popular revival in his tours of the 1920s, though even this late acclaim was offset by concurrent critical defamation in the writings of the first wave of Canadian modernists (particularly those of A.J.M. Smith and F. R. Scott). Over the ensuing decades, his writings have been viewed—when considered at all—with the kind of bemused embarrassment that academics usually radiate when confronted with the evidence of their own undergraduate attempts at poetry. The British novelist Martin Amis has remarked of the problem of literary popularity: ''When success happens to an English writer, he acquires a new typewriter. When success happens to an American writer, he acquires a new life.'' When success happens to a Canadian writer in America, his old typewriter receives a lucrative oiling. He writes more and for greater rewards, but always to be accused of slickness and shallowness at home. Or so the example of Bliss Carman would lead us to conclude.

At least in the United States and England success is recognized, even celebrated, by the writer's audience, if with characteristic hyperbole in the former and understatement in the latter. In Canada, success remains a problem for critics and public alike. Assertions by detractors of the "world-famous-all-over-Canada" crowd to the contrary, success continues to be recognized at home only after recognition abroad, and even then it is viewed with the dispositional reservation that is at once such an attractive and troubling characteristic of Canadians. More to the point, popularity often ruins the writer's reputation posthumously. It takes a long time for the writing to be recuperated, the reputation to be fairly assessed, and the literary record to be righted. Consider the examples of Thomas Chandler Haliburton and Stephen Leacock: despite their continuing popular and critical acclaim abroad, they have had to be reappraised at home in an ongoing effort to resist the enduring collective urge to relegate them to the realms of popular and topical phenomena, or to assign them the status of literary lightweights. Thus the continuing need in Canadian publishing for a series that is intent upon reappraising the writings of our literary predecessors. The present volume and its contributors are devoted to beginning this process of recuperation for Bliss Carman.

It would be naive, though, to assume that Carman's problematic status in Canadian literary history is simply a result of the deleterious effect of wide popularity on a writer's claim to serious attention. The problem is also one of literary valuation and, more precisely, of the ignorance and/or deceptiveness of the evaluators; or, if that is too strong, the problem devolves from the sort of willed blindness to the continuum of Canadian poetry that has led at least twice in this century (in a kind of inversion of Mark Twain's joke) to belated announcements of the birth of Canadian literature. Carman's initial popularity only made it easier for the anxious, the ideologically correct, and the theoretically fashionable to dismiss him either unsympathetically or unread, whether that dismissal arose from the envy of a contemporary, from the Bloomian need to clear space, or from the biases in a theoretical system that purports (paradoxically) to demystify bias. Carman has suffered from all three. In the early part of the century his popularity drove William Wilfred Campbell to accuse him of high poetic plagiarism. This first shot in the War of the Poets led to the ignorant treatment of the Confederation poets by modernists such as Smith and Scott, and in recent decades to the near total eclipse of Carman and his contemporaries by the growing body of post-structuralist commentary. (It is curious that Anglo-American post-structuralists have commented so perceptively upon the writings of the English Romantic period, whereas their Canadian counterparts ignore the closest Canadian equivalent, the Confederation poets, and write instead about their contemporaries, or about themselves writing.) Such a critical history of neglect and bemused dismissal has made it necessary for many of the contributors to this volume to do some pushing aside, some tearing down and redressing, some dusting off and shining up of the subject. For instance, a number of contributors recall Carman's considerable literary influence: we are reminded a few times of Ezra Pound's willingness to salvage only Carman from a relished imagined drowning of all "American" poets, of Wallace Stevens' chanting of lines from Carman like a poetic mantra, of Carman's influence on Robert Frost, Edwin Arlington Robinson, and others.

Generally, the present volume is designed to progress from biographical concerns, through bibliographical, to theoretical, and finally to more practical criticism. An overview of Carman's literary life is provided by Mary B. McGillivray, though other contributors such as James Doyle and Laurel Boone also draw attention to different aspects of his biography. In "The Popular and Critical Reputation and Reception of Bliss Carman," McGillivray surveys her subject while drawing upon an impressive range of sources. She charts the vicissitudes of Carman's career and reputation, providing compelling reasons for the changes in critical and popular responses to the poet and the poetry, and focuses finally on what a number of contributors describe as the enduring "haunting" quality of Carman's poetry. James Doyle outlines Carman's relationship with the American literary milieu at the turn of the century, especially with regard to the literary magazine scene and particularly the influential Boston periodical the *Chap-Book*. Laurel Boone cautiously establishes a lineage of modern dance that begins with François Delsarte and includes the hitherto unrecognized contribution of Carman's and Mary Perry King's schools of personal harmonizing.

Three poet-critics share their views of Carman's influence as Canadian poet-predecessor. Al Purdy will doubtlessly surprise some readers with the revelation that it was the oft-maligned Carman who inspired him to become a poet, thereby confirming D. G. Jones' view that Purdy may well be the true inheritor of the Carman mantle. We all knew of Purdy's freight-riding Depression days, but little did we suspect that he clipped along clutching a copy of Carman's collected poems. Elizabeth Brewster offers a charmingly personal view of Carman's importance to her as poet and fellow Maritimer, providing along the way much interesting critical analysis, as in her close reading of "Ephemeron." Jones gives us a paradoxical Carman who occupies a literary niche between the classically stoic writer and the post-modernist ironic, a poet whose lasting image remains an evanescent one, a trace, best figured in the moth and the wind.

John R. Sorfleet contends that assessments of Carman's development by earlier critics are based on a false chronology of the poetry. He provides a new and more accurate record of Carman's development in phases based on an accurate chronology of composition, thereby offering scholars the opportunity to begin making more reliable analyses of the relation between developments in Carman's thought and work. In "Carman as Critic" Terry Whalen argues that Carman was essentially anti-modernist as both literary critic and philosopher of poetry. Drawing upon an impressive array of sources, Whalen finds the formulators of Carman's "intelligent modesty" in writers such as W. B. Yeats and George Santayana. Like Jones, Whalen considers Carman a transitional figure, but unlike Jones, he is unwilling to perpetuate, however sympathetically, the view of Carman as "fool-saint." D.M.R. Bentley looks at Carman's work in the context of the late nineteenth-century "mind-cure" movement, which was a therapeutic program designed to counter industrialized modernity's disabling effects on individual and collective sensibility. One route to mind cure involved withdrawal from the jangling city, rejuvenation in the countryside, and return to the world of men; another route was through reading, and Bentley, through metrical analysis of a *Sappho* poem, demonstrates how the poetry was composed to effect Carman's melioristic ends.

Subsequent papers turn to more particular facets of Carman's work. Tracy Ware presents an analysis of some specifically dedicated elegies in *By the Aurelian Wall*, establishing the influence of Romanticism generally and some of the major Romantic poets (Shelley, Blake, Keats) on Carman and Confederation poetry. Ware concludes with a fascinating look at the volume's concluding elegy—an elegy for the self. Drawing upon the evidence of numerous poems, ballads mostly, Louis K. MacKendrick investigates a heretofore ignored dimension of Carman's work, showing the strategic uses to which Carman put, and the fun he had with, the Gothic. A. R. Kizuk examines Carman's lyrics in terms of psychoanalytical-Lacanian theory, focusing on the impetus of desire in the poetry, its object in the absent Mother, and the importance of threshold imagery for drawing attention to the opposition between indoors and outdoors in Carman's poetic attitude. And in making her case for Carman's influence on modern dance, Laurel Boone establishes the importance of his pageants and masques, as well as his essays.

In their summary comments on the volume, R. L. McDougall, D.M.R. Bentley, and Douglas Lochhead consider the general tenor of the essays, focusing attention on such questions as "Whatever happened to Bliss Carman?" and "Why has it taken so long for this book-length reappraisal of Carman?" and on the need for a complete bibliography. In the hope of filling that need, John R. Sorfleet has generously provided a bibliography that should satisfy most teachers, students, and critics of Carman's work.

At the very least *Bliss Carman: A Reappraisal* should help foster an awareness among critics of the work being done in Carman scholarship and of potentially rewarding areas for future research. But the essays collected here should also give encouragement to those of us who hope for a lasting resurgence of interest in Carman's voluminous and varied writings and in writers of the nineteenth century generally. As the biases of modernism and post-structuralism are recognized as biases, and as the growing influence in England and the United States of material criticism and the new historicism begins to be felt in Canadian criticism, there is reason to hope that critics will be less hesitant to re-value Carman's work in the contexts of his time and place and intentions. Judging from the uniformly high quality of the papers brought together here, there is also sound reason to hope that Bliss Carman will find his true place in Canadian literary history.

I wish to express my appreciation to the Social Sciences and Humanities Research Council of Canada for its support of this project. Thanks are due to Lorraine McMullen, general editor of the Reappraisals series, and to Frank Tierney for advice and encouragement. Thanks also go to Janet Shorten and Jenny Wilson at the University of Ottawa Press, and to my colleagues in the Department of English at the University of Ottawa who read the papers and were generous with their time and advice: Glenn Clever, Robert Collins, Camille La Bossière, Seymour Mayne, John Moss, David Rampton, David Staines, and Peter Stich. Thank you, too, to Marie McKinnon and Julie Sévigny-Roy for administrative and secretarial assistance. Finally, thank you to Mary Jo and our children, Bryan, Meghan, and Maura, for much patient understanding.

The Popular and Critical Reputation and Reception of Bliss Carman

MARY B. McGILLIVRAY

Bliss Carman is a poet about whom the prevailing clichés have tended to be that he was some kind of effete Bunthorne,[1] posturing at readings, hair floating in the breeze, not taken seriously by anyone who mattered. In much of the criticism and analysis of the last couple of generations, this perception of Carman as lightweight has hindered sensitive, intelligent or even-handed reception of his poetry. It has been broadly assumed, in fact, that Carman is hardly worth the trouble of reading. But I have always been drawn to Carman's poetry, and I suspect that his contemporary reviewers and audience, the "positive" version of the "negative" we have now, might have been on to something that has been ignored or forgotten. Response to Carman, especially during his lifetime, is ground well worth exploring. It should prove useful to see if what used to draw readers to Carman is still discernible, and perhaps briefly to explore the relationship between the contemporary reception of Carman and my own response to him.

One of the first things worth mentioning is that Carman's audience consisted of more than luncheon clubs. For example, Ezra Pound had this to say in 1910: "Bliss Carman is about the only living American poet who would not improve by drowning."[2] In 1923, Odell Shepard, writer and professor of English, said: "Carman's [poetry] brought beauty back for me into God's world."[3]

The range of response to Carman, both during his lifetime and after it, is as extensive as his poetry is varied. In all our literary history, no one rivals his unique ability to inspire a powerful and enduring emotional response among readers both literary and otherwise. Carman's poetic career was followed with real interest by the publishing world, including reviewers and critics, the general public, who made some of his books the most popular after the turn of the century, and fellow poets.

Carman himself was chary of such response. In a letter to W. W. Campbell in 1890, he tells his disgruntled fellow poet not to mind being overlooked by the critics:

> —ah! my dear fellow. What does it matter? You have written your work; it is beautiful. That is enough. It would be better if *nothing* were ever said of us until we were dead. You who have all the fire and calm beauty of the lakes in your very heart, what is it to you whether this reviewer or that can see the beauty of it too? I say your *true self* is sufficient judge, sufficient audience, sufficient world of fame.[4]

Carman meant this and, to a large extent, I believe he lived it, at least if we can judge by the dedicated way in which he pursued his own vision of worthwhile poetry. Nonetheless, he kept several scrapbooks in which he retained many reviews and critical assessments of his work. And the trajectory of his fame, as well as the composition of his audience, traces a fascinating pattern.

The present volume is welcome evidence of the recent revival of interest in Carman, but it has been a long time coming. Carman's hope that nothing be said about him until after his death was not realized; he attracted far more critical and public attention during his life than he could have imagined possible in 1890 when he was consoling Campbell for being excluded from an anthology. And by the late 1920s he was creating a stir that would surprise even today's audience. What Carman would have seen as an ironic twist, however, is that after his death less and less was said about him. Until he was rescued by Sorfleet's efforts of the late 1970s and Gundy's of the early 1980s, Carman was regarded by many critics as beneath notice. After a flurry of activity just after his death in 1929, one that included James Cappon's useful—if uneven— *Bliss Carman and the Literary Currents and Influences of his Time* (1930), critical assessment of Carman's work was sporadic and frequently negative. It was fashionable for about forty years to use Carman as a kind of straw man. No doubt many of the contributors to this volume have had to defend their interest in Carman against the indifference, even the incredulity, of their fellow scholars. Nonetheless, in the decades of his disrepute he has had a loyal following of educated and sensitive readers, some academics like Desmond Pacey and Malcolm Ross, and other poetry lovers who continue to feel what Carman's contemporary audiences felt. In this paper, I want to present or re-acquaint the reader with the ebb and flow of the tide of Carman's reputation and reception, and ultimately to suggest what it is about Carman's poetry that has *allowed* it to survive.

It is difficult now to imagine or credit the magnitude of Carman's reputation early in the century. His first book of poems, *Low Tide on Grand Pré* (1893), was warmly received by reviewers in such respectable journals as London's *Athenaeum*, which noticed Carman's gift for the mystical and evocative, and which, Carman felt (in spite of other less glowing observations), was "ruinous" in its praise.[5] In the first two years, this volume went into three editions. Carman had arrived. In one of his scrapbooks, he made a special note of a review that he clearly thought expressed something of what he was trying to convey to his readership: "Every poem gives us a picture," says the reviewer, "and not the mere picture which would strike the superficial observer, but the vision of one who sees the forms, but also penetrates into the meaning of things."[6] The elusive draw of Carman was recognized early.

When in 1894 he and Richard Hovey published the first volume of their *Songs from Vagabondia*, the book was received with wild enthusiasm, both critical and popular. It was reviewed in literary magazines and in daily newspapers across the continent and overseas. The *New York Times* reviewer gushed:

> Hail to the poets! Good poets, real poets, with a swig of wine and a lilt of rhyme. . . . Who would have thought that good fellowship and the free air of heaven could fan such fancies as these into a right merry woodland blaze in dry times when satyrs . . . lie hid under the dead willows till great Pan should come again.[7]

The *Chicago News* for September 29, 1894, said:

> [T]o have a volume of the richest poesy drop from satin wings into the lap of every-day formality is like the opening measures of a spring song, and a boyish desire to crow "finders keepers" stirs prosaic tempers at the sight and melody of *Songs from Vagabondia*.[8]

The more staid *Athenaeum* allowed that writing poetically distinct, cheerful verse was "far harder" than to succeed at writing "in slow metres to mournful airs" and said: "Both these young writers . . . have that charm, rare in writers of verse, of drawing the reader into the fellowship of their own zest and contentment."[9]

But even this early there were loud negative voices, as has been quite typical of Carman's reception. In Canada, Carman's good notices were offset by controversy. William Wilfred Campbell, himself newly arrived on the literary scene, issued a kind of challenge to Carman. In the pages of the Toronto *Sunday World*, June 16, 1895, Campbell anonymously accused Carman of literary plagiarism. He went more public with the issue the following week in a signed article charging that collusion and self-promotion existed among Carman, Roberts and Lampman.[10] Writers and critics across the country entered the fray throughout the summer, until, between the reviewer in the *Globe*, who called Carman a "poet's poet,"[11] and writer Peter McArthur, who pointed out that many similar accusations could be made of Campbell,[12] Carman's reputation was restored—or, at least, left alone. Campbell was not impressed with or touched by Carman's elusive lyric charm, and since Carman's death, most critics have been almost as dismissive as Campbell of the vagabond mode. But there was no doubt in the minds of the reading public. They loved it. Within fourteen months of its publication, *Songs from Vagabondia* went into its third edition. Both Carman and Hovey were widely recognized from that point on.

At this stage of Carman's career, he enjoyed a high profile indeed.[13] Perhaps because of Pacey's dismissal in the 1950s of the vagabond mode as "a pose"—and of the poetry of that style as "alien to [Carman's] own temperament"[14]—the enormous impact made by the Vagabond poems has been forgotten. But there can be no doubt of the breadth and depth of this appeal for some—the "Vagabond Song" from this book has been anthologized almost as frequently as "Low Tide on Grand Pré."

Carman's public at this time did not, as we may sometimes assume, consist only of jaded critics who responded to positive thinking. One of Carman's admirers was the young Robert Frost, who thought so highly of Carman's work that when, in 1894, his poem "My Butterfly" was accepted by the *Independent* and praised by Carman, he bound it into a four-poem booklet and presented it to Elinor White as part of his campaign to marry her.[15] And Frost did not entirely lose touch with Carman's work as his reputation waxed and waned; Mary Perry King mentions in a letter to Carman of January 14, 1924 (thirty years later), that Robert Frost had dropped by looking for him.[16]

By the early part of this century, Carman had published numerous volumes of verse, some in the vagabond mode, but many in various moods from the elegiac to the symbolic to what may loosely be called the "philosophical." Although of course the reviews and assessments of his work were not uniformly wonderful—the *Athenaeum*, for example, which had so enjoyed the rollicking tunes of *vagabondage*, was sick of Carman's positive and joyful spirit by 1904, and called his optimism a "facile thing"[17]—on the whole, Carman's work always found an appreciative audience. Each volume—and by 1905 there were seventeen—was widely reviewed in both the public and literary press in England and in the United States.

While the most prolific phase of Carman's poetic career was largely over—or at least in a rather long lull—by about 1910, he had become increasingly the public figure of the poet. When President Theodore Roosevelt returned from a safari trip in 1909 (the same year in which the opportunely named *The Rough Rider and Other Poems* appeared), Carman was invited to compose and read a poem at a welcome-back dinner in Teddy's honour in New York.[18] In 1915, when his poetic production was at a virtual standstill and he was scratching out a living by publishing various prose works on nature, art and personality, Carman secured a position at the Elizabethan Club at Yale through Roosevelt's influence. In exchange for the occasional talk on poetry, this position would guarantee him an annuity of $500.00 for life.[19]

Carman had long since been noticed by another readership—one anticipated much earlier by the Toronto *Globe*, when it had called him "a poet's poet such as Keats was,"[20] a readership joined early on by Robert Frost. At about the same time as he was being fêted along with Teddy Roosevelt, Carman was also the object of the quiet admiration of Ezra Pound and Wallace Stevens. The remark by Pound in 1910 about Carman's being worthy of living was not just a quip: Pound had begun to read Carman sometime around 1903. When he first approached a publisher in London, it was Elkin Mathews, the same house which for some time published Carman's verse in England. Pound was an admirer of Carman's and Hovey's *Songs from Vagabondia*,[21] as is evident, for example, in his "A Rouse" from *A Lume Spento* (1908). This poem opens with the lines, "Save ye, Merry gentlemen! Vagabonds and Rovers / Hell take the hin'most / We're for the clovers!" The *Sappho* poems, too, first widely published in late 1904, seem to have struck a chord which resonated in Pound's early work. "Threnos" ("Lo the fair dead!") in *A Lume Spento* and Δώρια in *Ripostes* (1912) are just two poems which demonstrate this influence.[22]

Carman's poetry was also instrumental in the shaping of some of Wallace Stevens' work. In his letters of January 1909 to his fiancée Elsie Moll, Stevens tells how he hummed one of Carman's spring songs all day long as he composed his own verse. He also mentions browsing through volumes of Carman's poetry in the library, lingering especially on the cheerful nature lyrics and on the *Sappho* poems. He mentions specifically the magic of Lyric LXXXII, "Over the roofs the honey-coloured moon . . . ."[23]

I find it interesting that these *Sappho* poems, which got little notice and less praise when they were published in 1904, persisted in the minds and hearts of men who were to be among the next generation's most important poets.[24] Even when he wasn't being reviewed or lionized, Carman was still being read.

His readers, however, were not prepared to follow him when he left poetry completely behind. By about 1906, the surge of poetic creativity upon which Carman had been drawing seemed to ebb. He wrote to his friend and fellow vagabond Tom Meteyard in late December of that year: "There is no poetry now, but quite a lot of prose, eventually to make a volume, *The Making of Personality*."[25] In spite of the notion that has persisted right up to the present of Carman as some kind of laughable figure from whom an undiscriminating public would accept almost anything, Carman's publishers, critics and readers were not prepared to pay the kind of attention to his joint projects with Mary Perry King (of which *Personality* was one) that he would have wished. In mid-career—or at least in mid-life—Carman's public profile began to have an unexpected effect. In order to get *The Making of Personality* published in 1908, Carman had to agree to leave Mary Perry King's name as co-author entirely aside and to re-write the volume almost completely.[26] I suspect that this had something to do with the mild scandal that surrounded the relationship between Carman and Mary Perry King. (It also had something to do with her appalling prose style.[27]) Carman was pleased enough with the sales of *Personality* in 1908, but although it did go into a second edition in 1913, it was not nearly as widely acclaimed or reviewed as his poetry had been; later editions were brought out only in the 1920s when his reading tours precipitated renewed interest in his work overall.[28]

As I have already noted, Carman's poetic creativity during the early part of this century waned, as did the acclaim for his work by critical journals. In 1905, the *Pipes of Pan* series, for example, got mixed reviews in the United States and quite poor ones in Britain.[29] By 1911, when it came time to publish the masques or the "Lyrical Pageants," of which Carman was proud and which were a kind of dramatization of the Carman–King unitrinianism that had been delineated in *Personality*, Carman had the unfamiliar experience of being rejected outright by some ten periodicals and more than half a dozen publishing houses.[30] When he tried to take the first of the pageants, *Daughters of Dawn*, on a kind of lecture and performance tour to California with Mary Perry King, he was told by his friend Irving Way that he had better not because of the gossip their appearance would fuel.[31] In the end, another friend, Mitchell Kennerley, undertook to publish both pageants at his own expense in 1912 and 1913. They were not re-issued, and they did not sell. Carman published one book of poems, *April Airs*, after the war (1916), which received rather lukewarm reviews. In 1919, Pelham Edgar reminded the public that Carman was still around, only to regret that Carman had "beaten out his philosophy [so] very thin."[32]

Although Mary Perry King's effect on Carman's life was not entirely positive, inasmuch as she kept him perhaps too focused on unitrinianism for the good of his poetry and too restricted in his movements for the good of his independent development, in the end it was she who engineered the re-emergence of Carman from the ashes of his apparently vanished fame in 1920. After World War I, Carman's finances—not for the first time[33]—were in a sorry state, and when in October 1919 he was stricken with tuberculosis, he could not afford to pay for the treatment and convalescence he needed. It was Mary Perry King who pulled strings, writing to poets and journalists in the United States and Canada to stir up interest in raising funds for the stricken poet. She personally staged benefits in New York. The public rallied. An American journalist, Dr. Frank Crane, who was in the editorial department of a huge news bureau in New York, wrote a heart-rending article entitled "Sick and in Prison" which ran in nearly all the bureau's papers across the United States and Canada. He informed his readers that Carman—whom, for discretion's sake, he did not name outright—was "struggling with the Great White Plague [tuberculosis]" and that he ". . . has no money, for poetry is not the road to wealth. All his life he has gone his way, singing his songs and cheering us all up." Crane appealed to the public not to let pass the "privilege" of giving "our material goods in return for the benedictions of beauty," and he reminded the lovers of poetry of the debt they owed Carman for "those elusive elements of the beautiful that haunt all of our minds."[34]

The response to Crane's and Mary Perry King's efforts demonstrated that Carman had not been forgotten—thousands of dollars poured in, from scholars, politicians and office workers all over the continent. In Toronto Peter McArthur, a writer and columnist, organized a benefit dinner at which Siegfried Sassoon spoke; Carman even heard from Vincent Massey who, as President of the Arts and Letters Club in Toronto, sent him a bank draft.[35]

Mary Perry King's efforts were timely; in fact, Carman's illness was timely. When his plight put him back in the public eye, a number of writers and other Carman loyalists in Canada seized the opportunity to invite him to return "home." Peter McArthur organized a reading tour for 1921. Later, he wrote to Pierce that, in arranging this, he "had the advantage of the publicity due to his recent severe illness. [Carman] appealed to the public as one returned from the dead."[36] At all events, Canada was more than ready to embrace the returned poet, and for the next four years Carman was transformed into the kind of matinée-idol figure which most of us know. In fact, his image as "the Bard" crowned with maple leaves by the Canadian Authors' Association is the one that too many students of Canadian literature still retain.

It is difficult for us to imagine the splash Carman made on the reading tours of early 1921 and 1921–22. He was able to command audiences whose numbers were staggering. In Guelph in early February

1921, he filled the hall *twice* to its 400-person capacity. In Toronto he read for an audience of 1,500. The faculty of the University of Toronto's English department turned out for a private reading at Hart House. In the fall, 600 people turned up for Carman's appearance at Winnipeg; so many were turned away that a second reading was scheduled. The tours included midwest and west-coast Canadian and American cities and, not to put too fine a point on it, at $1.00 a person Carman made a bundle from the western excursion. His tour in 1923–24 met with equal success.[37]

It is well known that this lionizing of the newly dubbed "Poet Laureate" was part of what led the McGill school of poets and critics, with A.J.M. Smith in the fore, to dismiss Carman as a contemptible, jingling optimist who wouldn't know good poetry if he tripped over it. In "A Plea for Original Sin" in the April 1922 issue of *Canadian Forum*, Douglas Bush notes that "a mass of Canadian poetry consists of apostrophes to dancing rivulets that no doubt give considerable pleasure to the author's relatives." Later, in "Wanted: Canadian Criticism" in the April 1928 issue of *Canadian Forum*, Smith complained, "If [the serious Canadian writer] chooses to work out his own salvation along lines which cannot be in keeping with the prevailing spirit of pep and optimism he finds himself without an audience. . . ."

Wilson MacDonald, too, objected to the glorification of Carman. In an article entitled "Is Carman Supreme?" in the Kingston *British Whig* of March 1925, MacDonald stirred up much the same hornets' nest as W. W. Campbell had some thirty years earlier by challenging Carman's right to the name he had acquired, that of Canada's best poet. This time, J. D. Logan, R. H. Hathaway and even E. J. Pratt came forward with corrections, opinions and counter-opinions. Pratt's letter concludes, "It might be considered sacrilege to question the place of a deity in our little world; still, it must be remembered that our throne is one we build with our own hands."[38] In spite of any objections, however, Carman's public profile remained high for most of the rest of his life. On the strength of his new prominence he at last published a collection of poems in Canada, and subsequent volumes of verse won favourable reviews.

When he died in 1929, he was still very much the public figure. It is perhaps another indication of the double edge to the "reputation" Carman had acquired that Mary Perry King, having helped him back into the role of "acknowledged servant of beauty," was reluctant to sacrifice her private and personal hold on him. Upon Carman's death, one of his neighbours enlisted Canadian Padraic Colum to help with the funeral arrangements. To the surprise of Colum and the neighbour, Mary Perry King refused to notify Charles Roberts and the rest of

Carman's family. When Theodore Roberts did hear the news from the neighbour, he wired that the city of Fredericton and the province of New Brunswick wanted a ceremonial burial in Fredericton. Mrs. King again refused, and in the end the Canadian delegation came to New Canaan. They were misdirected, ended up at the wrong church, were finally rushed past Carman's body in the King house, and at the funeral itself were seated behind Mary Perry King who, "simply swathed" in "the deepest of crepe," was the self-styled chief mourner.[39] It took some two months—and the intercession of Premier Baxter and Prime Minister Mackenzie King—for Mrs. King to release Carman's ashes for his public interment in Fredericton.[40] But this anecdote, besides being funny, is also significant because it shows how easily Carman himself, rather than his poetry, becomes the issue.

Upon Carman's death there was a flurry of critical and public attention, most notably James Cappon's book mentioned above, and Muriel Miller's overly laudatory *Bliss Carman: A Portrait* (1935), but within a few years recognition of Carman's talent had virtually vanished. The decades since have produced little in the way of even-handed criticism, in spite of the occasional reminder from Pacey or from Malcolm Ross to take a closer look.[41]

It has been too easy to forget the kind of influence and power Carman had over both literary and general audiences during his life-time. In spite of the sinking of his critical stock for so many decades, the emotional response he inspired in his audience was as enduring as it was powerful. I don't believe that the nascent Canadian patriotism of the 1920s entirely accounts for this; nor does Carman's deliberately crafted reliance on the effect of sound or rhythm in his verse, although such effects are real enough. There is something more than mass hypnosis involved here.

There is a common thread in what led me to Carman and what drew his appreciative audience in the past. Although not all critics or reviewers are drawn by the same works, there is one description that recurs in the response to Carman that hints at what I believe to be of enduring value in Carman's best work, at what, in fact, merits closer consideration: that is, the "lingering," or "haunting," quality of his lyrics. The reviewer for the *New York Sun* in 1894 said of "Marna" that it has "sentiment and music to satisfy and to linger."[42] In the same year, the *Nation*'s reviewer called Carman's poetry "haunting."[43] Crane used the same phrase when he publicized Carman's troubles. Bliss Perry, Harvard professor and editor of the *Atlantic Monthly*—though he dismissed the beautiful *Sappho* poems in the same manner as did nearly all the critics—bemoaned the loss of "something that [he] felt in the nostalgic and Vagabond modes, . . . [something] really memorable."[44]

Wallace Stevens, entranced, quoted a line from one of the *Sappho* lyrics and hummed a spring song. Desmond Pacey, deaf like Perry to the *Sappho*'s quality but alert to much else in Carman, gave special mention to Carman's ability to create an effect of "haunting melancholy" through image.[45] This whole issue of the memorable and the haunting is indicative, I think, of the power to which all of Carman's audiences responded, and to which I respond. And this lingering quality is invariably linked to the mystical and spiritual elements implicitly present in Carman's best lyric poetry.

Carman treasured the review which said that he reveals to his reader more than "the mere picture which would strike the superficial observer; [he also conveys] the vision of one who sees the forms, but . . . penetrates into the meaning of things." This goes some way, I think, towards suggesting the importance of the visionary in Carman's work: what Carman is consistently striving for, seeking to grasp even as it eludes him, even in what we may now call his less successful poetry, is the spiritual perception of beauty, eternal through its temporal manifestation. It is this experience that infuses Carman's best work with those qualities which have so frequently been characterized as "haunting" and "memorable."

The Carman of "How soon will all my lovely days be over /And I no more be found beneath the sun," or the Carman who sees Robert Louis Stevenson's remote island grave as a seamark set

> High on a peak adrift with mist,
> And round whose bases, far beneath
> The snow-white wheeling tropic birds,
> The emerald dragon breaks his teeth
>
> ("A Seamark," ll. 149–152)

or the Carman who watches as

> A breath of wind comes ruffling the smooth lake
> And strews the white plum-blossoms on the grass,
> Stirring old transports, and is still again
>
> ("Sorcery," ll. 12–14)

—that Carman is not a poseur. He offers the reader a portal into his own spiritually charged world, by contemplating and creating images of beauty evanescent and mutable.

Lyrics such as these suggest that Carman's reputation had some solid ground beneath it; they are evidence that Carman's work is well worth retrieving. The rescue of the *Sappho* poems from their undeserved obscurity has begun, and I believe that a number of the essays in the present volume will re-introduce us to other lyrics and elegies. There is more. And this brings me to my final point—which is really more of a beginning. One of the effects of the enthusiastic response Carman met near the end of his life was that he returned to the lyric mode of poetry from which he had drifted away in the last half of his career. Perhaps an echo of Bliss Perry's lament over the loss of his lyric power remained with him, or perhaps his audience re-kindled in him the wish to convey his gospel of nature by means of metaphor rather than "rational speech." In any case, I think the poetry of Carman's later life (for example, that in *Wild Garden*, and the aptly-named *Sanctuary*, from which "Sorcery" comes) is also worth another look. In the later works the lyric and the rational or philosophic modes are fused, as Carman attempts to offer, by means of a presentation of nature as sanctuary, another instance of the paradoxical riddle of "the measure of beauty / Fleet yet eternal." Carman's admirers knew something worth knowing.

NOTES

1. H. Pearson Gundy also uses this image in his "Lorne Pierce, Bliss Carman and the Ladies," *Douglas Library Notes* XIV, 4 (Autumn 1965), p. 24.
2. Ezra Pound, cited in Noel Stock, *The Life of Ezra Pound: An Expanded Edition* (San Francisco: North Point Press, 1982), p. 81.
3. Odell Shepard, *Bliss Carman* (Toronto: McClelland and Stewart, 1923), p. xii.
4. Bliss Carman to W. W. Campbell, March 23, 1890. In H. P. Gundy, ed., *Letters of Bliss Carman* (Kingston and Montreal: McGill-Queen's University Press, 1981), p. 36. Hereafter I shall refer to the *Letters* as Gundy.
5. Carman to Gertrude Burton, August 1894. In Gundy, p. 74.
6. Anon., *The Week*, December 22, 1893. In Carman Scrapbook, Queen's University Archives.
7. Anon., *New York Times*, September 30, 1894. I located this clipping in Carman Scrapbook, Queen's University Archives.
8. Anon., *Chicago News*, September 29, 1894. In Carman Scrapbook, Queen's University Archives.
9. Anon., the *Athenaeum*, April 6, 1895. In Carman Scrapbook, Queen's University Archives.
10. Gundy provides a brief and useful note about this series of events in the headnote to a letter from Carman to Peter McArthur, June 22, 1895. Campbell went so far as to call Carman "perhaps the most flagrant imitator on this continent" (Gundy, p. 99).
11. In the Toronto *Globe*, June 19, 1895. See Lorne Pierce Collection of Carman papers, Queen's University Archives, for this and the article by Peter McArthur cited below.
12. Letter to the Toronto *Globe*, June 25, 1895.
13. *Low Tide on Grand Pré* appeared in its second edition six months after the first, for example, and by 1895 was in its third edition; between 1894 and 1921,

Songs from Vagabondia appeared in no fewer than fifteen editions, most of which had print runs of 750 copies; one (1911) had a run of 1,000.

14.   Desmond Pacey, *Creative Writing in Canada, A Short History* (Toronto: Ryerson, 1964), pp. 54 and 47.

15.   W. H. Pritchard, *A Literary Life Reconsidered* (New York: Oxford University Press, 1984), p. 5.

16.   In the Lorne Pierce Collection, Queen's University Archives.

17.   Anon., the *Athenaeum*, January 9, 1904. The reasons for this shift in the *Athenaeum*'s perspective are difficult to ascertain. Tastes may have altered, or there may simply have been a change in reviewers.

18.   Gundy, p. 176.

19.   Gundy, p. 215.

20.   Toronto *Globe*, June 19, 1895. In Carman Scrapbook, Lorne Pierce Collection.

21.   Eric Homberger, ed., *Ezra Pound: The Critical Heritage* (London: Routledge & Kegan Paul, 1972), p. 3.

22.   See also Noel Stock's *Poet in Exile: Ezra Pound* (Manchester: Manchester University Press, 1964), pp. 8–9, where Stock compares Carman's "Will not men remember us / In the days hereafter" (XXXVIII) to Pound's "Let the gods speak softly of us / In days hereafter" in Δώρια [Doria], *Ripostes* (1912).

23.   Wallace Stevens to Elsie Moll. In Holly Stevens, ed., *The Letters of Wallace Stevens* (New York: Knopf, 1970), Letters 147 and 148.

24.   In fact, it has only been in the last few years that the *Sappho* lyrics, thanks in part to Malcolm Ross's having kept them alive in his *Poets of the Confederation*, have been given serious consideration by scholars and critics. D.M.R. Bentley's important article, "Threefold in Wonder: Bliss Carman's *Sappho: One Hundred Lyrics*," in *Canadian Poetry* 17 (Fall/Winter 1985), pp. 29–58, was a significant contribution to the re-introduction of Carman to careful reading.

25.   Carman to T. B. Meteyard, December 29, 1906. In Gundy, p. 157.

26.   See Gundy's note to the above-mentioned letter, p. 157.

27.   Mary Perry King's letters reveal a rather woolly mode of expression: at one point, she explains rather clumsily to Carman that "people aren't grown to move so as to *help* nature in attunement with natural laws of preservation of growth— and they allow clothes to destroy their bodies and their being" (April 24, 1913). Throughout her correspondence with Carman she indulges in the most objectionable childish talk—one letter (October 27, 1914) tells him, "I dess caught a ille mouse wight here"—but even when she does not do this, her style tends to be histrionic and flowery. In Lorne Pierce Collection.

28.   *The Making of Personality* appeared in further editions in 1921, 1925 and 1929.

29.   Examples of these reviews are in the Carman Scrapbooks in the Lorne Pierce Collection, Queen's University Archives; they are also fully and usefully documented in Hugo McPherson's unpublished M.A. thesis, "The Literary Reputation of Bliss Carman: A Study in the Development of Canadian Taste in Poetry," University of Western Ontario, 1950, pp. 40–43.

30.   See Carman to Irving Way, August 27, 1911. In Gundy, p. 185.

31.   See the headnote to Carman to Irving Way, September 26, 1911. In Gundy, p. 188.

32.   Pelham Edgar, "Canadian Poetry," cited in McPherson, p. 84.

33.   After Dr. Morris King, Mary Perry's husband, discovered the nature of his wife's relationship with Carman, sometime in 1905, he forced a separation between them by demanding that Mary join him in Japan for an extended tour. When the Kings returned in 1906, Dr. King called in the money Carman owed

him—$592.00. Such was Carman's sorry financial state that he could pay only $15.00 of this—and that $15.00 represented one third of all he had in the world. See Carman to Muriel Carman Ganong, February 28, 1906, and Morris Lee King to Carman, March 29, 1906, Lorne Pierce Collection, Queen's University Archives.

34. A clipping of "Sick and in Prison" is in the Lorne Pierce Collection, and with it is a letter of Frank Crane (February 6, 1920) which indicates that the syndicate to which Crane belonged fed copy to dozens of newspapers in the United States and Canada. The column ran in January 1920.

35. Massey to Carman, November 13, 1920. In Lorne Pierce Collection, Queen's University Archives.

36. Peter McArthur to Lorne Pierce, April 20, 1923. Typescript copy in Lorne Pierce Collection, Queen's University Archives.

37. The information about the audiences for these tours is compiled from the correspondence between Carman and Peter McArthur during the winter/early spring tour of 1921 (e.g., February 20 and 22, March 14 and 31), and during the second tour in November/December of the same year (November 7 and 13, December 5), and from the correspondence between Carman and his doctor at the Lake Placid Sanatorium (e.g., February 13, 1921). In Lorne Pierce Collection, Queen's University Archives.

38. MacDonald's article was reprinted in Toronto's *Saturday Night*, March 28, 1925. The debate continued in its pages throughout the spring; Pratt's letter was published on April 25, 1925.

39. Mrs. W. Whitman Bailey to Mrs. M. Mitchell, undated. Copy in Lorne Pierce Collection of an original at the University of New Brunswick Library, Fredericton.

40. In Gundy, p. 336.

41. The welcome critical efforts of John Sorfleet, Terry Whalen and David Bentley have only—but at last—begun to rescue Carman's work in the last decade or so. Malcolm Ross's essay "Bliss Carman and the Poetry of Mystery" in his *The Impossible Sum of Our Traditions*, Introd. David Staines (Toronto: McClelland and Stewart, 1986), adds further to this effort, and Raymond Souster's and Douglas Lochhead's selection of Carman poems, *Windflower* (Ottawa: Tecumseh, 1985), has recently given readers further access to Carman's poetry.

42. *New York Sun*, October 27, 1894. In Carman Scrapbook, Lorne Pierce Collection.

43. Cited in McPherson, p. 25.

44. Bliss Perry to Bliss Carman, November 21, 1905. In Lorne Pierce Collection, Queen's University Archives.

45. Pacey, p. 50.

Three Poets Read Carman

AL PURDY
ELIZABETH BREWSTER
D. G. JONES

On Bliss Carman
Al Purdy

For the last dozen years or so I didn't think anyone but me considered Carman to have much value. Most people who've written about him recently have sounded negative; few would admit they enjoyed him for fear other people would think they had no taste or modern sensibility. By contrast, many of those who wrote about him when he was alive were worshipful and embarrassing in their praise.

And now I am—let me admit it at the outset—quite surprised at the interest in Bliss Carman demonstrated by this volume. It seems I am not alone in my ambiguous admiration and less than unstinted praise for the man. And I wonder if my careful ambiguity about him resembles yours—

I was thirteen in the early 1930s when I first read Carman's "Peonies." I don't have any of his poems before me at this moment while I process these words with two fingers on my manually operated Olympia typewriter, but the poem goes like this:

> Arnoldus Villanova
> Six hundred years ago
> Said peonies have magic
> And I believe it so.
>
> There stands his learned dictum
> Which any boy may read
> But he who learns the secret
> Will be made wise indeed.

> Astrologer and doctor
> In the science of his day
> Have we so far outstripped him
> What more is there to say?

And et cetera. But you know, that poem stiffened me, enchanted me if you like. The words hummed through my head like hydro wires in winter, when you first realize the whole countryside is alive and talking under the snow. And I realized other people were talking to me as well— in books I'd never seen—when I read that one poem of Carman's. All this wasn't conscious thought, of course, but it was there just the same.

I'd read a lot of books before this happened, but none I remember in the same way. And I suppose it was Carman who led me to R. L. Stevenson ("Home is the sailor, home from the sea / And the hunter home from the hill''), G. K. Chesterton ("Old Noah he often said to his wife as they sat down to dine / I don't care where the water goes if it doesn't get into the wine''), W. J. Turner ("I have stood upon a hill, and trembled like a man in love / A man in love I was, and I / Could not speak and could not move"), and eventually to Oliver St. John Gogarty ("I will live in Ringsend / With a red-headed whore / And the fan light gone in / Where it lights the hall door / And listen each night / To her querulous shout / Till at last she streels in / And the pubs empty out"). . . .

And I'll bet some of you don't know at least one of those names. I could quote much more, but I'll spare you that ordeal, though I am tempted, since this selective memory of loved poems is something I treasure.

I wrote my own first poem right after Arnoldus Villanova. It was certifiably awful, but got published in our high school magazine, *The Spotlight*. I got paid a buck for it, thought it an easy way to make a buck, and kept on writing.

All because of Bliss Carman? I think yes, it was; but that story gets mixed up with the one about me playing football and not getting enough attention—so I wrote a poem. They've both become personal anecdotes of mine; the truth in them varies, according to the accuracy of my memory.

At the end of grade nine I was still writing, publishing poems in *The Spotlight* and the local newspaper, the *Trenton Courier Advocate*. I was committing book-length effusions about the Norse myths and Robin Hood, using a neighbour's machine to type them; and I stapled them together with leather covers into small books. I was hooked on the stuff— poetry, I mean. And all because of Bliss Carman? I'm not sure.

I became, of course, the "school poet" at Trenton High School. And came close to regretting this cultural status when one Wilson

MacDonald visited us to read his own poems. I was solemnly ushered into his presence in the principal's office—another unfortunate who had contracted the metric disease.

MacDonald was in his fifties in the early 1930s. I remember most his long thin nose and black hair brushed sideways across a bald skull. I forget what we said to each other—but that MacDonald was a great poet was taken for granted by everyone. He admitted it himself.

In the school auditorium with a captive audience, he read "Whist a Wee"; something about tug boats in English Bay, Vancouver; and "Song of the Ski": "Norse am I when the first snow falls / Norse till the ice departs / The fare for which my spirit calls / Is blood of a thousand Viking hearts." (I don't have MacDonald's poems in front of me either; but if I make mistakes, who would know?)

Anyway, the point is: Bliss Carman, whom I never met, is probably responsible for me meeting Wilson MacDonald. Visiting the Soviet Union in 1976, I came across a Russian edition of MacDonald in a Moscow bookstore—and expostulated mildly to my hosts. Still later, when they translated some of my own stuff there, I wondered if they'd compared me to MacDonald and Joe Wallace—the latter also Russian-published.

Reverting back to the mid-1930s, I was playing football at high school and enjoying the twin status of poet and athlete (I was a lousy football player, too), reading novels concealed inside textbook covers in class. Not surprisingly, I failed to pass into grade ten.

But I liked football, weighing about 180 pounds and being more than six feet tall; and I liked poetry. Therefore, I stayed another year at school to play football and write poems. You can see immediately the deleterious effect of Carman on young minds.

In the mid-1930s I quit school for good, and rode the freight trains west at age seventeen during the Great Depression. At one point I left the boxcars in Toronto and picked up a copy of Carman's *Collected Poems* at a second-hand bookstore. The book was bound in maroon leather, and probably marked the beginning of my bibliographic obsessions. I hugged it to my bosom as the train's wheels imitated Carman's iambic pentameters or dactylic hexameters or whatever the textbooks say they are.

As you've undoubtedly noticed, all this has been very personal. But I've never attempted to analyze my feeling for Carman until this moment, and I don't think I'll do that at this moment either. Strangely enough, W. H. Auden has something relevant to say relating to feelings about Carman:

> Time that is intolerant
> of the brave and innocent,

and indifferent in a week
to a beautiful physique,

Worships language and forgives
everyone by whom it lives . . .

Bliss Carman is an integral part of the history of Canadian writing. Beyond that, he lives for me as incantation; and I can't possibly escape him even if I wanted to—and I don't want to. His music shadow is in my head—"The Shambling Sea," "Make Me Over Mother April," "The Nancy's Pride," and so on.

Carman's mysticism and solemnity I consider nonsense. Two paragraphs inside those three prose books he did with fancy titles, and I can read no further. They bore hell outta me. But his poems echo in my mind, like a remote counterpoint to what I write myself. And that sounds ridiculous to me, even as I get it down on paper.

I carry his stuff with me into the future, as possibly someone else may carry what I write into a more distant future. All of us do that, of course—update the past into the present. And Earle Birney once made Carman's past even more contemporary for me. He told me a story about Carman in New Canaan, which I believe is a town somewhere in New England.

It seems Carman had a mistress named Mary Perry King. She lived with her husband in New Canaan; Carman too lived, rather fortuitously, in the same small town. And each of these three must have made generous allowances for the other two.

Carman used to walk to his mistress's house every morning. And Doctor King walked to work as well, at the same time and on the same street. They would pass each other on opposite sides, each with different objectives. Carman's personal objective need not be explored further. But as they passed each other in that small New England town, is it possible that Doctor King lifted his doctor's hat or Carman the poet's sombrero he affected? Did either sneak a look sideways as they passed, or Doctor King snort, "Ridiculous poseur!"? And did Carman ever consider including his mistress's husband in a romantic poem?

Not to quote Auden again, I doubt that time will be any more intolerant than it has been already of Bliss Carman. It's unnecessary to mention his shortcomings—we all have some of those; he is still in the company of Eliot, Dylan Thomas, Yeats, Lawrence and the rest. They will not be snobbish about his intellect, even though most writers are very noticeably snobbish about such things. They will all be silent together, those famous writers, for obvious reasons.

Haunted by Bliss
Elizabeth Brewster

I'm beginning with one of my own poems, "For Bliss Carman." This poem says in concentrated form much of what I have to say about Carman—or to Carman, as the poem is addressed to him, or to his ghost.

FOR BLISS CARMAN

Surely, old Bliss, you would choose to be read
on such a summer day: late July
with sunshine and clouds, some white, some sullen,
shifting and dappling the sky,
and green trees casting greener shadows
on greenest grass

far though this garden is
from your Acadie (and mine).

You too might have sat here
in a nook of the grass
your eyes on the orange lilies
by the white picket fence;
imagined yourself the ephemeron
swaying in the great golden heart
of one of those daisies,
or the white butterfly flitting
over the roses
(not, probably, the hurrying industrious ant
    on little black feet).

You might have strolled to the edge
of the vegetable garden,
picked a handful of raspberries,
cracked open a pea-pod
to eat the sweet green peas raw

might have looked up and heard
startled

wings flutter above you
(Ah, there's a tiny bird
totally yellow—
gone now)

To wait patiently to hear
what the silent flowers might say,
daisies, bluebells,
the nasturtiums around the corner,
that one white shadow
of a dandelion now
swaying in the wind:
yes, you would have enjoyed
such a long afternoon,
heard who-knows-what whispers

may still enjoy it
for all I know,
your tall, stooped ghost
grey-cloaked
swinging open my garden gate,
advancing down my walk,
leaning over my shoulder
to see what poem
of yours I am reading.

Your hair flops in your eyes,
your cape flaps in the wind.
In your hand you hold
a windflower from another season.
At your heels there follows
your red wolf   despair

tamed now, perhaps?

You're just as likely to haunt
this spot, I suppose,
as that old graveyard
overlooking the river
where the land we both know
will soon be full of August.

"I am no-one," you wrote once,
"not even a name or a signature";

and again, "There is such delusion
in the Muse."
You told a friend,
"I have given my life for the poor verses,
and have nothing left me now."

A waste, did you think? A failure?
those old-fashioned poems? the prolixity
you deplored but could not avoid?

                    No, not a waste,
I want to reassure you.
Your poems delight sometimes,
as the small anonymous birds
delight, perching on my gate, heads cocked
meditating song

or the sturdy, half-wild rose-bush
at my kitchen door,
putting forth once more
this quintessential rose,
small, thorny, silken, blood-purple
smelling of summer

unimproved since Eden.

This is a poem that attempts to catch something of Carman's personality, gentle, dreamy, rather indolent, with a touch of melancholy and a touch of mysticism, a tenderness for the natural world. It alludes in a glancing way to several typical Carman poems: "Ephemeron," "Windflower," "The Red Wolf," "In a Garden," "Marigolds," "Daisies," "The Ships of St. John." It is also a poem that uses some of Carman's strategies. Carman himself addresses poems to other writers (Shelley, Browning) or writes elegies for them (Keats, Stevenson). Carman's poems often contain an "I" addressing a "you" who is dead or absent: writer, lover, friend. And the natural background, the place, is important in many of Carman's poems, as it is in this poem of mine, where the Saint John River Valley in August, and the graveyard where Carman is buried, are present in the same space as my back-yard garden in Saskatoon.

If I were asked, most days, what poets had influenced my work or were most important to me, I probably would not hit upon Carman to begin with. Yet his poetry was a part of my growing up, and it is not, after all, surprising that his ghost, along with other ghosts, has haunted me from time to time. Like other Canadian school children of my generation, I encountered some of his poems in the schoolbooks: "Daisies," "The Gravedigger," "The Ships of St. John" (with that marvellous stanza—

> Fair the land lies, full of August,
> Meadow island, shingly bar,
> Open barns and breezy twilight,
> Peace and the mild evening star.

—a stanza that I loved because it captured so perfectly the feeling of the landscape where I grew up). And, of course, "Low Tide on Grand Pré," where the remembered landscape of elms and dusk must be, or so I have always thought, the river valley near Fredericton, a remembered landscape superimposed upon the Grand Pré landscape. From 1942 to 1946 I attended university in Fredericton, a town still haunted by the ghost of Carman. Roberts and Carman were unfashionable as poets then; nevertheless I bought Roberts' *Selected Poems* and Carman's *Pipes of Pan*, all that was available by either writer in Fredericton's only bookstore; and I looked up other volumes in the university library. I always thought of Roberts and Carman together, Roberts as the successor of Wordsworth, Carman as a latter-day Coleridge. Roberts' sonnets about back pastures and potato fields and mowing appealed to my solid and practical tastes, the part of me that loved *Robinson Crusoe*. But "A Northern Vigil" and "Windflower" and "The Eavesdropper" appealed to my sense of the mysterious, to whatever made me admire "The Ancient Mariner" and "Christabel" and Poe's "To Helen." Also Carman, when he was lucky, could create lines that lingered in the mind:

> The windows of my room
> Were dark with bitter frost

or

> A fleet and shadowy column
> Of dust or mountain rain,
> To walk the earth a moment
> And be dissolved again

or

> High on a peak adrift with mist,
> And round whose bases, far beneath

> The snow-white wheeling tropic birds,
> The emerald dragon breaks his teeth.

Perhaps what mattered most to me at that early stage was that Carman had lived in the place where I lived, that I could walk past the house where he had lived and visit the graveyard where he was buried. Poe had written about southern vigils, but Carman wrote about a *northern* vigil, and I recognized that dark frost on the window pane, the wintry forest, the longing for April and its fragile flowers. If he had written out of his place, which was also my place, so could I. Carman's name had a practical effect on my early career: as a student at the University of New Brunswick I was twice awarded the Bliss Carman poetry prize. I wrote Lorne Pierce, who was responsible for the prize, a letter of thanks at the time; and later it was Lorne Pierce, Carman's friend and editor at Ryerson Press, who edited my first small chap-book, *East Coast*, for publication.

When I first left New Brunswick, it was to study at Harvard, where Carman had also studied, though I was luckier than he was and earned a degree there. Like him, I have lived at some distance from what I still think of as home, though my vigils have remained northern. When my thoughts have turned towards home, I have seen Carman as one of its guardian spirits, a modest and perhaps whimsical local deity.

Through the years I have come back to Carman's poems. I ran into his *Ballads and Lyrics* and *Last Songs from Vagabondia* in second-hand bookstores. I was pleased when Souster and Lochhead edited their selection, *Windflower*, and I could share some of Carman's poems with a class of students. It's true, many of his poems go on too long, and he wrote too many of them. Nevertheless, they continue to appeal to me. Why? Maybe because, when I was a child of eight to twelve, I lived in a haunted house and recognize a tenacious ghost, and a creator of tenacious ghosts. Maybe because the contradictions in Carman—his peculiar mix of despair and hope, melancholy and bravery—arouse my admiration.

Here is a poem which is typical of what I like in Carman. This is "Ephemeron: To a Belated Moth," from *The Green Book of the Bards*, which I had marked in the copy of *Pipes of Pan* that I bought as an undergraduate. (That subtitle isn't in *Pipes of Pan*, but is in *Windflower*, from which I take my version.)

EPHEMERON

> Ah, brother, it is bitter cold in here
> This time of year!
> December is a sorry month indeed
> For your frail August breed.

I find you numb this morning on the pane,
Searching in vain
A little warmth to thaw those airy vans,
Arrested in their plans.

I breathe on you; and lo, with lurking might
Those members slight
Revive and stir; the little human breath
Dissolves their frosty death.

You trim those quick antennae as of old,
Forget the cold,
And spread those stiffened sails once more to dare
The elemental air.

Does that thin deep, unmarinered and blue,
Come back to you,
Dreaming of ports whose bearing you have lost,
Where cruised no pirate frost?

Ah, shipmate, there'll be two of us some night,
In ghostly plight,
In cheerless latitudes beyond renown,
When the long frost shuts down.

What if that day, in unexpected guise,
Strong, kind, and wise,
Above me should the great Befriender bow,
As I above you now,—

Reset the ruined time-lock of the heart,
And bid it start,
And every frost-bound joint and valve restore
To supple play once more!

This poem is one in which the speaker addresses a moth, a tiny summer creature caught by a December frost, appearing almost dead as it rests numbly on the window pane. It's called an *ephemeron* because its life is only a day, or at least a very short span, like the speaker's own. The speaker calls the moth "brother," thus recognizing the kinship of man and moth. (If the moth is "frail" and "slight," so is the man.) The moth has sought "a little warmth" at the window of the human house, and the man, by means of "a little human breath," revives it from its apparent "frosty death." Although the man plays an almost godlike part in the miracle, the double use of "little" applied to the human suggests the modesty of the speaker. The "frail" moth, on the other hand, revives "with lurking might," and has the power and daring of an airplane or a sailing ship, spreading its "stiffened sails." The moth is a voyager on strange seas, and Carman, recognizing another similarity between them, addresses it as "shipmate." If the moth isn't exactly a vagabond, at any rate it's a traveller, and one in the same ship—one might say the same boat—as Carman. This miracle is, of course, a temporary one. It's December, after all. Both moth and man will some day fall victim to the "long frost" of death. This shiver at the approach of death is typical of Carman: the sense of human frailty, the body so easily "ruined." The poem might have ended with that shutting down of the "long frost"; but Carman goes on to a "What if?" Will the "great Befriender" revive the man, as the man has revived the moth? He is not sure; he merely speculates, with the hopefulness which is the other side of his melancholy. But the "great Befriender" shares some of the nature of the man, as the moth does. Like the man, the god is tender to fragile, ephemeral creatures. I find myself imagining an immense, shadowy Being who looks rather like Bliss Carman.

It is a poem in a tradition, of course. One can't help thinking of Burns's "To a Mouse." But Carman has his own distinct, recognizable voice, creates his own personality, has his own phrasing and imagery. This may not be a great poem, but it is a genuine one, movingly expressing those ambiguous feelings many of us have towards our own mortality and the mortality of other creatures in the universe. That ambivalence is often expressed by Carman, and is the source of some of his most felicitously expressed lyrical passages. I'll give Carman the last word by finishing with another such passage from the concluding stanzas of "Non Omnis Moriar: In Memory of Gleeson White":

> There is a part of me that knows,
> Beneath incertitude and fear,
> I shall not perish when I pass
> Beyond mortality's frontier;
>
> But greatly having joyed and grieved,
> Greatly content, shall hear the sigh
> Of the strange wind across the lone
> Bright lands of taciturnity.
>
> In patience therefore I await
> My friend's unchanged benign regard,—

> Some April when I too shall be
> Spilt water from a broken shard.

It's the "lone / Bright lands of taciturnity" that I especially admire here—a line connecting with Carman's epitaph, "Success is in the silences."

Carman: *Animula vagula blandula*
D. G. Jones

> *There is dust upon my fingers,*
> *Pale gray dust of beaten wings,*
> *Where a great moth came and settled*
> *From the night's blown winnowings.*

The significance of Carman is, at least in part, his difference from his predecessors and his contemporaries, and this difference is headlined in the word "vagabondia." Some readers miss the point, as when Donald Stephens tends to dismiss Carman as an armchair vagabond. We must, I think, take Carman seriously.

The vision of an organic society that informed much English-Canadian poetry between 1820 and 1880 is a settler's vision. It is a vision of life rooted in space and affording a continuous intimacy with the particulars of that space or place—the region, the village, the landholder's own fields and orchards, house and family. It is centred; it generates a series of concentric circles and a list, a catalogue, a kind of lover's inventory of lakes, woods, animals, what Dennis Lee later calls "the quirky particulars," the most central being the settler's wife. It ensures stability as well as intimacy, linking public and private, one generation to the next, through surveys, titles, marriage contracts, wills and other settlements.

Carman's night, the world of "Pulvis et Umbra," is hardly stable. The moth deposits a bit of dust on the speaker's fingers and, by the end of the poem, this "light guest" is seen "[r]acing seaward in the gloom." As well as any, this text defines the moment of intimacy and the meaning of settlement in Carman's work. It is one measure of the *écart* or swerve from the work of his predecessors.

It marks a swerve from his contemporaries as well. For, while Roberts and Lampman turn their backs, at least in their poetry, on the rising village, as being no longer a domestic but an imperial centre, generating, not concentric circles of intimacy, but more linear lines of power (of the kind one sees in the later poems of E. J. Pratt), these Confederation poets cultivate much the same vision of an intimate community, though without benefit of society, private property, or wife and children. The solitary woodsman or the poet or some anonymous speaker now marks the centre of a personal space, generating a list of intimate particulars, moose-bush, cornel bunches, grey moss, owl and chipmunk, blue jay and partridge, waterbugs and daisies, hornets and mullein stalks, with only the occasional potato-picker or waggoner to give a human dimension to the scene. Such texts discriminate nouns, articulate them metonymically, and tend to freeze them into a "picture."

A typical Carman poem is different. It does not present a finely discriminated list; things tend to be presented more generally; the space is more vague or blurred. Indeed, it is not concerned to articulate things in space but events in time, which are figured metaphorically. The typical event is transitional, like a change in the weather or the season, or it is a brief epiphany. Unlike events in a pioneer narrative or an E. J. Pratt narrative, it settles nothing, establishes no stable centre, ensures no projection of a line (or break in such a line). Carman's vision is the nomad's vision; the lines are unpredictable or discontinuous. A centre may appear anywhere, another centre, and each may wander or disappear.

Let me be so gauche as to talk about the author. Carman moves from Fredericton to Oxford to Edinburgh; to Cambridge, Massachusetts; to New York, to Washington, to Philadelphia; to New Canaan, Connecticut, to Haines Falls, New York. He later tours across Canada, goes to California, Santa Fé, Tucson. He covers the continent. Does he ever buy a house or a single piece of real estate? Does he ever have a fixed residence? Perhaps, in a manner of speaking, he does—between Sunshine House in New Canaan and Moonshine House in the Catskills, or, let us say, his "own" cottage, called Ghost House.

When Carman is so rash as to propose marriage to Jessie Kappeler, the family is naturally suspicious of a young man with no fixed income and no fixed address and quashes the arrangement. A true poet, Carman remains be-Mused for the rest of his days. On one occasion he writes that he has not married because he would be a failure as a father. But, he is against marriage, not only for himself, but for most of the young women he knows who inform him of their intentions of marrying. They will be confined, stunted, if not enslaved.

What sort of man is this, with no sense of property, no sense of marriage and family? A vagabond, clearly, if not a bounder.

Still, Carman's view of things saves him from the hypocrisy or the schizophrenia of some of his peers: Charles G. D. Roberts, who lives in New York and writes about the noble animal in the wilderness, where he leaves his wife and children while he pursues more urban game; Lampman, whose wife cannot be his muse and whose muse cannot be his wife and who exhausts himself paddling his canoe from the Rideau Locks to Lake Temiscaming and back.

Carman's view is unsettled and unsettling. Nothing is stable, not even the subject, the name.

Carman signs himself inconstantly. He is Bliss; he is Blissie; he is Blissikins. He is Hillborn to Jessie Kappeler's Seaborn. He is Dear Daddy or D. D. to his dearest Atom, Gladys Baldwin. He is Moonshine to Frederika Milne's Wayside.

He was christened William Bliss. And sometimes he actually uses the name of the father, as a kind of comic alter ego, or id, or astral self, which may also be a parodic imitation of W. B. Yeats. He sometimes writes about, and signs, little Monkey Willy and Willy Truly. To his friends the Fickes he signs Felipe. And to the serious Margaret Lawrence, who thinks he is a Villon, he signs François. Earlier, joking about his fall from poet to prosateur, the need for even King Arthur's fool to have his cakes and ale, he signs himself Dagonet.

This is, of course, a kind of epistolary game. In an early letter from England, following a walking tour, he signs himself Leggy. But it is a persistent game. In 1927 he writes to Margaret Lawrence, declining her demand for an autobiography:

> O yes, Margaret, I love being "Carman" to you. Or anything else you choose. My first name (of the two usual ones) I was always called at home as a boy, and often since by certain intimates. . . . But I don't care for it much simply as a name. . . . I have had many familiar more-or-less intimate names. But what I often think I need is a new name. . . . Where does one get it—(if not in being admitted to some Indian tribe)? . . . Ah me! (Gundy, 347)

A year earlier he writes to his Atom:

> My dear and perdurable: As ever it is i (lower case, not even capital I) who am delinquent, and as infrequent in correspondence as a returning planet or a wandering comet. But who shall say that we are not all—stars, suns, moribund worlds, and our glimmering selves—ruled and revolved by love, from which there is no escape? (Gundy, 334)

A lover's game, yes, but altogether suggesting a profound sense of the relativity, not only of the name, but of the subject, the presumably substantial centre of the world of individual particulars. Even his Atom is merely "perdurable."

This does not mean that his Atom has no value, that individual creatures or things cannot be recognized and celebrated for their ephemeral identity—the self or the "glimmering selves." But there is no doubt that they are ephemeral.

Nor does it mean there is not something more permanent, a larger order or process which Carman refers to above as "love," of which the "glimmering selves" are only local manifestations in constant transformation. Carman speaks of the soul. In a 1927 letter to Lawrence he makes a nice use of the comma: "The soul must condescend, to live"

(Gundy, 350). The world is a moving condescension—of some larger and largely ineffable process, love or soul or whatever—poignant, but also, perhaps, risible.

Which may explain Carman's insouciance towards survey lines, national boundaries, family titles, even the authority of the "onlie begetter." He does, at times, worry about copyright and suffer anxieties about his achievement as a man and as a writer. But he has little sense of the "egotistical sublime." In another letter to Lawrence he writes:

> Of course, I have always realized that any artist's work, when it is excellent, is not of his own rational devising. He knows not at all *how* it happens. It simply comes to him. (Gundy, 344)

One may, perhaps, sympathize with a Donald Stephens when he complains that Carman seems to have no distinctive identity, as a man or as a writer—that so many echoes or influences run through his work that it is impossible to say just what precursors, major or minor, author the author named Carman. Carman is a vagabond to himself. As a writer, one might argue that he condescends too much. He fails to become a major poet because he fails to take on the full anxiety of influence that Harold Bloom ascribes to the major poet; he lacks the Oedipal aggression necessary to become the father, the maker, displacing this precursor as the great original. And one might note that the figure in Carman's poems tends to be that of the child before the great mother. (He never does become a father—though, unlike an Émile Nelligan, he appears to have no difficulty enjoying and recommending sexuality.) No, for better or for worse, it is this happy humility, this confident naiveté, that is distinctive in Carman. It disencumbers him in advance of the impossible ambition to be the Original. And though very much "of his time," it allows his work or his "world" to seem oddly like an anticipation of the post-Modern, one in which he condescends, with all things, to being a trace, to being intertextual, a concatenation of texts as of little Monkey Willy and Bliss, of sun and wind and snow. Though it might be better to avoid that anachronism and suggest that his view of the writer and of the world is oddly Classical—sufficient to justify borrowing, from Marguerite Yourcenar's *Memoirs of Hadrian*, the line of an emperor for the title of this article: *animula vagula blandula* or, as Yourcenar translates it, "Little soul, gentle and drifting."

Neither, of course, is quite right. The world of Hadrian is too stoic, the world of Derrida too ironic. Carman's originality lies in the difference.

Carman identifies and delights in the moth, the windflower, the rain and the foam. His texts are all oxymoron: what is permanent is change; what is delightful is ephemeral; what we fear is the fount of desire.

The intimate encounter is a marvel, but is never decisive or final. All is metamorphoses. There is no settlement. Carman hates partings, but he is always parting. The Janus-faced character of "Low Tide on Grand Pré," its poignant alterity (communion/isolation, joy/grief), marks Carman's *oeuvre*. It modulates at times from a calm acceptance of mutability to an exuberant complicity to a boastful identification, an eerie, because both ominous and triumphant, ecstasy.

> O Mother, I have loved thee without fear
> And looked upon the mystery of change,
> Since first, a child, upon the closing year
> I saw the snowflakes fall and whispered, "Strange!"
> —"The Great Return"

> In the beginning God made man
>   Out of the wandering dust, men say;
> And in the end his life shall be
>   A wandering wind and blown away.
> —"The Vagabonds"

> We are the vagabonds of time,
>   Willing to let the world go by
> —"The Vagabonds"

> And we are overlords of change,
>   In the glad morning of the world
> —"The Pensioners"

> Then I leaned far out and lifted
> My light guest up, and bade speed
> On the trail where no one tarries
> That wayfarer few will heed.

> Pale gray dust upon my fingers;
> And from this my cabined room
> The white soul of eager message
> Racing seaward in the gloom.

> Far off shore, the sweet low calling
> Of the bell-buoy on the bar,
> Warning night of dawn and ruin
> Lonelily on Arrochar.
> —"Pulvis et Umbra"

There is a good deal more strangeness or originality in such lines than most readers are ready to recognize. One obvious source is the local Maritime toponymy: names like Grand Pré, Acadie, Minudie, Manan, the "eerie Ardise Hills." Is there a Maritime Arrochar? (The only Arrochar in my atlases is in Scotland—a long way for a moth!) But the real strangeness in the last verses is in the way that a frail creature racing to its doom becomes the "soul of eager message," the way a bell-buoy's presumably ominous calling is said to be sweet and low. Literally it warns the night, not the moth, of "dawn and ruin." We may still want to insist that "night" is a metonym of the moth, the container for the contained, whose ruin we must anticipate—more wreckage from the night's blown winnowings which dawn will reveal, leaving us temporarily more lonely. Yet there is an ambiguity, another possibility: that night will be ruined by dawn, the message of the moth will take us out of a benighted world into a new dawn.

Certainly the poet uses clichés, knowingly when he speaks of the convention whereby God made man of the wandering dust. But our own familiarity with the poetry, our very assumptions about its conventionality, often blind us to its ambiguities, its strangeness, its originality. What does it mean to say that we are vagabonds of time? Do we recognize the peculiarity of these lines in "The Eavesdropper"?—

> And the lost children of the wind
> Went straying homeward by our door.

If they are lost, how do they go homeward? Well, they find their way home by straying. For surveyors and road-builders, this has a disturbingly Taoist ring.

We might end by examining one of his simpler, if still memorable, poems, "Love, by that loosened hair," presumably inspired by Seaborn, Jessie Kappeler. It is simple in that it is another list or lover's catalogue and enumerates only three features in three symmetrical stanzas, the symmetry reinforced by the use of anaphora.

> Love, by that loosened hair,
> Well now I know
> Where the lost Lilith went
> So long ago.
>
> Love, by those starry eyes
> I understand
> How the sea maidens lure
> Mortals from land.

Love, by that welling laugh
Joy claims its own
Sea-born and wind-wayward
Child of the sun.

The initial line of each verse, descriptive and metonymical, leads into an allusive, narrative, and overwhelmingly metaphorical figuration. By virtue of a name in the first verse, two lines in the second, the poem engages two rich intertexts, the world of Lilith and the world of mermaids, sirens, undines. Eminently brief, the poem speaks volumes, or millennia, sweeping us from the Creation to the present, from myth through romance to an apparently contemporary realism.

The Canadian reader may be a little surprised to find a poet of the Confederation celebrating a woman by virtue of her resemblance to the lost Lilith or to the sinister undines. But I presume most readers quickly recognize its conventional nature, at least in the first two verses. Carman here follows the Pre-Raphaelite and broadly Symbolist conventions of the late nineteenth century, whereby images of loosened hair, of Lilith and the Mary Magdalene, not to mention Rossetti's model, Elizabeth Siddal, all become icons of an ambiguous, slightly perverse but often sanctified eroticism. The real surprise comes in the last turn, where an exuberant laughter shatters the air of grave decadence, dismisses the theology, negates the sinister in what appears to be a purely natural outburst of joy.

Of course, Lilith and the starry-eyed water sprites continue to define the lover, but they have undergone a paradigmatic sea-change. No longer substitutes for negative sexuality, divine error, thanatos, they have become substitutes for eros, life and joy—for the figure of Aphrodite or Venus Anadyomene, who rises from the text almost unnoticed in the metonym ''Sea-born.''

There is nothing quite like this in Lampman, or the other poets of the Confederation. It is not Whitman. It is an odd moment, an innocent moment, between Rossetti and Dowson and, say, T. S. Eliot. It is original Carman, reworking the conventional to produce a sudden freshness, a seemingly immediate voice or laughter—another metamorphosis of wind and wave and sun, another foam-born creature, ruled and revolved by love.

No, Carman is distinctive. His metaphoric bent, his nomadic vision of a world de-centred and dynamic, his childlike blithe confidence in the midst of mutability, all serve to differentiate him from his peers—and, perhaps, to link him to that figure discriminated by Canadian criticism, the fool-saint, and by extension to certain later poets.

I, for one, hear an echo of Carman in Raymond Souster's early poem "The Nest," where, following the war, the speaker defines the necessary haven for himself and his love:

> There must be a high, strong roof
> so the rain-children will not break
> the step of their marching above us.

More broadly, one may suggest Carman anticipates the Leonard Cohen of "As the Mist Leaves No Scar" and "Suzanne Takes You Down." Even the Irving Layton of "The Fertile Muck," where the speaker turns his back on the builders of suburban bungalows as he and his love make a meditation in the garden, butterflies rising around them with tiny wrist-watches on their wings. Perhaps Carman himself suffers a major meta-morphosis in that equally peripatetic, if decidedly more raucous fool-saint, Al Purdy, for whom the land is hardly solid, the moment hardly stable, for whom fences, buildings, people appear and dissolve and reappear transformed, the speaker himself none too stable as he sinks into earth, into another time, slides with his only recently alienated love down craters of the moon, or becomes a sister to a herd of cows. Purdy marries metaphor and metonymy, the precise list with the sudden dizzying dislocation. Unlike Carman he actually owns a bit of land, built an A-frame, married, and fathered a child. He shoulders more Oedipal aggression, shrugs off more anxieties of influence. But he is no imperialist, and no settler. His vision too is the nomad's vision of a poignant but exuberantly transitory world, where all the glimmering selves, Beothuks and Dorset Eskimos, dinosaurs and Cariboo horses, Annettes and terrible uncles, not to mention versions of Al, Alfred and A. W. Purdy, are ultimately ruled and revolved by love: eros, Aphrodite, the White Goddess, who may be his wife or the farmer's daughter or the melting imprint of one of the Annettes, her buttocks making Purdy angels in the snow.

This is a difficult thesis, since Purdy continues that interest in particulars and place, running back through Birney to Lampman and Roberts to the earlier nineteenth-century poems of Kirby and Howe. Yet it pleases me to see him as a transmogrified Carman, de-centred and always centred, be-Mused amid mortality, as in "Ten Thousand Pianos," where the speaker drifts through an arctic spring, attentive to the melt-water of the drifting icebergs, and concluding:

> I am an elderly boy come here
> to take piano lessons
> realizing one should be born
> in silence like a prolonged waiting

after the first death-cry
knowing this music
is what silence is for
in a canoe in Cumberland Sound
waiting among the white islands
for summer's slow departure

(Purdy, 230)

Carman's tombstone, I gather, bears the lines, ''Success is in the silences / Though fame is in the song.''

WORKS CITED

Brown, Russell, ed. *The Collected Poems of Al Purdy.* Toronto: McClelland and Stewart, 1986.

Gundy, H. Pearson, ed. *Letters of Bliss Carman.* Kingston and Montreal: McGill-Queen's University Press, 1981.

Pierce, Lorne, ed. *The Selected Poems of Bliss Carman.* Toronto: McClelland and Stewart, 1954.

Yourcenar, Marguerite. *Memoirs of Hadrian.* New York: Farrar, Straus, 1963.

Bliss Carman and the American Literary Milieu of the 1890s

JAMES DOYLE

In the fall of 1889 Bliss Carman wrote his sister Muriel from Cambridge, Massachusetts, where he was enrolled as a student at Harvard. "Some fellows in Boston are starting a new review," he informed her, "and have asked me to take the management of it. . . . It is hoped to make the thing first class in every way. A weekly paper on Literature, Art, Sociology, chiefly."[1] The fellows in Boston finally got a literary magazine going a few years later, but nothing came immediately of the 1889 project. By February of 1890, in fact, Carman had abandoned Harvard, and had moved to New York to begin work as assistant editor of the mass circulation magazine the *Independent*. After two years on the *Independent*, he spent two years as a free-lance and part-time editor and writer for various American magazines. In 1894 he moved back to Cambridge to become founding editor of the *Chap-Book*. By 1897 he was back in New York, after more time spent in free-lance work, to briefly associate himself with a revamped periodical entitled—in suggestive anticipation of a later British publication—the *Criterion*.

Carman spent over half his life in the United States, and did most of his professional writing for American publication. Although he retained his regional and his British imperial loyalties, of the many Canadian writers living in the United States in the late nineteenth and early twentieth centuries he developed particularly extensive and durable connections with the American literary milieu. His close friends included the Massachusetts poet Louise Guiney, and the Illinois-born poet Richard Hovey, with whom he co-authored three volumes of *Songs from Vagabondia*. His taste in modern literature encompassed a wide range of American writing, from the sentimental doggerel of James Whitcomb Riley to the experimentalism of Walt Whitman.

But it was especially the early years and the first contacts of this long residence in the United States that helped shape Carman's literary career. As he moved on from Harvard to professional activity in New York and Boston, he developed from a somewhat naive and idealistic provincial poet to a knowledgeable professional writer and editor. By the end of the century, his success as a poet and man of letters was solidly established in both the United States and Canada, and his mainly free-lance activities consisted of writing new poems for publication in the major periodicals of both countries, and preparing many successive volumes of his work for book publication. But for about ten years, from the time he first thought of taking on the editorship of the review proposed by the Boston group, he was constantly learning and developing as a member of one of the most lively and prolific artistic communities of the nineteenth century.

The American literary milieu of this time was dominated especially by periodicals. The quality and editorial focus of the hundreds of magazines publishing creative writing in the post-Civil War United States were extremely varied, ranging from popular family magazines to short-lived experimental publications. Carman was involved with almost every kind of American publishing venture imaginable in the 1890s. His activities as an editor and writer south of the border had important consequences for the international reception of Canadian literature, since he was often responsible for the publication and critical recognition in the United States of the work of other Canadian writers.

Although in the late 1880s Carman shared his Boston friends' dreams about experimental literary periodicals, he was ambitious and practical enough to want to break into the affluent mass-circulation American magazines. The early appearance of his work in such outlets as *Current Literature*, the *Atlantic Monthly*, and the *Century* helped him to qualify for the position on the *Independent*. But although it offered the opportunity of a steady salary and national exposure, the *Independent* was foreign to Carman's romantic, individualistic ideals and life style. As the editor of his letters has observed, he must have had reservations about signing an employment memorandum testifying to his agreement with the magazine's views on "temperance, smoking, card playing and . . . matters of Social Reform."[2] But like many other young writers in his situation, he was glad to have on any terms a regular salary and a connection with an established publication. Although the literary pages of the *Independent* were usually relegated to the back of the paper following the more abundant religious and political coverage, the editor W. H. Ward, to his credit, seems to have given Carman a free hand with the literary content. Before Carman's advent, the magazine featured the work of such popular poets as Ella Wheeler Wilcox and Frank Dempster

Sherman; besides printing submissions from his many younger American friends, Carman published the work of Charles G. D. Roberts, Archibald Lampman, Wilfred Campbell, Duncan Campbell Scott, and Gilbert Parker.

Carman's employment with the *Independent* also introduced him to the cosmopolitan social and cultural world of New York. A provincial by sentiment and habits, Carman at first could not admit to liking the city. "New York is so beastly big it makes me tired," he wrote his friend Maude Mosher a couple of months after joining the *Independent*.[3] But he came to enjoy the easy sociability of the groups of young writers to which his genial personality readily gained him access. Over the next few years, increasing numbers of Canadian expatriates joined him in the search for literary success in the metropolis and, although Carman's residence in the city during the 1890s was broken by interludes of varying length spent in Boston, Washington, and New Brunswick, he repeatedly returned to the genteel Bohemianism of the publishing offices, artist's garrets, rooming houses, and restaurants of lower Manhattan. As his letters indicate, he was equally at home in the more conservative cultural circles of Boston and Cambridge, but his years in New York epitomize his busy and sociable early literary life. Carman as the centre of a Canadian literary community in New York became the subject of memoirs by other expatriates, including Charles G. D. Roberts, Arthur Stringer, the Englishman Mitchell Kennerley, and Frank L. Pollock, a young would-be writer from Toronto. Pollock tells of gatherings in the Bodley Head publishing offices, of which Kennerley was manager, and of convivial (and presumably bibulous) meetings at a place called Maria's Restaurant in Greenwich Village.[4]

But above all, New York meant the opportunity for working steadily and accumulating experience in the literary trade. The *Independent* job was a good opportunity for a young writer to learn the practical aspects of editing and publishing, and to become more widely known in the United States. On the negative side, however, the salary was minimal, the heavy workload left little time for his own writing, and there were problems with the abstemious publisher. "I am going to leave the *Independent* soon," he wrote his sister in May of 1892; "I hope to do better. Several good things are in prospect."[5]

The immediate prospect involved part-time or temporary work with a succession of popular magazines, including *Current Literature*, the *Cosmopolitan*, the *Atlantic*, and the *Literary World*, work which made him better known to influential magazine editors as well as to American readers, and exposed him to a still wider range of literary activity. His most noteworthy activity following his experience on the *Independent*, however, involved a comparatively obscure periodical.

A version of the publication projected in Boston in 1889 finally appeared in the summer of 1892, under the editorship of the brilliant architect, essayist, and bibliophile Ralph Adams Cram, with Carman as one of three associate editors.[6] The *Knight Errant*, a "quarterly review of the liberal arts," was an elaborately illustrated 9-1/2" x 14" review devoted to poetry, essays, some fiction, literary news, and information for book collectors. Its contributors were mostly young would-be writers and artists associated with the intellectual and creative circles of Boston and Cambridge, including Carman, Cram, Louise Guiney, Bernard Berenson, Cram's architect partner Bertram Goodhue, Herbert Copeland, and others.[7]

Although these people represented a variety of creative and intellectual affinities, they were united in their subscription to a kind of *fin de siècle* neo-romanticism that was gaining currency in the United States. This tendency was inspired by various sources, including French symbolism (especially the poetry of Verlaine), the Whitman cult, the aestheticism of Oscar Wilde and Aubrey Beardsley, and a general urge among the new generation of writers to revolt against both older literary traditions and what they considered the excesses and trivialities of contemporary trends in realism and naturalism.

Although his participation in the editing of the periodical was probably substantial, Carman contributed only two signed items to the *Knight Errant*. "In the Wayland Willows," printed in the third issue, is a playful ballad describing the poet's flirtation with a "soncy maid," with wording ambiguous enough to shock Richard Hovey, although it was eventually admitted to the 1899 Carman–Hovey collaboration, *More Songs from Vagabondia*.[8] The more interesting item appeared in the first issue of the *Knight Errant*. "A White Cauldron," a short story of about fifteen hundred words, is possibly Carman's only significant published work of prose fiction, apart from three very brief sketches, really prose poems, that appeared in 1897 in a little Boston magazine, *Time and the Hour*. "It's vile," Carman insisted to Louise Guiney about "A White Cauldron"; "I wish I could do prose like some of my betters." Guiney, however, was loyally enthusiastic: "The descriptive passages [are] fresh and glorious, and the flesh-and-blood element vague and episodical."[9]

In fact, the story is a moderately successful blend of atmosphere and melodramatic incident, suggesting that Carman might have profitably continued to experiment with prose fiction. Probably asked by Cram to contribute something distinctively Canadian, Carman ventured on a story rather than a poem, to illustrate the sublimity and fear inspired by the vast northern wilderness. By the 1890s this idea was relatively familiar in American literature. Henry Thoreau had based some of his transcendental meditations on similar concepts; the theme was a recurrent staple of popular magazine writing; and Charles G. D. Roberts was to make his greatest success in the United States with short stories and novels about the north.

In "A White Cauldron," Carman's nature descriptions rely, like those of Thoreau and other American romantics, on metaphors of human pomposity and power:

> [The snow storm] came with tumult and the blare of victory. There was no hope of quarter in the sound of those trampling legions. Captained by caprice, all night these teeming forces of the world, with the terror of music in their van, streaming from the gorges of the outer dark, would drive across the deserted fields, wasting in their track; and when the calm dawn should return with golden flutes to re-possess his harried dominions, there might perhaps be revealed, skulking upon the flying rearguard of the storm, the wolfish and inescapable camp-followers of death.[10]

This rather overworked figurative language develops the situation of a lover who falls through a hole in the pack ice while braving the storm to visit his sweetheart. But if Carman relies on a rather stale plot, some of his descriptive language has a colloquial quality that indicates a concern for authenticity of observation and directness of presentation, unexpected in a writer who was impatient with the realist fiction of the time:

> When the ground grows as hard as stone and the brooks and ponds are already hushed, then the big rivers begin to freeze. One still night falling in a week of cold seals them down for their long sleep, and you hear nothing more from them but the muffled groaning under the iron blanket, until spring comes by that way. But sometimes they do not freeze so quickly; if they are coated from bank to bank one night, the next day may bring a strong wind and rain, and break the fetters and give the prisoners another respite.[11]

But Carman's flirtation with prose fiction was as abortive as the *Knight Errant* itself. Plagued with production delays and financial problems stemming especially from the costly graphics, the magazine expired after four issues. The experience did not dampen Carman's enthusiasm for the idea of an independent, avant-garde literary periodical, however. In 1894 he accepted an invitation from Cambridge, Massachusetts, to edit a new periodical currently being established there. The *Chap-Book* was the first and most important of dozens of small, limited-circulation and usually short-lived literary periodicals that flourished in the United States through the late 1890s and into the first decade of the twentieth century. One of Carman's contemporaries identified Carman as the prime mover in the whole evolution of these periodicals. "It was, at the early dawn," wrote Walter Blackburn Harte in an 1897 article on "The Chap-Book Movement in America," "the happy idea of the poet Bliss Carman, this revival of the pamphlet."[12] But the impetus for the pamphlet periodicals actually came from a variety of sources and influences, including prior publications such as the *Knight Errant*, as well as the iconoclastic aesthetic theories of Herbert Stone and H. I. Kimball, the two young Harvard undergraduates who published the *Chap-Book*. The British *Yellow Book*, which began to publish only a month before the first issue of the *Chap-Book*, was not an influence so much as a parallel development growing out of impulses and ideas that were moving back and forth across the Atlantic in the 1890s.

The *Yellow Book*, in fact, was never very popular with most young American writers of the period, because of its association with "decadence." This term seems to have encompassed a multitude of sins, seldom defined, although Carman clarified his own thoughts on the subject in an 1896 article for the *Boston Evening Transcript*: "Anything that is commonplace is decadent," he insisted. "All popular, commercial art which is merely pretty and is supplied to fill a demand is decadent. . . . Magazine poetry, for instance, . . . is thoroughly decadent. It is admittedly ephemeral; it is intended for the average man, and is intended to last until the next number of the magazine can come to press—about thirty days."[13] By these criteria, the *Chap-Book* was to be the very antithesis of decadence, for the primary aim of the magazine was, quite simply, literary excellence. This was to be, however, a literary excellence independent of social, moral, or economic considerations: unlike the mass-circulation family magazines, the *Chap-Book* carried no advertising except from the publishing trade, and catered neither to the reading tastes of the lowest intellectual level of society nor to the moral assumptions of the more prudish or sensitive reader. As Wendy Clauson Schlereth has shown in her history of the *Chap-Book*, the magazine over its four-year existence adhered to no narrowly consistent editorial policies, apart from giving special consideration to untried younger writers and occasionally proclaiming a broadly defined romantic idealism.[14] The work of Henry James, Hamlin Garland, and Stephen Crane appeared side by side with that of Eugene Field, Thomas Wentworth Higginson, and Ella Wheeler Wilcox, along with dozens of untried young poets, some subsequently forgotten, others such as W. B. Yeats at the beginnings of distinguished careers.

Carman was editor for only the first four issues, but he remained associated with the editing of the magazine until it moved to Chicago in the fall of 1894; and as Schlereth reports, over the whole four years he was by far the most frequent contributor. As he did on the *Independent*, he made sure that his fellow Canadians were well represented: Roberts' poem "The Unsleeping" was the first work in the first issue, and regular contributors included Lampman and Gilbert Parker, as well as Ethelwyn Wetherald and the young New Brunswicker Francis Sherman. Almost all the Canadian contributions were lyric poems, but Carman seems to have tried to modify the popular American notion of Canadian poetry as dominated by images of the forest wilderness or the lakes and fields of New Brunswick and Ontario. Roberts' "The Unsleeping" sets the tone with its tentatively mystical, symbolic exploration of the reciprocal relationship between the poetic imagination and a cosmic creative principle. Carman's own "Prayer in the Rose Garden," in the second issue, attempts to relate an Emersonian notion of spiritual evolution to a principle of natural order and beauty. Gilbert Parker's "There is an Orchard," in the issue of November 1, 1894, involves a similar image, incorporated into a romantic love lyric; and Archibald Lampman's "Inter Vias," of January 15, 1895, is a Poe-like withdrawal to a visionary land of supreme beauty.

The *Chap-Book* thus offered Carman, as contributor and editor, freedom in his own poetic composition and the opportunity to bring a more comprehensive view of Canadian literature to an American audience. Yet in the long run, he expressed considerable dissatisfaction with the *Chap-Book*. "The *Chap Book* takes up a lot of time and is of doubtful profit," he wrote Henrietta Hovey shortly after the first issue appeared. And to Richard Hovey he complained that the publishers, Stone and Kimball, were "good fellows but *boys*. They have no business methods or manners whatever."[15]

Besides being inefficient businessmen, Stone and Kimball were perhaps a bit too solemn for Carman, who had a streak of literary mischief in him, as is illustrated by his "Wayland Willows" poem as well as some of his contributions to the *Chap-Book*. As his correspondence shows, he was a friend and admirer of Gelett Burgess, editor of the irreverent *Lark, Enfant terrible*, and *Petit Journal des Refusées*.[16] Although he could not bring himself to join Burgess's all-out burlesque of literary magazines, he was not above occasionally using the pages of the *Chap-Book* to poke friendly fun at his contemporaries. His tribute to the western poet Eugene Field in February 1895, signed with the anagram "Slim Barcans," begins:

> O lean Eugene,
> Evergreen Eugene,
> Dear bard of the wooden-doll mien, Eugene![17]

As he wrote to Louise Guiney in 1895, "*The Chap-Book* . . . does not sate my thirst for editing. I want something like a half-grain *Atlantic* which should be light, not silly, devoted but not without humor, sane and gentlemanly, and never up to date unless the date were worth being up to.''[18] Carman never found quite what he was looking for, however. He continued to do occasional editorial work for various magazines, served as reader and advisor to a book publication venture of Stone and Kimball, and in 1895 entered into a similar relationship with Lamson Wolffe of Boston, another partnership of young avant-garde publishers.[19] But by the late years of the decade, Carman obviously felt that the American publishing business had little to teach him, and was merely consuming precious writing time without bringing him a significant financial return. In 1897 he joined an association of literary and theatrical people in New York who were publishing a magazine called the *Criterion* in conjunction with the Criterion Independent Theatre. But although Charles G. D. Roberts was also a member of the association and a frequent contributor to the magazine, Carman seems to have been no more than nominally associated with it.[20]

By the turn of the century, Carman was devoting more and more of his literary energies to the preparation of his poetry in book form. By the mid-1890s his reputation was adequately established to guarantee ready acceptance by the well-paying popular magazines, and he continued to write for *Scribner's, Munsey's, McClure's,* the *Century,* and others for the rest of his life.[21] He submitted occasional work to various little magazines: "The King of Is" appeared in *Town Topics* (1894), "The Paupers" in the *Lotus* (1896), "In Philistia" in *The Philistine* (1897), and "Three Prose Idylls" in *Time and the Hour* (1897). But by 1900 his apprentice and early journeyman service in the American literary milieu was effectively over.

Carman was always proud of his descent from New England Loyalist stock and his distant kinship with Ralph Waldo Emerson. Throughout his life he was amiably pro-American, having no fear of cultural or economic domination, no anxieties about Canadian identity. He had no objections to being assigned by a journalist to ''a new school in American literature,'' or to finding himself included in Jessie B. Rittenhouse's 1904 critical study *The Younger American Poets.* ''I favoured Reciprocity myself,'' Carman wrote to a British admirer in 1911, ''but then I am a free trader.''[22] He was ambitious and practical enough to see that, if Fredericton and Grand Pré were important sources of literary inspiration for him, the vibrant and cosmopolitan worlds of New York and Boston were far more congenial environments for pursuing the literary profession. This life of exile, furthermore, created no tensions in him, as comparable experience did for such a person as Henry James; nor, in the long run, was he any less a Canadian writer for the experience.

It could be argued that Carman and other Canadian writers might have exerted themselves to encourage a domestic publishing industry;

but such easy hindsight glosses over the formidable cultural indifference of nineteenth-century Canadian entrepreneurs, bureaucrats, and readers. The United States certainly had its own anti-cultural biases, but it also had diverse and democratically accessible publishing outlets which could make it possible for the talented unknown to acquire much-needed experience, to reach a substantial audience, even to make a respectable living from writing. In the United States of the 1890s, Bliss Carman found the best available environment for pursuing his literary career.

NOTES

1.   Bliss Carman to Muriel Carman Ganong, October 3, 1889. In H. Pearson Gundy, ed., *Letters of Bliss Carman* (Kingston and Montreal: McGill-Queen's University Press, 1981), p. 31.
2.   Gundy, *Letters*, p. 35.
3.   Carman to Mosher, April 9, 1890. In Gundy, *Letters*, p. 37.
4.   Frank L. Pollock, "Canadian Writers in New York," *Acta Victoriana* 22:7 (April 1899): 434–39; see also Arthur Stringer, "Canadians in New York: America's Foremost Lyrist," *National Monthly of Canada* 4:1 (January 1904): 3–5, Charles G. D. Roberts, "Some Reminiscences of Bliss Carman in New York (1896–1906)," *Canadian Poetry Magazine* 5 (December 1940): 5–10, and H. Pearson Gundy, ed., "Kennerley on Carman," *Canadian Poetry: Studies/Documents/Reviews* 14 (Spring/Summer 1984): 69–74.
5.   Carman to Muriel Carman Ganong, May 17, 1892. In Gundy, *Letters*, p. 46. See also Muriel Miller, *Bliss Carman: Quest and Revolt* (St. John's, Nfld.: Jesperson, 1985), pp. 81–83, according to which Carman was finally squeezed out by the publisher.
6.   No editors were listed in the magazine, but the *Independent* announced in June 1892 the forthcoming appearance of the *Knight Errant*, with Cram as editor and Carman as associate (Clipping, Carman Scrapbook, Lorne Pierce Collection, Queen's University).
7.   For an account of the beginnings of the *Knight Errant*, see Ralph Adams Cram, *My Life in Architecture* (1936; New York: Kraus, 1969), pp. 84–88.
8.   Carman to Hovey, July 5, 1896, Lorne Pierce Collection, Queen's University: "I should quite agree with you as [sic] in the Wayland Willows, if he did anything but kiss the girl."
9.   Carman to Guiney, March 8, 1892, and Guiney to Carman, May 3, 1892, Lorne Pierce Collection, Queen's University.
10.   Carman, "A White Cauldron," the *Knight Errant* 1:1 (1892): 21.
11.   "A White Cauldron," 20.
12.   Walter Blackburn Harte, "The Chap-Book Movement in America," *Criterion* 16 (October 23, 1897): 17.
13.   Carman, "The Modern Athenian," *Boston Evening Transcript*, August 8, 1896 (Clipping, Carman Scrapbook, Lorne Pierce Collection, Queen's University).
14.   See Wendy Clauson Schlereth, *The Chap-Book: A Journal of American Intellectual Life in the 1890s* (Ann Arbor: UMI Research Press, 1982), especially chapter 1, "Misconceptions of a Mind and a Magazine."
15.   Carman to Henrietta Hovey, June 4, 1894, and to Richard Hovey, January 7, 1895. In Gundy, *Letters*, pp. 67, 83.

16.   See correspondence between Carman and Burgess, Lorne Pierce Collection, Queen's University.
17.   Carman, "To a Portrait of a Western Poet," the *Chap-Book* 2:15 (February 1895): 320.
18.   Carman to Guiney, March 14, 1895, Lorne Pierce Collection, Queen's University.
19.   See James Doyle, "The Confederation Poets and American Publishers," *Canadian Poetry: Studies/Documents/Reviews* 17 (Fall/Winter 1985): 65.
20.   See Editor's announcement of Criterion Theatre, *Criterion* 16 (October 23, 1897): 22; see also J. E. Bender, "The Criterion Independent Theatre," *Educational Theatre Journal* 18 (October 1966): 197–209.
21.   For a partial list of Carman publications in the large-circulation American periodicals, see A. R. Rogers, "American Recognition of Canadian Authors Writing in English, 1890–1960," Diss., University of Michigan, 1964.
22.   Carman to H.D.C. Lee, September 29, 1911, Lorne Pierce Collection, Queen's University. Carman is described as one of the "new school" in an unidentified newspaper clipping, headed New York, July 7, 1896, Lorne Pierce Collection.

On Analyzing and Editing Bliss Carman's Work: The Critical Question

JOHN R. SORFLEET

The development of Bliss Carman's work has long interested Carman critics.[1] The differing critical opinions range from those of H.D.C. Lee, Carman's first book-length critic, to those of Odell Shepard, James Cappon, Muriel Miller, Desmond Pacey, and Donald Stephens, his later ones. Thus Lee, writing his dissertation on Carman in 1912, states:

> The work of Bliss Carman considered as a record of the evolution of his thought falls easily into three periods. The early poems of *Low Tide on Grand Pré* show the poet at one with Nature; conscious, as Mr. Stopford Brooke remarks Browning was at times, of being "a living piece of the great organism, having his own rejoicing life in the mightier life which includes him; and feeling with the rest the abounding pleasure of continuous life reaching up through growth to higher forms of being, swifter powers of living." The poems of *Behind the Arras* mark a temporary rupture of this close intimacy with Nature and a period of depression and doubt. Having once, however, known joy and confidence, the poet believes in their existence and works towards their recovery. He analyses his former experiences, and on the results of this builds up a philosophy of life. The following volumes indicate that this philosophy has stood the test of practice, and are all more or less expository of its principles.[2]

Odell Shepard, in his 1923 book on Carman, also writes that Carman's work ranges "through three distinctly marked periods," though his description of those three periods differs somewhat from Lee's. The first period, including *Low Tide on Grand Pré* (1893) and the *Vagabondia* poems of 1894 and 1896, Shepard describes as "strongly Romantic, even 'gothic' in its obscurity and wilful idiosyncrasy." The second period, beginning with *Behind the Arras* (1895) and continuing into *From the Green Book of the Bards* (1903), is "one of equally excessive rationalism," where "obstinate questionings begin to disturb the poet's mind so that much of the grace . . . of the earlier style is sacrificed to the lucidity demanded by rapidly increasing didacticism." The third and final period, beginning with *From the Book of Myths* (1902) and *Sappho* (1903), joins the extremes of the first two periods, wedding imagination and reason into "a new poetic unity."[3]

James Cappon, in 1930 the third of Carman's early book-length critics, took a position mid-way between Lee and Shepard. Comparing Carman's early and later poems, Cappon states:

> In his later work there are new notes of course, and the vague romanticism and visionary elevation of his first songs become a closer reflection of his real experience. But the form of vision which gives him wings does not change. It is always transcendentalist exaltation of experience, often a little mystical yet always trying to maintain itself on a foundation of rational thought.

Nevertheless, Cappon also sees three periods to Carman's work and thought: the early period of "vague romanticism and visionary elevation," a middle period where his "cosmic philosophy is busy moulding this mystical symbolism into more definite forms of thought and vision," and a later period where "the mystical light was fading into that of common day."[4] For Cappon, the first period roughly corresponds with *Low Tide on Grand Pré* (1893), the second with *Behind the Arras* (1895) through the *Pipes of Pan* series (ending 1904), and the third with *The Rough Rider* (1909) and subsequent volumes. His grouping is very approximate; many of Carman's poems are seen as exceptions or as reversions or, like the four prose volumes, as transitions. Cappon's general feeling is also that Carman's work evidences a steady qualitative decline beginning from towards the end of the second period.

Though these three early critics tend to see Carman and his works differently, they have one thing in common: they base their division of Carman's work into periods of development upon an incorrect assumption. Grouping his work by published volume, they try to prove development from one volume to another. Had Carman published his work chronologically, this would have been a valid procedure; unfortunately for his critics, he did not. Instead, his method was to print some of his work in magazines and then, when he had enough poems on the same general theme, to publish a volume composed of previously printed and unprinted items written over many years. From the time of his first volume of poetry, *Low Tide on Grand Pré*, Carman followed this procedure, saying in his Preface:

> The poems in this volume have been collected with reference to their similarity of tone. They are variations on a single theme, more or less aptly suggested by the title, *Low Tide on Grand Pré*. It seemed better to bring together between the same covers only those pieces of work which happened to be in the same key, rather than to publish a larger book of more uncertain aim.[5]

Carman confirmed his method a decade later in his letter of July 16, 1902, to Miss M. E. Cramer, observing that his poetry

> has almost all been printed sooner or later in the magazines and newspapers. Then whenever I wished to make up a volume, I would select all the poems of a certain kind and issue them with the most appropriate title I could find.[6]

Similarly, each prose volume collects essays, written and printed over a period of years, around a unifying theme.

What Carman's publishing procedure means is that the date upon which a book was published is an inaccurate indication of when the poems or essays collected therein were written. A good illustration is provided by *From the Green Book of the Bards* (1903); the poems it contains range from 1887 to 1902. Similarly, the poems in *From the Book of Myths* (1902, rev. 1903) extend over a ten-year period dating from the summer of 1892. Each volume embraces all three of Lee's and Shepard's periods of development and two of Cappon's periods. As this kind of time-spread is common for most of Carman's books, it is clear that any analysis of chronological development based upon dates of book publication can only be misleading. This is the major defect of the early critical studies of Carman and perhaps also the reason for their divergent opinions.

Carman's later critics realize that his method of publication creates difficulties for any attempt at developmental analysis of his work and thought. Each of them tries to respond to the difficulty in a different way. The earliest and most scientifically valid response was that of Muriel Miller, writing in 1935. In her *Bliss Carman: A Portrait*, Miller uses the evidence of an index to Bliss Carman's poetry scrapbook, edited by Dr. Morris King and Lorne Pierce and printed in 1931,[7] to ascertain the dates of first printing for those poems which Carman had clipped from magazines and had pasted into his scrapbook. Correlating this information with the dates of his books of poetry, she attempts to determine and list Carman's poetic output by year of first publication. Her chronology leads her to draw certain conclusions about Carman's development in poetry and life, and she sees six periods to his work. The first, from 1861 to 1886, she sees as formative years of "prentice work." The second period, from 1887 to 1892, is one of mystical lyricism. The third, from 1892 to 1896, she sees as the "pivotal centre of Carman's poetic career," the period in which he shows his versatility in many kinds of poetry. The fourth, from 1896 to 1902, she describes as a largely transitional period, "scanty of output and relatively poor in quality."[8] The fifth period, on the other hand, is one of spiritual recovery, of poetry of love, and extends from 1902 to 1905. The last—and longest—period, from 1905 to 1929, is one of decline, the result of an increasingly didactic attitude.

Miller's chronology provides a more valid basis for a discussion of development, but it is marred by four serious defects: first, she relies strictly upon dates of printing (rather than those of writing); second, she clusters the poems in twelve-month periods without any attempt to determine further the specific date or order of composition; third, she confines herself to Carman's poetry and ignores its relation to his prose; and fourth, her listing, at various points, is both incomplete and incorrect. (For example, "A Friend's Wish," from *More Songs from Vagabondia*, is omitted, as are a number of Carman's early poems; the printing of *Last Songs from Vagabondia* is dated at 1901 rather than 1900; "Premonition" is erroneously credited to Carman rather than Hovey; poems such as "At the Portal of Spring," "An Autumn Song," and others assigned to 1904, are actually retitlings of various poems published between 1895 and 1903; "The Tidings to Olaf" and "Olaf Hjorward" are confused with each other with a resultant dating error of eight years; and the first printing of many poems is attributed to a later year, such as 1931, than was actually the case.) In addition, information from some corollary sources (for example, Carman's letters) was probably unknown to her at that time. Nevertheless, her work has the merit of at least recognizing the problem of chronology and attempting to deal with it.

As well, Miller recently published another book, a biography entitled *Bliss Carman: Quest and Revolt* (Jesperson Press, 1985). Though not a book of literary criticism in the sense of the other works I am discussing, this biography is interesting and useful insofar as it follows the sequence of events revealed in Carman's correspondence, diaries, and the memoirs of his friends. However, Miller also uses extracts from approximately fifty of the poems as passages directly commenting on the poet's own life, as she explains in an appendix:

> Because I wanted it to appeal to a far wider reading-public than biographies usually do, I decided to do a direct reconstruction of Carman's life with live scenes in it built up out of fact and using direct quotations from the poet's verse and letters in permitting the poet to speak for himself.

Unfortunately, this procedure, especially the use of extracts from the poems as biographical "facts," sometimes leads to questions when the dates of poem extracts and the events they supposedly depict do not jibe. Further, the possibility of erroneously confusing the poet with a poetic *persona* is real, and the danger is increased by this method.

A different response to the question of chronology was that of Desmond Pacey in 1958. Though his is a chapter on Carman rather than a book, that chapter in *Ten Canadian Poets* was quite influential, and Pacey's procedure requires some examination, if only for what he doesn't do. He simply decides that Carman's "peculiar method of publication precludes a strictly chronological approach to his poetry." Instead, Pacey tries to "group Carman's books and consider them as exemplifying the various aspects of his poetic personality." He divides Carman's volumes into four groups: the *Vagabondia* series, the *Pipes of Pan* series, the books of brief lyrics, and a miscellaneous group. Pacey realizes that his groupings and even his choice of volumes in each grouping are open to objections, so he uses his groupings only to organize his discussion of certain poems. He does not claim that his is a valid analysis of the development of Carman's writing; nevertheless, he does say that Carman's later work puts "greater stress on the didactic and rational elements in poetry."[9]

The next book-length study of Carman was Donald Stephens' for the Twayne series in 1966. Stephens presumably felt that the chronology of Carman's work was irrelevant, since he contends that "there is no development or growth in Carman's poetry." He makes this statement because he feels Carman was an extremely derivative poet, easily influenced by others and almost without a mind of his own. He says that the periods of poetic development mentioned by other critics are rather "patterns of style and thought" illustrating influences which remain unsynthesized. He states that "all the primary elements of Carman's poetry were with him at the beginning of his career," and that, when Carman "found anything that he thought was one of his 'bests,' he used it again and again until it became stagnant and odious to the reader."[10] Aside from being aesthetically questionable, Stephens' statements lack a rational basis, for such statements about lack of development, as well as those about development, can only have logical validity if founded upon a reliable calendar of Carman's writings—which Stephens' book is not. Indeed, in terms of both methodology and critical understanding, his book—notwithstanding its comparatively recent date—is probably the weakest of all the studies on Carman.

Thus, though the critical opinions of Carman's work range from sympathetic to antipathetic, from contending development to denying it, the defect common to all these analyses is that they were not based on a sound chronology of Carman's work. Similarly, the anthologies of his poetry by Rufus Hathaway, Lorne Pierce, and even, most recently, Souster and Lochhead[11]—following Carman's own procedures—were organized by theme or mood rather than by date of composition. As such, these anthologies are interesting introductions to his work, but they don't really help the reader to understand properly the development of Carman's thoughts, themes, and techniques.

The alternative course, and the one I chose to follow both in my critical work and in the anthology I compiled for the New Canadian Library, was—by consulting dated manuscripts, letters, and other sources in various archives throughout North America—initially to ascertain when each poem (or prose piece) was written or, where that information was lacking, when it first appeared in print in any form. Only after constructing the most detailed and reliable chronology did I feel it valid to proceed to any analysis of the correlation between Carman's work and thought. Chronological analysis of his work reveals that it falls into a series of phases which correlate with developments in his life or thought: 1861–1886, a formative period when Carman developed a transcendentalist outlook; 1886–1892, years when Carman, after a mystical experience which inspired his "first poem"[12] of any consequence, showed the continuing influence of that experience in his work; 1892–1899, a period when Carman's idealism incorporated evolutionary elements; 1899–1910, a phase when Carman added a unitrinian theology to his thought; and 1910–1929, a late period when unitrinian dogma was given less prominence in Carman's poetry and was better merged into his overall outlook. I have discussed these periods in more detail in the article "Transcendentalist, Mystic, Evolutionary Idealist: Bliss Carman, 1886–1894"[13] and in the Introduction to the New Canadian Library edition of Carman's poetry,[14] so I will merely note here that subsequent criticism has tended to accept the procedures and analysis outlined above.[15] I have also been working on a book-length critical work and on a more comprehensive chronologically organized anthology of Carman's poetry —easier to do now that his work is in the public domain and the previously widely scattered copyrights no longer pose a problem.

During the last twenty years, Carman criticism has come a long way; during the next twenty, it should advance still further. This volume represents a survey-point, a point from which the past can be viewed, the present can be enjoyed, and the future can be anticipated. In all directions the outlook is a better one than it would have been two decades ago.

NOTES

1. The following paragraph prefaced my oral presentation of a version of this paper at the Bliss Carman Symposium (University of Ottawa, April 28–29, 1989).

> Before beginning my paper, I'd like to recall an episode that epitomizes what the academic community can ideally mean. Many years ago, in 1972, I wrote a lengthy article [for *JCF* I:2] reviewing the New Canadian Library as it existed at that time. In the course of the article I stated some serious reservations I had about the abridgement of various nineteenth-century texts in the series, and, after pointing out in considerable detail that many of the poems by Carman in Malcolm Ross's *Poets of the Confederation* were abridged without the alterations even being indicated, I laid the responsibility at Ross's door. I subsequently learned that he had simply ordered the reprinting of many of the poems previously included in Lorne Pierce's anthology, and that it was Pierce who had made the silent excisions from Carman's work and who therefore bore the main responsibility. However, Professor Ross took no offence, and later, when he had the opportunity, he convinced Jack McClelland to publish an anthology of Carman's work to compensate for the errors. And then—this is the notable part—he asked *me*, the person who had criticized his own anthology, to assemble and introduce it. He also made some very complimentary remarks, in *Canadian Literature* #68–69, about my article "Transcendentalist, Mystic, Evolutionary Idealist: Bliss Carman, 1886–1894." These actions, to me, were not only magnanimous, but they also showed me then, and remind me now, what the scholarly life can be: not petty, not political, the way we all observe it at times, but a calling dedicated to the unselfish pursuit of knowledge, a calling which recognizes mistakes but doesn't let criticism fester and instead builds towards new insights, the way I had thought it would be before entering the profession and becoming slightly disillusioned. So, I would like here to commend Malcolm Ross for his generosity of spirit and his contribution, in my mind at least, to the ideals of academia.

2. H.D.C. Lee, *Bliss Carman: A Study in Canadian Poetry* (Buxton: Herald Printing, 1912), p. 35.
3. Unless otherwise identified, all quotations in this paragraph are from Odell Shepard, *Bliss Carman* (Toronto: McClelland & Stewart, 1923), p. 33.
4. James Cappon, *Bliss Carman and the Literary Currents and Influences of his Time* (Toronto: Ryerson Press, 1930), pp. 36, 211, and 199.
5. Bliss Carman, "Preface" to *Low Tide on Grand Pré* (Cambridge & Chicago: Stone and Kimball, 1893 with additions in 1894), n.p.
6. Rufus Hathaway Collection of Canadian Literature, University of New Brunswick, Fredericton, N.B.
7. *Bliss Carman's Scrap-Book: A Table of Contents*, ed. Morris L. King and Lorne Pierce (Toronto: Ryerson Press, 1931). 19 pp.
8. Muriel Miller, *Bliss Carman: A Portrait* (Toronto: Ryerson Press, 1935), pp. 17 and 71.
9. Desmond Pacey, "Bliss Carman," *Ten Canadian Poets* (Toronto: Ryerson Press, 1958), pp. 86 and 87.

10. Donald Stephens, *Bliss Carman* (New York: Twayne Publishers, 1966), pp. 91 and 92.

11. See my "A Primary and Secondary Bibliography of Bliss Carman's Work" later in this volume.

12. Carman to H.D.C. Lee, September 29, 1911 (Edith and Lorne Pierce Collection of Canadian Manuscripts, Queen's University).

13. In George Woodcock, ed., *Colony and Confederation: Early Canadian Poets and Their Background* (Vancouver: University of British Columbia Press, 1974), pp. 189–210.

14. John Robert Sorfleet, ed., with an Introduction and Notes, *The Poems of Bliss Carman* (Toronto: McClelland and Stewart, 1976). 169 pp.

15. See, for example, Terry Whalen's *Bliss Carman* in the "Canadian Writers and Their Works" series (Downsview, Ont.: ECW Press, 1983).

Carman as Critic

TERRY WHALEN

> . . . *I perceive that if criticism does not bring compensation to the critic,*
> *a mental stimulus, a satisfaction and a joy, it is indeed the sorriest of trades.*
> (BLISS CARMAN, *"The Modern Athenian," May 8, 1897*)[1]

In an 1899 column titled "Marginal Notes: Criticism and Construction," Bliss Carman half-humorously said that "If all our busy, well-meaning critical babble could be blotted out for a single decade, the benefit to art would be incredible" (n.p.), and some critics have assessed Carman's own criticism as itself little more than "well-meaning . . . babble." Donald Stephens, in *Bliss Carman* (1966), views Carman's criticism this way, and Louis Dudek sees the limitation as a national one, saying, "Canadian novelists and poets don't often write serious criticism. The books of Bliss Carman on the nature of poetry are deplorable—self-indulgent, vague, and maudlin-mystical" (182). With these two assessments in mind, and also with the "reappraisal" spirit of the present volume in view, I intend to relate the basis of my higher regard for Carman's criticism, and my judgement that some of it is a pleasure to read.

While the usual assumption is that we have a fair representation of Carman's criticism in his books of prose, *The Kinship of Nature* (1903), *The Friendship of Art* (1904), *The Poetry of Life* (1905) and *The Making of Personality* (1906), I think these books do not really represent his critical skills at their best, especially his critical reviewing skills—and they contain very few of the many more durable literary commentaries he wrote over a period of two decades for close to two dozen newspaper and periodical publications.[2] His columns for the *Commercial Advertiser*, titled "Marginal Notes," and those he wrote for the *Boston Evening Transcript*, usually titled "The Modern Athenian," contain some of his best critical journalism, and while the four books of prose do contain a number of literary-critical pieces—and for my taste *The Poetry of Life* is the best of

62

them because of this—they are essentially repositories for Carman's more powdery essays on how average citizens might refine their sensibilities without getting weighted down with thoughts too heavy to handle.

If some of Carman's collected prose pieces are given to a hyper-solemn tone about their purposes, a spitting response to their limitations as journalism still seems to me to be beside the point. As readers of Terry Eagleton's *The Function of Criticism* (1984) can appreciate, the history of literary criticism is one in which late nineteenth-century critics were awkwardly torn between the conflicting roles of literary "sage" and literary "hack" (60), and this meant they had to do their best in the midst of a hurried journalistic world. As Carman put it in "The Modern Athenian: A Note on Style,"

> The beauty of style is like the beauty of nature, achieved through infinite care of results, with infinite carelessness of time. The successes of journalism are achieved through infinite care of time, with infinite carelessness of the manner in which results are expressed. (n.p.)

Carman knew the perils of the literary trade, and in individual instances he managed to overcome them and produce more well-crafted and careful results than the formula above might suggest. "Criticism achieved security by committing political suicide; its moment of academic institutionalization is also the moment of its effective demise as a socially active force" (65), says Eagleton, and at least Carman had a kick at the can. Nonetheless, it is still my claim that Carman's most interesting critical writing is the uncollected material written in the period from approximately 1890 to 1905—and it is almost entirely on British and American writers.[3]

Carman in his best criticism is an amiable writer who values love, peace and goodwill to others, so in some of his reviews he appears to lack that cringe-inspiring, authoritarian forcefulness of will that is sometimes mistakenly assumed to be the mark of a first-rate critical mind; but he could be sharp, discriminating, steady in his judgments, and his even-tempered stance is one he thought out quite carefully, as a few quotes from his literary columns will show. Like the currently fashionable M. M. Bakhtin, he had nothing but contempt for what Bakhtin has called the "authoritarian word in general, with its indisputability, unconditionality, and unequivocality. . . . This is the word that retards and freezes thought" (133)—or, as Carman would have it, in "Marginal Notes: On Criticism II," in "matters of art there can be no constituted body of authority, with power to approve or disapprove. And it is not desirable that there should be" (n.p.). More elaborately, in a column titled "The Artist and His Critic," he states his view of the ideal critical posture this way:

> [The critic] will not allow himself to be clever at the expense of truth nor jocose at the expense of tolerance. He will be a very different person from the average American reviewer. . . . He will never lose his temper; he will neither bark nor gobble; for he will be constantly aware of the greatness of truth and how it must prevail in the end. He will hold his doctrines lovingly but lightly, ready to change them with a moment's notice on the bidding of conviction. He will have a generous hospitable mind, delighting to entertain strange new thoughts—even though they may be only vagrants. He will seldom mistrust his own impressions; he will keep his sensitiveness too bright and alert for that. He will almost always mistrust his own judgements, particularly when he finds himself thinking they are final. (n.p.)

He disliked barking dogs and gobbling turkeys, perhaps because he had been bitten and gobbled at himself, but he was always trying to define the virtues of creative humility anyway,[4] and it shows up here and elsewhere in his critical writing as a very likable and flexible self-scepticism. In "The Artist and His Public," he quips, "There are really only two people who can speak with cocksureness in matters of aesthetics —the genius and the ignoramus; and the chances are that we none of us belong in the former category" (n.p.). We can all think of at least a dozen imperial critics who would disagree.

For Carman, intelligent modesty is the first requirement in the critic, and it is for this reason that he holds up G. K. Chesterton as a model of how "'not to do it.'" In Carman's review of Chesterton's *Robert Browning*, he says,

> Mr. Chesterton delights in taking liberties with men and manners, with letters and logic. With all the exuberant confidence of youth, nothing pleases him better than to take a fall out of any one. That seems to be his idea of criticism. He must be unusual at any cost, not for the sake of novelty of phrase, but rather for the titillation that comes with paradox. Hesitation is unknown to him, omniscience itself could hardly be more prompt and sure in its opinions. (303)

Carman disliked what he called in "The Modern Athenian" (February 13, 1897) the "Corinthian style, the style whose aim is 'to prevail, to be admired, and to triumph' . . . it is a style very typical of our great metropolitan journalism" (n.p.). It is also a style he attacked in another version of that column (November 14, 1896) as the "too frequent 'slangwhanging' '' (n.p.) of the newspaper and magazine world, and in "Marginal Notes: On Criticism II," as "the censorious, the patronizing, the furtively malicious, the acrid, the snarling, the insulting, the brutal" (n.p.). He disliked criticism as the pursuit of power, described it in "Marginal Notes: The Provincial Note in Art" as "the afterthought of spirit" (n.p.), and he saw its first duty as the sifting out of the good.

In his poetry Carman sometimes appears too good, too gentle for this world; and his comments on the ideal temperament of the good critic might make him appear to be too nice for the rigours of discrimination and judgement. But this is not really the case; he was highly conscious of his taste or preference for positive, mystical, buoyant, edifying literature—and he could be quite rigorously analytical of his reasons for not liking the literature of defeatism or any literature of any hue which was, in his view, poorly written. It is nice to be nice, but critics also have to be candid and argue for what they believe in; examples of his wit and candour as a reviewer and critic are many, but I will cite especially his entropic comments in a November 1894 issue of the *Chap-Book*, in which he reviews Francis Thompson's first book of poems. He says of Thompson,

> The immediate phrase and the memorable cadence are alike beyond him. He is no little wooden Wordsworth; to read him is like chewing sand. (5)

And:

> Imagination he certainly has, as several of his lines attest, flaring and undoubted; but it is an imagination uncouth and unschooled. It has never had its hair cut. He cannot depend upon it. (5)

And finally:

> No, I cannot feel that Mr. Thompson has yet written a single poem, I can only feel that he has allowed himself to put forth a premature volume of execrable verse, blotched here and there with an untutored though genuine fancy. (8)

Yet Carman never disparaged a contemporary simply because he thought it would play well with those he wished to influence, and he almost always found some minor value—sincerity, for example—in writers he otherwise disliked.

He treated the major writers of the past with the same strict standards he applied to his contemporaries. He commonly stressed, even in his early years, a unitrinian requirement that poetry should embody feeling, thinking and sensuality in a healthy equipoise, and he often upbraided established literary figures for their excesses or limitations in this regard. Carman, that is to say, was unintimidated by the canonical figures, the great tradition writers, and he constantly held to his claim, expressed in "The Modern Athenian" (October 10, 1896), that "madness, idiocy and debauchery [are] the three diseases of the mind" (n.p.). In the same context he would proclaim that "to abound in emotional and sensuous traits and to be lacking at the same time in mental qualifications is to exhibit the taint of idiocy" (n.p.). It is for this reason that he sees limitations in the work of, among many others, Henry Wadsworth Longfellow, Ralph Waldo Emerson, Alfred Lord Tennyson and William Wordsworth.[5] Of Wordsworth, for example, he says (in "The Modern Athenian," October 10, 1896):

> You will grant me, he is a great poet. He is so by virtue of a small and very excellent body of work left to us. But with him his excellence was very rare, so rare that you may almost say it was evidence of divine inspiration. So very occasional were his excursions beyond the jingle of imbecility. (n.p.)

For Carman, ". . . it takes something besides sanity and wholesomeness to make art of the very first order, to make a poem of the very first order. It takes thought" (n.p.). In Ezra Pound's lingo, poetry must also be intelligent. (In January of 1910, by the way, Pound, as quoted by Noel Stock in *The Life of Ezra Pound* [1970], suggested that "Bliss Carman was about the only living American poet who 'would not improve by drowning' " [225].[6]) Carman was suspicious of art that was merely emotional and he was simultaneously aware of the destructive nature of fixed ideas in poetry. He much admired the work of Thomas Hardy, for instance, but he thought him governed by an intolerant determinism, just as he felt John Davidson's aesthetic sense was injured by social ideology, and Rudyard Kipling's by what he names in a November 28, 1896, column of "The Modern Athenian" a "moth-eaten" theology (n.p.).[7] His entire canon of criticism is tissued throughout by his careful attempts to adjust his judgements to the legitimate claims of the intellect, and to measure carefully its foibles and pitfalls.

For Carman, all manifestations of intellect that are ignorant of the wonder of life—and of the struggles and needs of others—lack an essential generosity of spirit and are therefore morally limited. His instincts told him that wit and irony are often despoilers of gladness and wonder, and he knew—as did Wordsworth, as did D. H. Lawrence— that a coldly cerebral glance at life is narrow and self-defeating. He claimed that Adam and Eve left the Garden of Eden with a twin affliction—the sense of shame and a knowledge of irony. In his "The Modern Athenian" (October 10, 1896) column, he says,

> Evil is the irony of the universe, the giant sarcasm of existence, the titanic gibe in the teeth of good. It was when Eve tasted the apple that she first saw the point of the joke. And when she was forced to sew fig leaves together, she did not know whether to laugh or cry. Before the catastrophe neither laughter nor tears had been heard in Eden, but humor and shame were the two shadows that followed the man and woman out of the Garden . . . you might say that art, in its highest ambition, would attempt to lead us back into the Garden, leaving our shadows behind us. (n.p.)

Art is at its highest level *anti*-ironical for Carman, since he felt that humour is at its best an equivocal compensation. Irony gave him the existential fantods, so to speak, and at the reading lamp level he very much preferred the traditional goodwill and healthy wit and humour of his friend James Whitcomb Riley to the more cynical, puncturing irony of modernists. He was to say of Riley (in *James Whitcomb Riley*) that, "With all of his breadth of humor and appreciation of rustic wit, he never acquired any of the cynicism and effrontery that so often characterize so called men of the world" (20). In "Riley Just As He Is," he was also to say:

> [Riley] has nothing of the recent spirit of skeptical mockery, which likes to indulge its brilliancy in endless epigrams and facetious flippancies, and holds nothing too sacred for its acrid jest. . . . He has not imbibed the acid of modern thought, and feels no call to doubt the excellence of the word or the validity of old-fashioned notions. . . . His poetry has no trace of the incredulity and unrest which form so large a part in the thinking and feeling of many men today. . . . His humor is sheer gladness and exuberance of spirit. Irony and satire have little part in his genial nature. (n.p.)

Such comments might make Carman appear light-minded to those readers still mired in modernism who adhere to a singular view of twentieth-century literary history. But his words grow, in fact, out of considered thinking about the limitations of the ironic persona.

As a transitional figure, a nostalgic modern, Carman had the unco-operative perspicacity to see that cerebral humour is narrow, and often limited by what Geoffrey Thurley (in *The Ironic Harvest* [1974]) has called "the sclerosis of irony" (191), a hardening of the heart and mind which reduces the poet to *manqué*-artist, one who can express little more than the sterility of self-hatred and despair. It is for this reason that he would say in a *Toronto Star* interview (November 5, 1923) that he much prefers the "ancient sweetness of Sappho" to the "nitric acid of Ezra Pound or the nitro glycerine of T. S. Eliot" (18). He seems always to have been aware of the way in which being too smart for one's own good is just another form of spiritual imbalance. As he grew older, Carman certainly became more concerned with the demands of the intellect, and he became more philosophical—but he was always aware of the dampening, diminishing effects of intellectual severity. In this regard he anticipated later, revisionist literary historians (like Thurley, like Wayne C. Booth) who would in more detail—and with the advantage of hindsight—note the thinness and conventionality of the ironic harvest in twentieth-century literature.[8] Carman contributed to both the production of and the criticism of modern literature, and it is a contribution which is in constant discussion with the new.

In "The Beginnings of the Modern Movement in America," chapter six of his *A History of Modern Poetry* (1976), David Perkins credits Carman for his contribution to the decline of what he calls (after George Santayana) "The Genteel Tradition" (101) in American poetry, seeing him as a precursor of more avant-garde literary impulses, more modern ones. Speaking of the poetry written during the period of 1890 to 1912, Perkins notes:

> The Genteel Tradition was obviously prevalent, but opposition movements were strong. If the former monopolized prestige, the latter aroused more interest and hope. Markham, Hovey, and the Canadian Carman were read far more eagerly than their genteel contemporaries, for they conveyed a greater reality and zest. They illustrate the degree of rebellion for which publishers and an audience could then be found. (101)

Carman was not only considered by Louis Untermeyer—as late as 1919—a poet "with a buoyancy, new to American literature," one who was "frankly pagan as contrasted to the moralizing tributes of many of his predecessors" (130), but he wrote many literary commentaries that advocated the work of Hovey, and other poets of pagan crispness who had gone past the confines of "The Genteel Tradition."[9] And as co-editor, with Richard Hovey, of the *Chap-Book* from 1894 to 1897 he was responsible for the publication of works by as various a group of writers as Hamlin Garland, Henry James, Theodore Wratislaw, Edmund Gosse, Louise Imogen Guiney, Stéphane Mallarmé, John Burroughs, Kenneth Grahame, John Davidson, Max Beerbohm, H. G. Wells and Stephen Crane, to mention only a few. As a transitional modern, Carman participated in the literary currents and discussions of his day.

Another measure of his transitional identity is his engagement with the challenge of George Santayana's views on art and religion. It was through his knowledge of Santayana's works that he was able to move yet further past a simple taste for twilight romanticism and into the somewhat colder light of a modern thoughtfulness. Speaking of Santayana's place as a transitional figure between traditional, antique and more modern modes of art and thought, Perkins suggests in *A History of Modern Poetry*:

> [The Genteel Tradition] became one of the great, valued roads always open to the human spirit. In this prestidigitation no one was more adroit than Santayana, who would argue that there is, after all, no compelling reason why a poetry or a philosophy must express the life either of the author or of whatever time and place it happened to be composed in. If Santayana was in some moods a materialist and a naturalist, in other moods he was more a Platonist and pursuer of unchanging essences. And so he could say that one's allegiances are spiritual and ideal and that one should live in eternity. Although he was the most penetrating of the many critics of the Genteel Tradition, Santayana was also, in some respects, its greatest exponent, both as a philosopher and as a poet. In him the Genteel attitude purged itself of most of its timidity and soft-headedness, which he brilliantly satirized, and presented a permanent intellectual challenge to the self-consciously American and Modernist movements that were soon to dominate poetry in the United States. (103)

Philosophical influences on Carman's aesthetic definitely included the work of George Santayana, and of Josiah Royce, both of whom he was taught by at Harvard University in the years 1886–1888. In the work of both philosophers—and particularly in Santayana's *Poetry and Religion* (1900)—Carman was to find a stress on the value of reason in matters of art and religion which encouraged him in his organic view of art as at its best the embodiment of an expansiveness of thought, particularly as it relates to matters of religion and poetry. It was primarily because Carman agreed with Santayana that he had strong reservations about Leo Tolstoy's views on art and religion;[10] and it was definitely

Santayana he had in mind when he wrote, in "Marginal Notes: Scribes and Pharisees," that:

> Opposed to Scribes and Pharisees, you may have not only the great and faithful few, the masters and sustainers of the spiritual life, the seers and prophets, but the loving skeptics as well. There is more virtue in a devout agnosticism than in most of our smug professional churchianity (as it has been well named). And if we cannot be intense and fiery upholders of righteousness, let us be gentle free believers. The large, slow smiling certitude of indifference,—I fancy there may be much salvation there, particularly for our feverish modern mercurial selves. (n.p.)

Santayana's example encouraged Carman to differentiate between religion as the pulpit-trafficking in bourgeois fictions of transcendence, and the more rugged requirements of an honest spiritual life. He valued the intellectual authenticity of Santayana, and valued him the more because, in addition to the "materialist and naturalist" moods in Santayana, he also found in his work the "Platonist and pursuer of unchanging essences" of which Perkins speaks. To Carman, Santayana was an explorative pessimist who sought after spiritual sanity in something more durable than either "churchianity" on the one hand or nihilism on the other.

In a review of Santayana's *Poetry and Religion* in "Marginal Notes: Poetry and Religion," Carman was to say of Santayana:

> He is eminently the advocate of sanity, of severe thought, of intelligence; and the critic of all those misty semi-emotional creeds which are ever lacking in followers.
>
> Considering the sort of critical writing we are accustomed to in current literature, the inane and false and hurried judgements that prevail on every hand, one must admit that a good deal of Mr. Santayana's book will be profoundly novel; to the few who care for the stability of logic and truth, however, it will be a welcome discovery to be treasured with the *Essays in Criticism* and *Religious Aspects of Philosophy*. (n.p.)

Anyone who doubts the dialogic relationship between these two writers should take a look at Carman's copy of Santayana's *The Life of Reason* (1905), in which almost a third of the book's contents are underlined and discussed in its margins; on the inside blank page is a quote, written in Carman's handwriting, from page 24 of the book, which reads, "The hunger for facile wisdom is the root of all false philosophy.''[11] Carman worried constantly that his early poetry was facile because unintellectual and, while he felt that it was the duty of the poet to be joyful, to be glad, he lived in a context at the turn of the century in which many of his contemporaries viewed life as more of a sarcastic joke than as grounds for joy; but he was ultimately to come to terms with his new intellectual scepticism, for the most part, and his literary criticism was to embody that process.

Ironically, while Carman felt that he had gone past "facile wisdom," had found mental maturity by way of his discovery of the demands of reason, many commentators—most recently, Malcolm Ross —have assessed that his new regard for "the stability of logic," combined with the influence of Delsarte and Mary Perry King, pretty much ruined his poetry after 1905. As Ross stated in 1985, "Carman's almost desperate effort to clamp thought on sensibility" (28) cost him in his poetry "most of his magic and much of his music" (29). But this struggle with thought is the edge that sharpens and focuses much of his best literary criticism, and informs it with a searching curiosity he otherwise wouldn't have had. At least that much of a compensation comes into play.

All of the above notwithstanding, he always managed to sustain his essentially pragmatic conviction that artists should keep the happiness of their audience in mind. His tendency was consistently to praise writers who sustained an alertness to beauty, and he sometimes excitedly endorsed those writers particularly who managed to show an affirming existential faith in spite of their knowledge of competing reasons for despair. As he matured, he widened the scope of his literary taste because he wished to find reconfirmation of his life-faith in the writing of his contemporaries, and this required that he find new terms for his likes and dislikes. He began to value all contemporary writing which, to borrow a phrase from Eliot, managed "to keep our metaphysics warm" (56). In his commentaries on Emily Dickinson, Stephen Crane, Maurice Maeterlinck and William Butler Yeats, among others, he focused on the religious feeling in their writing, and found it to be different from, but still related to, the metaphysical warmth he felt when he had read the older writers who had engaged his attention in his youth.

Carman had a high regard for Yeats's literary criticism because he could see in Yeats a toughness of intelligence and, simultaneously, a fine artistic sense of the need to go past the merely intellectual. In "The Modern Athenian: A Note on Style," written in 1896, he uses Yeats's essays on Blake as a thinking point around which he can focus his own hunger for a literature of religious feeling:

> Now Mr. Yeats closes the first of his papers with a very wise sentence. After remarking that "the errors in the handiwork of exalted

spirits are as the more fantastical errors of their lives," he adds, "he who half lives in eternity endures a rending of the structures of the mind, a crucifixion of the intellectual body." That is very true. And so it was of Blake: he "half lived in eternity." His work had imagination and fervor. It had the traits of great intelligence and great spirituality. (n.p.)

Carman was sometimes a severe critic of modern literature—he disliked its imagination of disaster, its pessimism and despair. He considered Henrik Ibsen, for instance, a thoroughly unhealthy man; he upbraided Hardy for his modern gloom in spite of liking him; and we have already considered his brief comments on Eliot and Pound.[12] Interestingly, though, he had his own moments of existential doubt in poems such as "Windflower" and "The Eavesdropper"—such poems threaten to unwrite virtually *all* of his many other poems of fragile elation—so he was always, as a reviewer, on the lookout for contemporary writing that might keep a sense of the eternal alive. For Carman, all writers who half-lived in eternity were potential harbingers of existential good news. Yeats helped him think about this in some detail.

He was always an uneasy pragmatist, so he constantly guarded and reasserted the refreshing value of Robert Browning's optimism and the natural good health of Walt Whitman—and he valued in Emerson what he called in *Progress* "The exhilaration, the confident spirit—this is the great boon of transcendentalism as the Concord teacher gives it to us" (n.p.). He was a nervous pragmatist primarily because his increasing scepticism made him aware that optimism was facile unless sobered by an awareness of its opposite, and feckless unless one had at least stepped up to the abyss. In a letter to H.D.C. Lee in January of 1912 (see Gundy, *Letters of Bliss Carman*), he stated the terms of his own optimism:

I inherited the ancient traditions to the full, and I am sure their influence was wholesome and benign; yet I could not accept them without scepticism. They all had to be broken up, discarded, and made over, before I could be happy. That was a long, hard process. A student and devotee of Matthew Arnold could not remain easily optimistic; and a lover of Emerson could not remain in pessimism. So, here we are! An optimist with James and Royce. (193)[13]

This willingness to allow his predilections to be "broken up, discarded, and made over" informs the best of Carman's reviews, and it is the explorative edge that makes the more readable his critical writing during his most prodigious years as a critic, the years 1895–1905. These are the years during which he was to write about the value of the Symbolist movement in literature, and about the strengths and limitations of literary realism. The Symbolist movement pleased him because he saw in it a depth in its attention to beauty and a wisdom in its metaphysical impulses—and he was loudly to praise its manifestation anywhere he found it in the art of his contemporaries.

Carman had some reservations about literary realism, but when it came to the poetry and fiction of Stephen Crane he felt that Crane's particular, inspired brand of realism was interesting and valuable, for he could see in Crane's work that he, too, "half lived in eternity" and the suggestive indefiniteness (the term is Edgar Allan Poe's) of his symbolism was the register in his works which embodied that awareness. Crane might be an existentially disgruntled writer, but he did keep his metaphysics warm. In a comment on Crane's *The Open Boat* (in "Marginal Notes: The Higher Journalism") he says:

> I confess it seemed to me a surprising masterpiece in its way; faithful, picturesque, realistic to a degree, and yet at the same time something more than all this. . . . there was one peculiarity that struck me—a sort of transcendent realism, realism used to become no longer incidental and particular, but typical and universal. (n.p.)

Carman compares Crane's dialogue with that of Maeterlinck's plays, saying:

> In each case the writer's object is to create an atmosphere, to make a powerful spiritual impression: and he has resorted to the weird haunting effect which repetition imposes on the mind. (n.p.)

And finally,

> The word of a mystical symbolistic writer might stand for the aim of the realist at his best . . . [Crane] has been a faithful contributor to the Higher Journalism, but he has also made a brilliant mark in the more exacting pages of literature. (n.p.)

Carman became quite animated in his literary columns when he began to perceive that the writing of his age, though preoccupied with the issues of literary realism, was also sustaining, through the Symbolist impulse, an affinity with Romantic and Transcendentalist concerns. When he reviewed, in 1896, an edition of Emily Dickinson's poetry in "The Modern Athenian: A Note on Emily Dickinson," he called her "A symbolist of the symbolists, she is a reviver and establisher of the religious sentiment" (n.p.), and he would go on to appreciate her healthy, whimsical humour as well. On the evidence of the work of Crane, Yeats, Dickinson and Maeterlinck particularly, he was to recognize that, social realism notwithstanding, poetry at the end of the nineteenth century was seeking, in words he borrowed from Yeats (see "Marginal Notes," September 3, 1898), "to create a sacred book" (n.p.). He added: "To create a sacred book is not only the ambition of art and letters today; it has been the true function of art and poetry in the whole history of the world" (n.p.). Carman was to write a series of more analytical commentaries on the Symbolist movement, and the warmth of its metaphysics became for him a sign that not all of modern writing was chilled by a terminal *angst*.

Symbolist writing came to represent for Carman a necessary broadening of religious feeling past the confines of "churchianity," a broadening that he had already witnessed in a more straightforward manner in the works of the great mystical writers of the past. In an August 14, 1897, version of his "The Modern Athenian" column he said of "all the symbolists" that they were "contributors" to "the larger religious feeling of the future" (n.p.). In "A Poet in Color" he was to conclude that "the spell of beauty is still beyond analysis" (n.p.), and he felt that this was particularly true of Symbolist writing. In its suggestion of other-worldly essences, and in its intelligent strategy of going past the intellect towards a sense of mystery, it gave Carman hope that all he treasured in the literature of the past would survive, hybrid-fashion, "broken up, discarded, and made over" in the modern tradition.

Yet he feared that its seriousness, its worth, its re-created existential message would *not* survive, would not be heard, given the unimaginative, anti-intellectual, materialistic and monopolistic social conditions he observed in the United States at the turn of the century. Many of his literary columns register a sense of crisis as they record the removal of the arts to the margins of society. He blamed the corruption of American culture on the veniality of its politicians, the monopolistic tenor of its industry, and the complacency of its bourgeoisie. In 1905, in "The Purpose of Poetry," he states his view from the margins:

> It may seem at a superficial glance that the arts are all very well as a pastime, for the employment of the few, but can have no imperative call upon busy men and women in active modern life. And if the average American should be told that in his country there was no widespread love of beauty, no popular taste in artistic matters, he would not, I believe, take the accusation very much to heart. He would probably admit it, and with pride point to the wonderful material success, the achievements in the realm of trade and commerce, the unmatched prosperity and wealth. But that answer will not do.

> You may lead me through the streets of the great cities, and fill my
> ears with stories of uncounted millions of money, unrivaled advance
> among the nations; but that will not divert my soul from horror at
> the state of society, where municipal government is a venial farce,
> where there is little reverence for law, where Mammon is a real God,
> and where every week there are instances of mob violence, as revolting
> as any that ever stained the history of the Emperors of degenerate
> Rome. The soul is not deceived. She sits at the centre of being,
> judging severely this violence, this folly and crime. (287)

In "Marginal Notes" (October 1, 1898) Carman suggests that informed
readers will have to get used to the "idea of a multiplicity of selves"
(n.p.), given the findings of psychology—and it is the man who authored
the above, the more ideological Carman, who is perhaps the least known
of the many, multiple selves that go to make up his total contribution
to writing. It is a sometimes moralistic, enraged self, but it is a surprising one, and implicitly it tends to diminish the critical fabrication that
he was disengaged, aloof, a quietist on the social-political issues of his day.

Carman, that is to say, seems to have been very much aware
of the American social, ideological environment; he viewed literature
as having a social function, not only as the embodiment of religious feeling and as a model for personal harmony, but also as the custodian of
the conscience of a people and as an agent of social reform. While he
is still often portrayed as a somewhat oblivious, literary fool-saint, his
attempts to connect literature to society were many, and he sometimes
showed up at the writerly, political barricades when he felt it was morally
imperative that he speak out.

He quite often lectured, even hectored, Americans for their slav-
ishness to inept politicians and to their myths of imperial and moral
superiority. He once cited the Japanese way of life as an implicit criticism
of the American,[14] and in "Marginal Notes" (September 10, 1898) he
saw the barbarism of American imperialist attacks on Cuba as outra-
geously possible only in a nation where political power was hegemonic,
consolidated at the very top. He saw 1898 as the year "the States were
infected with the Bacilus Imperialis" (n.p.), and he placed the blame
on the systemic absurdity of American government:

> . . . one thing is certain: as an executive machine the American form
> of government is a lamentable failure. That it should be cumbrous
> and rigid is bad enough in times of pace [sic] when its corruption
> and incompetence are less in evidence. In times of need its imper-
> viousness to public sentiment and the stings of national conscience
> becomes awfully manifest.

Think of your conduct of the Cuban war, your pestilent transports, your fever-haunted camps. It is disgraceful enough that your
troops should suffer in the stages of preparation; that they should
be perishing now by fever and famine simply through the stupidity
of your paid officials is a shame to you forever. (n.p.)

There is enough Yank-bashing in Carman to warm the cockles of almost
any Canadian nationalist's heart, and much of it, like that contained
in the above, is on the level of anger.[15] But Carman was analytical as
well, making comments that go swiftly to the heart of familiar American
political realities. Further on in the same column he claims that England
provides an example of real, as opposed to ostensible, democracy, and
asks:

How long, you American people, do you think a British Minister
could retain his control of power while ship after ship of dying soldiers
came into Liverpool from a foreign war, while battalion after battalion
was dumped in a malarial swamp sick, wounded, fever-stricken, to
sleep on the naked earth, to feed on ship's biscuit and drink its own
drainage?
Not twenty-four hours. (n.p.)

When accounting for the abuse of power in the United States, he charges
that it is only possible because

[T]he United States is not governed by the American people. You
think you govern yourselves, but you see you do not. In a crisis you
are powerless. You have resigned your freedom to your chosen officers
for a term of years. Your Constitution is an inferior one. It pretends
to safeguard your liberties: in reality it commits you without redress
to the greed of the partizan and the bungling of the demagogue. (n.p.)

It gets worse—and could even be read as unconsciously humorous were
it not for the co-presence of a genuine moral rage:

Listen to me. The first time you see your flag with its honorable
stripes lolling in the wind, look at it well. Its stars are sullied, its
stripes are stained. All the winds of heaven can never blow it clean
of the mould of those Cuban transports and the germs of those miser-
able camps. Go to Washington and ask your grocery-store government what is the matter with "Old Glory." Perhaps you had better
get a new flag.
And the first time you have a silver half dollar in your hand,

look at it well. Whose image and superscription are there? What comely features are these? Liberty. Well, your liberty is a courtesan. You have sold her to the bosses. Your *Res Publica* is a public thing. And the superscription, "In God we trust." Well, my friends, I can tell you one thing. God won't save you from the politicians. You will have to save yourselves. Perhaps you had better get a new emblem for your coinage. A typical boss's head would be appropriate—the familiar features of your President's manager, or one of the leaders of Greater New York's municipal factions. These ornaments of the rogues' gallery are your true lords and masters. (n.p.)

Quite a number of Carman's political commentaries are vitiated by his righteous, liberal-cum-leftist social indignation—they have almost a self-parodying effect as a result of their earnest diction. But they are evidence of his social involvement.

By the turn of the century, Carman came to realize that American society was losing the conditions that would make it possible for bottom-dog citizens to become fully human, to fulfill their physical and spiritual needs. This annoyed the impressively proto-hippie side of Carman, and rather than settle for simply writing his essays on spiritual improvement and personal mental hygiene, he chose also to write about the causes of social wrongs. In "Marginal Notes: The Rights of Labor," he defends a controversial miners' strike and says that "the present strike, for all its wastefulness is productive of one priceless good; it has shown people the absurdity and moral wrong in private ownership of natural mono-polies" (n.p.), and he concludes with, "Until we reach a grade of intel-ligence and honesty the more strikes we have the better" (n.p.). Gentle but not aloofly genteel, he was unafraid of taking on the American economic establishment.

In "Marginal Notes: The Soul of Socialism," he sees socialism as "after all only an ingenious device for putting in practice the generous impulses of the human heart" (n.p.). He liked sanctioning progressive movements by dipping them in traditional waters, and he therefore claimed that Christianity was (or should be) the soul of socialism, and he named the constitution of the United States a "socialistic document" (n.p.). He craftily advocated the women's liberation movement (in "Physical Freedom for Women") in part by casting it as a way of increas-ing "women's helpfulness" (n.p.). That hook to his audience makes it possible for him to get away with comments such as,

So it happens that woman's genius is not only deeper, more mystical, more impassioned and religious than man's, but is at the same time more actual, more sentient, and less irrelevant. (n.p.)

And:

> The whole question of personal or physical emancipation for women
> on equal terms with men would seem to be logically prior to their
> social and political equality; and failure to make use of the one would
> seem fundamentally to delay the realization of the other. (n.p.)

Some feminists might disagree with his typification of the sexes, but there
is no doubt that his views on women were far in advance of the prevailing
paradigms of his day. It is the centrality of Carman's concern for the
lives of all individuals, his natural sense that their potential should be
respected, that makes his social writing such a pleasure to read.

All of Carman's social-political writing is governed by a desire
that every individual be given the opportunity to live a life which is fully
human, and he came to think that progress on this front was not possible
in America unless its economic structures were dismantled. While literature could embody the suggestions of that fullness, it was doomed to
remain at the margins unless there were suitable social conditions in
which it could be read. In "Marginal Notes: Subsidized Art," he said:

> . . . we shall never have any general national sense of the beautiful,
> any widespread feeling for art, any universal appreciation of the best
> things in literature until we rectify our miserable slave-making indus-
> trial conditions. (n.p.)

If social realism in literature made Carman nervous because of its proxi-
mity to journalism and its occasional neglect of aesthetic standards, he
nevertheless shared with realists such as Frank Norris a recognition that
the capitalistic philosophy of greed was threatening to undermine any
possibility of a socially responsible modern world. In his generally positive review of Norris's *The Octopus* (1901) in his "Marginal Notes: Two
Books," he appreciates the "rude strength" (n.p.) of that novel and
agrees with Norris that "in our life of to-day there are intolerable wrongs"
(n.p.), and says, "It is one of the great glories of art that it can accomplish easily what the preacher, for all of his lungs, cannot compass."
He could respond to Norris's analysis:

> Mr. Norris has written a powerful, almost unanswerable, exposition
> of the evil of a great monopoly. . . . I am sure we need just such
> expositions of the iniquity of things as they are. . . . The reader can-
> not help deducing from every page the truth that existing conditions
> are iniquitous. (n.p.)

And the fact that Norris had a co-present appreciation for beauty made the novel the more palatable for Carman. He did not like the way Norris blamed some of society's ills on nature, and he tired a bit of the novel's ponderousness—"It is clayfooted and does not hurry to its climax as a godlike piece of art should" (n.p.)—but he saw it as a novel that enacted a strong sense of pity and justice and beauty, a compelling work of radical humanism.

Carman appreciated the literature of social conscience, and he did not think that the only function of literature was the pursuit of an escapist, mystical-sublime. At its best, his was an analytical, socially committed literary criticism, and in it he tried to respond to the anti-spiritual tendencies of his time. Ironically, he did so with a generosity of spirit that is both sharper and more capacious than that of many literary critics who have written about his own career.

M. L. Rosenthal once said that "If there is, in fact, one distinctively modern quality in literature, it lies in the centrifugal spin toward suicide of the speaking voice" (7), and there is no denying the connection between this paradigm and the empirical and spiritual history of modern times. In a related key, speaking in the middle of our century, the poet Roy Fuller says, "Anyone happy in this age and place / Is daft or corrupt" (151). But cynicism can bring with it its own forms of (often political) complacency, and there is still some worth in the suggestion Carman made in his "Defense of Poetry" that "There is only one thing more important than to be strenuous," and "that is to be glad." This is the view of a cheerful pessimist, not a facile optimist, and it shares in the commitment of a small number of other twentieth-century writers who have realized that, all reasons for scorn notwithstanding, it still remains one of the main functions of the writer to celebrate, to give praise to life. The criticism of Bliss Carman will always make good reading for anyone who is a recovering cynic.

NOTES

1.   My sources for most of the material cited in this paper are the Lorne Pierce Collection at the Queen's University Archives, which contains 117 items of Carman's prose, and the Rufus Hathaway Collection at the Harriet Irving Library, University of New Brunswick, which is distinguished, in terms of Carman's criticism, for its selected assortment of the *Chap-Book* issues, and for its housing of Carman's personal copy of Santayana's *The Life of Reason*. Many of the items I have quoted in this paper are taken from newspaper clippings that are available at the Queen's University Archives, and the condition of the originals is such that some of the bibliographical information (usually page numbers) is missing. I have used the notation "n.p." where page numbers are missing, and "n.v." where volume and/or number information is not available. I wish to thank

George Henderson and Helen Cobb at the Queen's University Archives, and
Olive Cameron at the Harriet Irving Library for their kind help when I visited
their archives in search of some of the materials that are referred to in this paper.
2. These publications include: the *Book News Monthly*; the *Bookman*; the *Boston
Evening Transcript*; the *Chap-Book*; the *Commercial Advertiser*; the *Criterion*; the *Critic*;
the *Forum*; the *Independent*; the *International Interpreter*; the *International Quarterly*; the
Literary World; *Literary Miscellany*; the *Los Angeles Times Magazine*; the *New York
Times*; the *New York Times Review of Books*; the *New York Sunday World*; *Progress*;
Saturday Night; and *The World*.
3. Carman's commentaries on Canadian writers are very minor in comparison
to his other efforts, but examples of his writing on Canadians include:
"Contemporaries—V: Mr. Charles G. D. Roberts," in the *Chap-Book* 2.4 (1895):
163-71; "The Modern Athenian: XIX [on Joseph Sherman]," in the *Boston
Evening Transcript* (Dec. 19, 1896): n.p.; "Marginal Notes: A Forgotten Poet
[Isabella Valancy Crawford]," in the *Commercial Advertiser* (Feb. 11, 1899): n.p.;
"Marginal Notes: A Lover of Earth [Archibald Lampman]," in the *Commercial
Advertiser* (April 4, 1899): n.p.; and "Marginal Notes: A Canadian Lyrist
[Archibald Lampman]," in the *Commercial Advertiser* (Aug. 11, 1900): n.p.
4. See particularly his "Personality and Impersonality," in the *Forum* (June
1912): 642-48; and "Richard Hovey—My Friend," in the *Criterion* (n.d.): 11-13.
5. See his "Longfellow Through Modern Eyes," in the *Chap-Book* 8 (April
1898): 396-400, where he says of Longfellow that "His range was not wide, his
power was not varied, his insight was not deep; he had no passion and little force;
yet in spite of these incalculable defects, he had one of the chief traits of genius,
he had the charm of benignity, the serene composure of an untarnished mind"
(397). And in a comment which sounds like Carman having thoughts about his
own work, and his own context as a contributor to popular magazines, he says of
Longfellow, "He can never perfectly embody his new idea, never perfectly convey
it to his audience in all its freshness, since the only means of expression at his
command are conventional and already overworn. He must always compromise
between a freshness of expression which would completely satisfy himself, and
a triteness of expression which would completely satisfy his public. So that it
happens every artist, every poet, commands an audience whose size is directly in
proportion to this compromise" (397). Carman was very aware of the need to
make it new (the phrase is Ezra Pound's), but he knew from long experience that
many of the magazines he contributed to only wanted the same old stuff.
    For his comments on Emerson see especially his "Emerson," in the *Literary
World*, where he says of Emerson, "With him the main thing was not the creation
of a detached and finished mechanism in words embodying so much moral truth
or philosophic thought, but rather the expression of his convictions with the least
possible amount of reliance on language. He cared for his message more than his
medium" (120). And of Tennyson, he says, in "English and American Scholars
Celebrate Tennyson Centenary," that "He had none of Browning's sharp inquisi-
tiveness about the immediate drama of common life all around him, but found
himself rather a perplexed bystander in the confusion, aims, and crumbling beliefs
and new-sprung sciences of the nineteenth century" (n.p.).
    As most of the quotes in this note suggest, Carman tended to spend much
of his critical energy describing and measuring the kind of mind involved in the
works he discussed, but he was also very attentive to the artist's use of language.
Finally, part of his objection to Wordsworth was an objection to his language,
or use of speech, and in his "Marginal Notes: The Wind Among the Reeds,"
he compares Yeats's simplicity of language with the archness of Wordsworth's

diction, saying, "As a master of simplicity Mr. Yeats has no rival. In taking an every-day speech and making it a competent vehicle of poetic expression, he has succeeded where Wordsworth so often failed; partly, perhaps, because his Irish blood could not but save him from those grotesque banalities, those painful flatnesses of speech into which Wordsworth was betrayed by his lack of humor; and partly, indeed, through his Celtic instinct, the intuitive avoidance of those platitudinous vapidities to which the English mind is subject. It is their stubborn genius for platitude and cant that has made the English the slow, safe world-conquerors they are; and it is the Celtic abhorrence of these things that has given them their poetry" (n.p.).

6. For additional commentary of Pound's on Carman, see D.M.R. Bentley's "Preface: Minor Poets of a Superior Order," in *Canadian Poetry* 14 (Spring/ Summer 1984), where there are also interesting responses from Wallace Stevens recorded.

7. For commentary on John Davidson, see Carman's "Marginal Notes: John Davidson," where he says that "Mr. Davidson's genius is a curious blend of artist and revolutionary—of Tennyson and Morris. His devotion to beauty keeps him from being perfectly realistic; and his passion for humanity and the generalization of society keeps him from being thoroughly artistic. This is the dilemma of every artist, however, surrounded on every side with the tumult and distraction of modern life, so relentless and inscrutable . . ." (n.p.). For his views on Thomas Hardy, see "Marginal Notes: Poetry in the Provinces," in the *Commercial Advertiser* (Feb. 4, 1899): n.p.

8. I refer to Wayne C. Booth in this context primarily because I am thinking of his *A Rhetoric of Irony* (Chicago: University of Chicago Press, 1974), especially chapter nine ("Infinite Instabilities"), pp. 253-77. In *The Ironic Harvest*, Geoffrey Thurley claims that literary critics such as Eliot, I. A. Richards, F. R. Leavis and the New Critics have all overstated the virtues of the ironic persona, and they did so to the detriment of the scope of poetry in the modern world. Speaking of the "intellectualist critics" (36), he says that, "In fact, their greatest achievement was to rob poets of a sense of the importance of their task—of living the life of a poet in the sense which has been integral to Western poetry since Dante, if not earlier. They succeeded in making poets sceptical of a wide or exalted scale, in making them nervous of taking on the most important themes for fear of seeming portentous, above all in inhibiting the capacity for frank and full self-declaration which must in the last analysis form part of the poet's utterance. They destroyed the capacity for intense feeling by inculcating the fear of appearing naive: 'Am I being absurd? Am I deceiving myself? Do I really *feel* this?' These are the questions and doubts which are basically incompatible with the creation of 'the greatest kind of poetry'. This was the harvest of irony" (36-37).

For more relatedly Canadian revisionist literary history see: L. R. Early's *Archibald Lampman and His Works* (Downsview: ECW Press, 1983); my *Bliss Carman and His Works* (Downsview: ECW Press, 1983); and D.M.R. Bentley's "Remembering and Forgetting in Canadian Literature and Criticism," in *wh4t*, No. 4 (April/May 1986): 14-16.

9. The pagan poet he advocated the most was his friend, Richard Hovey. His criticism on Hovey includes the item listed in Note 4. See also, however, his "Contemporaries—IV: Louise Imogen Guiney," in the *Chap-Book* (Nov. 15, 1894): 29-36; and his commentaries on Richard Le Gallienne, "Marginal Notes: Young Lives," in the *Commercial Advertiser* (May 27, 1899): n.p., and "Marginal Notes: Two Books," in the *Commercial Advertiser* (June 22, 1901): n.p.

10.   For his views on Tolstoy see: "Marginal Notes: What is Art?," in the *Commercial Advertiser* (Aug. 13, 1898): n.p.; "Marginal Notes: Scribes and Pharisees," in the *Commercial Advertiser* (April 22, 1899): n.p.; "Marginal Notes: Poetry and Religion," in the *Commercial Advertiser* (April 28, 1900): n.p.; and "Marginal Notes: Tolstoi Once More," in the *Commercial Advertiser* (March 9, 1901): n.p.
11.   Carman's personal copy of *The Life of Reason* is available in the Rufus Hathaway Collection. Carman had also very thickly underlined the following words by Santayana, words which might have embarrassed him, given the eagerness of his own early mysticism: "The fanatic is, notwithstanding, nothing but a worldling too narrow and violent to understand the world, while the mystic is a sensualist too rapt and voluptuous to rationalise his sensations" (208).
12.   For his views on Hardy's pessimism see the item on Hardy cited in Note 7 above. His views on Ibsen are available in his *The Making of Personality* (1906; rpt. Boston: L. C. Page, 1908), pp. 55ff.
13.   Carman makes another reference to William James in his letters, when he writes to Irving Way, on July 24, 1911: "I don't read much except philosophy in the mountains. Just now, William James—*Will to Believe, and other essays*. He is a fine old faithful. And Royce is another. Royce, James, Santayana, three names that are Harvard's chief bid for immortality. America has probably given the world no finer piece of literature than *The Life of Reason*, no finer bit of thought than *The Spirit of Modern Philosophy*, and yet who ever hears of Santayana or Royce?" (Gundy, 185). It makes sense that Carman would respond favourably to James's pragmatic philosophy, and it might be that the continual references in his prose to the pursuit of happiness and the need for life-truths that can be related to human needs are further encouraged in his works by the example of James. The above is, however, about as explicit a reference to him as I can find.
14.   See, for example, his "Marginal Notes: Nomadie," in the *Commercial Advertiser* (Aug. 2, n.d.): n.p.
15.   In his *Chap-Book* article on Charles G. D. Roberts (see Note 3 above), he said of Roberts and his Canadian contemporaries, "The *ennui* of a closing age has not sapped their enthusiasm; the discouraging triumph of a corrupt plutocracy has not touched their country; and while they are cut off from the mental activity which underlies the scientific and socialistic philosophic speculation of London, they are also saved from the deadly blight of New York, that center of American letters, that gangrene of politics on the body of democracy. With their Loyalist traditions, their romantic history, their untold resource, their beautiful land, their vigorous climate, their future all to make, their days of immeasurable leisure, it is little wonder their songs should have all the genuine assurance of youth, the freshness of the fields" (169–70).

WORKS CITED

Bakhtin, M. M. "From Notes Made in 1970–71," in Caryl Emerson and Michael Holquist, eds., *M. M. Bakhtin: Speech Genre & Other Late Essays*. Trans. Vern W. McGee. Austen: University of Texas Press, 1986. 132–58.
Carman, Bliss. "The Modern Athenian," the *Commercial Advertiser* (May 8, 1897): n.p.
———. "Marginal Notes: Criticism and Construction," the *Commercial Advertiser* (March 4, 1899): n.p.

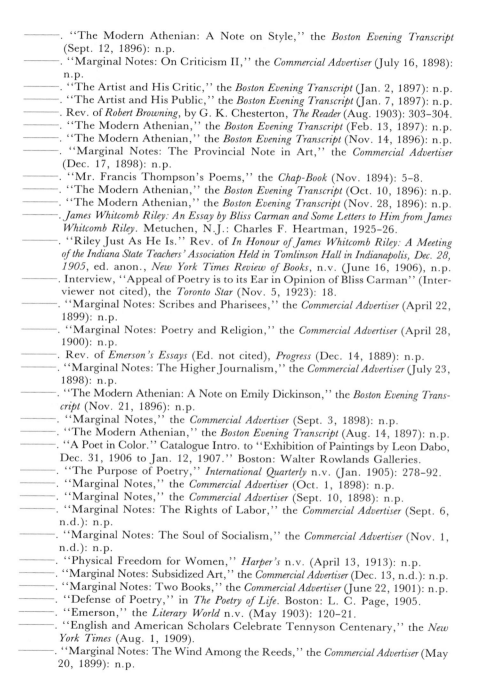

———. "The Modern Athenian: A Note on Style," the *Boston Evening Transcript* (Sept. 12, 1896): n.p.

———. "Marginal Notes: On Criticism II," the *Commercial Advertiser* (July 16, 1898): n.p.

———. "The Artist and His Critic," the *Boston Evening Transcript* (Jan. 2, 1897): n.p.

———. "The Artist and His Public," the *Boston Evening Transcript* (Jan. 7, 1897): n.p.

———. Rev. of *Robert Browning*, by G. K. Chesterton, *The Reader* (Aug. 1903): 303–304.

———. "The Modern Athenian," the *Boston Evening Transcript* (Feb. 13, 1897): n.p.

———. "The Modern Athenian," the *Boston Evening Transcript* (Nov. 14, 1896): n.p.

———. "Marginal Notes: The Provincial Note in Art," the *Commercial Advertiser* (Dec. 17, 1898): n.p.

———. "Mr. Francis Thompson's Poems," the *Chap-Book* (Nov. 1894): 5–8.

———. "The Modern Athenian," the *Boston Evening Transcript* (Oct. 10, 1896): n.p.

———. "The Modern Athenian," the *Boston Evening Transcript* (Nov. 28, 1896): n.p.

———. *James Whitcomb Riley: An Essay by Bliss Carman and Some Letters to Him from James Whitcomb Riley*. Metuchen, N.J.: Charles F. Heartman, 1925–26.

———. "Riley Just As He Is." Rev. of *In Honour of James Whitcomb Riley: A Meeting of the Indiana State Teachers' Association Held in Tomlinson Hall in Indianapolis, Dec. 28, 1905*, ed. anon., *New York Times Review of Books*, n.v. (June 16, 1906), n.p.

———. Interview, "Appeal of Poetry is to its Ear in Opinion of Bliss Carman" (Interviewer not cited), the *Toronto Star* (Nov. 5, 1923): 18.

———. "Marginal Notes: Scribes and Pharisees," the *Commercial Advertiser* (April 22, 1899): n.p.

———. "Marginal Notes: Poetry and Religion," the *Commercial Advertiser* (April 28, 1900): n.p.

———. Rev. of *Emerson's Essays* (Ed. not cited), *Progress* (Dec. 14, 1889): n.p.

———. "Marginal Notes: The Higher Journalism," the *Commercial Advertiser* (July 23, 1898): n.p.

———. "The Modern Athenian: A Note on Emily Dickinson," the *Boston Evening Transcript* (Nov. 21, 1896): n.p.

———. "Marginal Notes," the *Commercial Advertiser* (Sept. 3, 1898): n.p.

———. "The Modern Athenian," the *Boston Evening Transcript* (Aug. 14, 1897): n.p.

———. "A Poet in Color." Catalogue Intro. to "Exhibition of Paintings by Leon Dabo, Dec. 31, 1906 to Jan. 12, 1907." Boston: Walter Rowlands Galleries.

———. "The Purpose of Poetry," *International Quarterly* n.v. (Jan. 1905): 278–92.

———. "Marginal Notes," the *Commercial Advertiser* (Oct. 1, 1898): n.p.

———. "Marginal Notes," the *Commercial Advertiser* (Sept. 10, 1898): n.p.

———. "Marginal Notes: The Rights of Labor," the *Commercial Advertiser* (Sept. 6, n.d.): n.p.

———. "Marginal Notes: The Soul of Socialism," the *Commercial Advertiser* (Nov. 1, n.d.): n.p.

———. "Physical Freedom for Women," *Harper's* n.v. (April 13, 1913): n.p.

———. "Marginal Notes: Subsidized Art," the *Commercial Advertiser* (Dec. 13, n.d.): n.p.

———. "Marginal Notes: Two Books," the *Commercial Advertiser* (June 22, 1901): n.p.

———. "Defense of Poetry," in *The Poetry of Life*. Boston: L. C. Page, 1905.

———. "Emerson," the *Literary World* n.v. (May 1903): 120–21.

———. "English and American Scholars Celebrate Tennyson Centenary," the *New York Times* (Aug. 1, 1909).

———. "Marginal Notes: The Wind Among the Reeds," the *Commercial Advertiser* (May 20, 1899): n.p.

————. "Marginal Notes: John Davidson," the *Commercial Advertiser* (Jan. 14, 1899): n.p.
[Editor's Note: The above publications by Carman are listed in the order in which they are cited in the text of this paper.]

Dudek, Louis. "It's Good Broadcasting, But Is It Art?" Rev. of *The Creative Writer*, by Earle Birney. *The Gazette* n.v. (Oct. 8, 1966). Rpt. in Louis Dudek, *In Defense of Art: Critical Essays & Reviews*. Kingston: Quarry Press, 1988. 181–83.

Eagleton, Terry. *The Function of Criticism: From The Spectator to Post-Structuralism*. London: Verso Editions, 1984.

Eliot, T. S. "Whispers of Immortality." *Collected Poems: 1909–1962*. London: Faber and Faber, 1974. 55–56.

Fuller, Roy. "Translation." *Collected Poems of Roy Fuller*. London: Andre Deutsch, 1962. 150–51.

Gundy, H. P. *Letters of Bliss Carman*. Kingston and Montreal: McGill-Queen's University Press, 1981.

Perkins, David. *A History of Modern Poetry: From the 1890s to the High Modernist Mode*. Cambridge, Mass. and London: Harvard University Press, 1976.

Rosenthal, M. L. *The New Poets: American and British Poetry Since World War II*. London, Oxford and New York: Oxford University Press, 1967.

Ross, Malcolm. "Bliss Carman and the Poetry of Mystery: A Defense of the Personal Fallacy." *The Bicentennial Lectures on New Brunswick Literature*. Sackville, N.B.: Centre for Canadian Studies, Mount Allison University, 1985. 9–31.

Santayana, George. *Interpretations of Poetry and Religion*. New York: Charles Scribner's Sons, 1900.

————. *The Life of Reason*. New York: Charles Scribner's Sons, 1905.

Stephens, Donald. *Bliss Carman*. Twayne's World Authors Series, No. 8. New York: Twayne, 1966.

Stock, Noel. *The Life of Ezra Pound*. 1970 (Rpt. Harmondsworth: Penguin Books Ltd., 1974).

Thurley, Geoffrey. *The Ironic Harvest: English Poetry in the Twentieth Century*. London: Edward Arnold, 1974.

Untermeyer, Louis, ed. *Modern American Poetry: A Critical Anthology*. New York: Harcourt, Brace, 1919.

Carman and Mind Cure:
Theory and Technique

D.M.R. BENTLEY

> *Matthew Arnold in his poetry gave some expression to the soul-sickness of his time. But it may be that the poetry which is to cure that sickness has yet to be written. Is there not a large class of modern men and women who are most eager for something great in poetry, —something that shall deal strongly with their mental disquiet, something that shall help them to live, something that shall allay despair and reestablish their courage? Any adequate poetry ought to do this.*
>
> BLISS CARMAN, *The Poetry of Life*[1]

Although Carman's philosophical ideas and intellectual development have received considerable attention down the years, comparatively little space has been allotted to discussion of his poetic technique,[2] and to the now somewhat unfashionable issue of the relation in his poetry between form and content, manner and matter. On the assumption (shared, as it happens, by Carman)[3] that any account of a writer's means must take account of his ends, this paper will discuss technical aspects of an illustrative selection of materials mainly from before the First World War in the context of their author's participation in the mind-cure movement that flourished in New England around the turn of the century.[4] More specifically, the paper will argue that the poetry produced by Carman after he moved more or less permanently to the United States in 1890 reflects increasingly the same "mind-cure imagination"[5] that had since the late 1860s been spawning such popular books as *Mental Medicine* (1872) by Warren Felt Evans, *American Nervousness* (1881) by George Miller Beard, and *The Power of Repose* (1893) by Annie Payson Call. Once seen in the light of the mind-cure movement, most of Carman's attitudes and concerns during his American years—his "therapeutic" approach to "nature,"[6] his advocacy of the arts-and-crafts movement, and his near-obsessive promulgation of the Delsartean or unitrinian system of mind-body-spirit harmonization—become obvious for what they are: part of a coherent attempt that is also evident both thematically and technically in his poetry "to medicine the mind[s]" (Carman's phrase)[7] of that "large class of modern men and women" who were suffering from the psychological and psychosomatic consequences of their participation in what Arnold had long since diagnosed as the "strange disease of modern life."[8] To the extent that Carman assumed the role of "Physician of the iron age"[9]—a role earlier inherited by Arnold from Goethe, Wordsworth, and, of course, Emerson (a major influence also on Carman and other mind-healers)[10]—his writing asks to be seen, not merely as a form of therapy, but as a manifestation of the "therapeutic world view"[11] which, as T. J. Jackson Lears and others have persuasively argued, accompanies consumer capitalism as it develops from the nineteenth into the twentieth century.

Most therapists in the mind-cure movement, including Carman, agreed with Dr. Beard that "American nervousness"—the mental and physical exhaustion and dis-ease evident especially among the urban middle and upper classes of the Northeast—stemmed from one, single "predisposing cause": "modern civilization."[12] Among the factors which, in the opinion of Beard, Evans, Call, and others, were causing widespread "Americanitis" in such cities as Chicago and New York were loud and discordant noise, monotonous and specialized work, ease and speed of travel, rapidly changing ideas, and credit-buying.[13] Most of the items on this list are echoed and elaborated by Carman in his discussions of "modern life" and "civilization" in *The Friendship of Art, The Kinship of Nature, The Poetry of Life*, and elsewhere. "[O]ur modern world lies in a vast turmoil of excitement, battle, and doubt, beneath unlifting clouds of hesitation and dismay. We wear our hearts out in the ceaseless fret of affairs . . . " (*PL*, 194), he says in one essay, and in another: "Without being aware of it in the least, we become distraught, inefficient, and flighty, simply through the hurry in which we live. You may deny it as you please, but noise and haste are maddening. Watch the average businessman. . . ."[14] In other essays it is the "complexity of life [that] has begotten a perplexity of thought . . . ";[15] people are "distracted and uncertain . . . astonished with the many revelations of science" (*FA*, 110–111). Or the culprits are "specialization," "artificiality," "unnatural ugliness," "cramped garments," the "monotonous simplicity" of city streets (*FA*, 23, 172, 220, 221). Lears uses the terms "overcivilization" and "*embourgeoisement*"[16] to describe the root cause of the nervous exhaustion or neurasthenia diagnosed by Beard and others in urban Americans around the turn of the century; in Carman's analysis, astute enough for its times, American culture had become "overcentralized" (*KN*, 250) and its people "overmentalized" (*FA*, 27; *MP*, 26, 110, 220).

Of the many symptoms of "nervous 'goneness,' "[17] "tired nerves" (*MP*, 120), or, simply, "nerves" (*PL*, 92) as Carman calls neurasthenia, several have already surfaced in the poet's descriptions of the specific causes of the ailment: "doubt," "hesitation," "dismay," fretting, distraction, inefficiency, flightiness, "perplexity," astonishment. Among the other symptoms described by Beard—and these include "insomnia," "drowsiness," "atonic voice," "fear of responsibility, of open places or of closed places, fear of society . . . fear of fears . . . [and] fear of everything"—appears one that is of special relevance to the present discussion: "nervous dyspepsia."[18] This term is especially relevant to Carman, not merely because he uses variants of it at several points in his essays (along with less orthodox and more metaphorical terms like "mental rabies" [*KN*, 236], "modern plague" [*KN*, 47], "fever of power, [and] malaria of . . . soul" [*KN*, 43]), but because it also happens to be the particular form of neurasthenia that afflicted the poet in the aftermath of Richard Hovey's unexpected death on February 24, 1900. In March of that year, Carman was taken by Dr. George Hall, the physician with whom for a time he shared an apartment in New York, to a sanatorium "in the pines" in Thomasville, Georgia (*L*, 128) to undergo a rest cure.[19] "I am crawling back to normal from a slump of nervous dyspepsia," he told a correspondent in April 1900, adding that she should not worry because "I believe the Emersonian creed of sanity" (*L*, 130)—the creed, that is, of mental health through willed action ("self-reliance") combined, as often as not, with doses of the Over Soul as a cure for narrow "egotism."[20] Reflecting both his faith in the alignment of poetry and health and the blow to that faith registered by a mental breakdown partly induced by recent literary problems and doubts (see *L*, 127), Carman also observes from the "awful abyss of nervous 'goneness' " that Robert Louis Stevenson may not have been "altogether wrong" when he uttered "the supreme heresy" and "spoke of art as possibly a disease . . ." (*L*, 129). Little empathy is required to appreciate how dismaying a "slump" into "nervous dyspepsia" must have been for a poet who believed deeply that all worthwhile art—art that is "sane," "normal," and health-giving—must necessarily be "the product of great sanity and normal health" (*FA*, 136).

Carman's return to sanity and health in the Spring of 1900 was very likely due to a combination of factors that had for some time been elements in his own system of mind cure: Emersonian self-help and spiritual openness; a retreat from the city to the country for the dual purpose of counteracting the strain of modern life and permitting the "jangled" human organism to replenish its energy through rest and repose in a natural environment;[21] and—working in concert with these revitalizing processes—the ministrations of a good book. There is not room here to compare and contrast Carman's system of mind cure with the "multitude of [other] therapies . . . that had begun to swarm in the late nineteenth-century imagination,"[22] but it is necessary to refer his approach and assumptions to those generally current at the time if anything like a full understanding of his notion of book therapy is to be reached. As already intimated with reference to Beard's theories, most mind cures of Carman's day were based on the assumption that the "new functions" of "modern civilization" were causing a harmful concentration or channeling of nervous energy into one area, usually the mental or merely rational; the result, on the analogy of an electrical "circuit," was a lack of sufficient nervous energy to keep "all the lamps" burning actively: "those that are weakest go out entirely, or . . . burn faint and feebly . . . [with] an insufficient and unstable light. . . ."[23] The therapist's task was to recharge and rebalance the neurastheniac's system. At one extreme—the extreme of maximum external interference—a rest cure such as the one undergone by Carman in 1900 might be prescribed. At the other extreme—the extreme of complete self-reliance—the sufferer might be enjoined to effect his own cure through self-culture (to be "[Him]self the weeder and the weed," as Carman puts it in "Horticulture" [FA, 63]). Between these two extremes, and, in certain ways, partaking of both, lies the path to health advocated by Carman: a holiday in the country and/or in art during which the vacationer/reader who follows the poet-physician's regimen imbibes both tonics for the body and sedatives for the mind, the former through physical activities and artistic works that are vigorous[24] and the latter through those that are reposeful.[25] "The art most accessible to us all is folded between covers of cloth or paper, and may be carried with us to the mountains or the shore," says Carman in The Kinship of Nature; "[i]f it is well selected, it will serve to second the athletic recreations of the body, and put us in fine accord with the influences of nature and thought. If it is ill selected, our holiday may result in dyspeptic days of unprofitable idleness" (KN, 58–59).

A little less obviously than his notions of "[s]erenity as a sort of spiritual capital" (KN, 233) and "contentment" as an "ample balance in the Bank of Joy" (FA, 15), Carman's sense of a profitable and "unprofitable" use of leisure time indicates the complicity of his "mind-cure imagination" in the capitalist culture whose deleterious effects it both deplores and promises to remedy. Indeed, not only does the rhythm of repeated "creation and recreation" (KN, 54) in Carman's therapeutic scheme mimic the reliance of consumer capitalism on production and relaxation, getting and spending, but its ultimate aim—the return of the re-energized and rebalanced neurasthenic to the strenuous, work-a-day world of the city—actually serves to support the structure of modern civilization.[26] With his eye on the "American whose orbit lies between Wall Street and the park" (PL, 107)—the urban park being in itself an "anodyne"[27] for jangled nerves—Carman argues in The Kinship of Nature and The Poetry of Life especially that the poet can assist in encouraging a rhythmic and Spencerian alternation between strenuous "work" and peaceful "relaxation."[28] Since there is both Darwinian (or Spencerian) "strife" and Wordsworthian "calm" (*KN*, 18) in the natural world, why not also in the human one? Carman may not have been quite like Hovey, "whose tastes . . . [apparently] lay much more in the direction of a comfortable limousine and other similar resources of civilization"[29] than in the rough and ascetic pleasures of the outdoors, but he nevertheless enjoyed and endorsed the conveniences, "comforts," and "luxuries" (*PL*, 92) of modern life,[30] and sought to encourage a productive, spirited, and (more of this in a moment) honourable combination of the traditional American characteristic of masculine strenuosity[31] and the modern necessity of rejuvenating repose. "It is somehow possible, I think," he says at the conclusion of "On Being Strenuous," "to be as strenuous and efficient as nature herself in action, and yet to have in mind always, as a standard of normal being, the inflexible serenity of the sun" (*KN*, 20–21). In a twofold sop to "the captains of humanity"—that is, the captains of business and industry—Carman even goes so far as to assert that "stern struggle and victorious achievement can never be cramping to the soul"[32] and that those like himself who suffer from "unactive doubt," "lethargic torpor," and other sins against the work ethic will one day "be remoulded into something more trenchant and available for the forwarding of beneficent designs" (*KN*, 20).

Nor would anything but the tone of this analysis have dismayed Carman, for he was convinced that, with all its shortcomings, modern "[c]ivilization . . . is the best we can attain in our progress toward perfection" (*FA*, 232).[33] "[I]t is not altogether healthy, nor the mark of a strong man," he argued, "always to be setting one's face against the drift and tendency of one's own time . . ." (*FA*, 238). The "healthy" and "strong" artist must be both a part of and apart from his society—sufficiently a part of it to feel the sympathy necessary to assist its component individuals (and thus the society as a whole) towards higher levels of consciousness, and sufficiently apart from it—an "outskirter" (*FA*, 202)—to be attuned to the existence of such higher levels and alert to the shortcomings of present ones.[34] Prominent among these shortcomings, and urgently in need of redress in the interests of forwarding "true civilization" (*FA*, 232), were "overmuch" care for "wealth" and "business" (*PL*, 93; *FA*, 242) and "overlittle" concern for "loveliness" and "beauty" (*PL*, 13; *FA*, 242). Any poetry aimed at increasing the happiness and health of modern society by reforming[35] it in the direction of "loveliness and truth and charity" (*PL*, 13) would have to redress the imbalance between "business" and "beauty" by promoting "honesty" and "love" (for example) over "falsehood and greed" (*FA*,

273, 106), "vitality" and "permanence" (the hallmarks of genuine beauty) over ugliness and artificiality (*FA*, 167, 250, 172). Since beauty and goodness were closely linked in the moral aestheticism that Carman had inherited from Ruskin, Morris,[36] and their American disciple, Charles Eliot Norton,[37] to foster the former was to encourage the latter.[38]

Behind Carman's increasingly shrill and desperate attacks in the essays of the first decade of this century on the business-related vices of modern society[39] lies his growing awareness that in a world where art is regarded with "distaste" (*PL*, 113ff.) poetry cannot, as Arnold had suggested it would, take the place of religion. If beautiful objects are not seen or read, how can they generate good thoughts and so influence the progress of society for the better? Only a rebirth of morality could restore the efficacy of poetry as an ethical agent. "Poetry will return with religion" (*PL*, 123), not vice versa, and, in the meantime, Carman will "transfer much of [his] labour and allegiance to . . . prose" (*PL*, 214–215). In a sense Carman's disillusionment with the ethical component of his poetic and therapeutic program was inevitable for two reasons: the obvious one that a beautiful object does not necessarily generate a good thought and, perhaps less obviously, the displacement in the root assumptions governing mind cure of morality (a thief is a bad man who should be punished) by physic (a thief is a sick man who can be cured).[40] To the extent that Carman accepted the assumptions of mind cure, he substituted *soma* for *psyche* and diminished the ability of his poetry to perform as a substitute for religion. Obviously, his espousal of the arts-and-crafts movement (beauty breeds goodness) was one attempt to heal the rift between art and ethics. Another was his adoption of the Delsartean system of personal harmony whereby the energies and demands of the mind, the body, and the spirit (or emotions) were supposedly brought into balance as a means of achieving an equivalent harmony among the true, the beautiful, and the good and, in this way, creating healthier individuals and promoting a "higher civilization" (*FA*, 236). It barely needs to be said that Carman's use of "spirit" (or soul) and "emotion" interchangeably in his unitrinian writings was in itself an attempt to deal with the rift between *psyche* and *soma*, ethics and art, a rift that the poet never succeeded in doing more than paper over.

At the heart of Carman's therapeutic program, flawed as it was, lay two interconnected aims: to make his "artificial" modern civilization better because more beautiful and to make the "average" modern personality "normal" because well balanced.[41] One of the points at which these two aims converged, drawing as they did so both on Carman's moral aestheticism and on his Delsartean principles, was the artistic, balanced, and therefore "good" or "real" book. Such a book is a far cry from "[f]actory-made abominations of cloth and paper"; it has "vitality" and "soul" because it is a "living image"—a "sacramental" embodiment[42]—of the artist whose normalcy passes through it to bring balance, happiness, and health to the reader. Thus "the book, like the [artist], must be so true that it convinces our reason and satisfies our curiosity; it must be so beautiful that it fascinates and delights our taste; it must be so spirited and right-minded that it enlists our best sympathy and stirs our more humane emotions. A good book is one that leaves us happier or better off in any way for having known it" (*FA*, 166–167). Not only must the artist who creates therapeutic books be balanced and normal in the Delsartean sense (a man "capable of thought, capable of passion, capable of manual labour" [*PL*, 72]), but so too must be the critic: "To judge poetry one must be a man of affairs, yet without hurry; a religionist, yet without heat; a philosopher without system. One must be a generous lover, infatuated, but not insane; an unflinching logician, yet not inflexible; and one must be an athlete, also" (*PL*, 62). Needless to say, the best judges of poetry are found neither among "beery" sensualists nor among "overmentalized" academics— "those weedy, dyspeptic, ill-ventilated . . . creatures" who live with their "nose in a book" (*PL*, 61–62). Just as the narrow hedonist could profit from exposure to the asceticism of the "philosopher" or the "religionist," so the bookish don would benefit from a therapeutic dose of body and spirit, imbibed perhaps during an invigorating and uplifting holiday in the country or through a constitutional in the realms of art—a spirited stroll in the open air of Emerson, for example, or a hearty ramble along the open road of Vagabondia.

Even in these examples of possible book cures for the neurasthenic academic can be discerned the Delsartean aesthetic by which Carman judged various poets and poems (including his own) for their therapeutic value and, hence, overall merit. From a Delsartean perspective, both Swinburne and Pope are unbalanced, the former because his appeal is too much to the "senses" and too little to the heart and mind, the latter because he is "too purely mental" and thus deficient in tonics for the body and spirit (*PL*, 60). Francis Sherman "needs to be a little more burly" but *Songs from Vagabondia* "too often approaches the boisterous to be really very good" (*L*, 123, 74). Browning, more balanced than most poets, tends nevertheless to emphasize mind (thought) and spirit (beauty) at the expense of body (form).[43] The ideal Delsartean and therapeutic poet or poem would resemble Browning in "philosophic power combined with vigorous love of life," but to these two qualities would be added something of Arnold (social awareness), Morris (human sympathy), and Tennyson (self-possession),[44] together with the ability to "show us how to regain our spiritual manhood" (*PL*, 94–97). This is a tall order, and it inevitably raises the question of whether Carman himself succeeded in achieving his ideal of the fully-rounded physician-poet.

A glance back at the partial but representative list of Carman's poetic likes and dislikes in the preceding paragraph yields a point of entry into this question in the poet's perception that one of his own works—*Songs from Vagabondia* (co-authored, of course, with Richard Hovey)—had veered away from the ideal balance of elements appealing to the spirit, mind, and body towards the "boisterous," the "too purely physical." Was this merely Hovey's fault (certainly he wrote a number of the more "rollicking"[45] poems in the book) or was it a regrettable, inevitable, and even necessary consequence of the therapeutic aim of the book—its attempt to redress the imbalance of "overmentalized" readers like Carman's "dyspeptic" don by giving them a dose of the open road and the Over Soul? Probably the best support for this hypothesis lies in the structural shape of *Songs from Vagabondia*, for the poems in the book (and, indeed, the illustrations)[46] are arranged in a way that echoes the rhythm of "creation and recreation" (*KN*, 54) that Carman attributed to a therapeutic holiday in the country. Hovey's opening poem, "Vagabondia," establishes the mood of release from the constraints of the business world into a realm of imaginative freedom:

> Off with the fetters
> That chafe and restrain!
> Off with the chain!
>
>   * * *
>
> Here we are free
> To be good or bad,
> Sane or mad,
> Merry or grim
> As the mood may be,—
> Free as the whim
> Of a spook on a spree,—
> Free to be oddities,
> Not mere commodities,
> Stupid and saleable
> Wholly available,
> Ranged upon shelves;
> Each with his puny form
> In the same uniform
> We are not labelled
> We are ourselves.

> Here is the real
> Here is the ideal . . . .[47]

And so raffishly on into a masculine world of "boon companions," "wind," "sun," and "sea" in which "Laughable hardship [is] / Met and forgot" (*SV*, 34, 2–5). Although less boisterous and more stanzaically regular than many of Hovey's poems in *Songs from Vagabondia*, Carman's contributions to the opening pages of the book use similarly jaunty rhythms to suggest egress from the wintry city into the (re-)juvenescence of spring. Here are two of the closing stanzas of his "Spring Song":

> Let me taste the old immortal
> Indolence of life once more;
> Not recalling nor foreseeing,
> Let the great slow joys of being
> Well my heart through as of yore!
> Let me taste the old immortal
> Indolence of life once more!

> * * *

> Only make me over, April,
> When the sap begins to stir!
> Make me man or make me woman,
> Make me oaf or ape or human,
> Cup of flower or cone of fir;
> Make me anything but neuter
> When the sap begins to stir!

> (*SV*, 13)

Under the dual influence of "Indolence" and "April," the effects of "overmentalization" are alleviated and energy redistributed to the heart and body, with a corresponding rise or "influx"[48] of spiritual awareness and sexual vigour or "instinct"[49] (and note the pun on "Well" in the first stanza). The volume continues with a variety of poems celebrating wild nature and vibrant male companionship (both antidotes to the artificiality and effeminacy of modern life) and ends with Hovey's "Comrades," a somatic anticipation of the return of the regenerated vagabonds to a business world conceived, in Carman's words, as "a veiled yet ruthless encounter man to man,—a strife to the death" (*KN*, 167):

> Comrades, pour the wine to-night
> For the parting is with the dawn!

Oh, the clink of cups together,
With the daylight coming on!
Greet the morn
With a double horn,
When strong men drink together!

Comrades, gird your swords to-night,
For the battle is with the dawn!
Oh, the clash of shields together,
With the triumph coming on!
Greet the foe,
And lay him low
When strong men fight together![50]

(*SV*, 54)

After a week or a weekend imbibing relaxing drinks and invigorating poems in wayside taverns or, more likely, mountain- or lake-side cottages (a growing phenomenon at this time, as witness Carman's own beloved "Ghost House" and "Moonshine"),[51] previously nervous and flaccid businessmen will return to the financial world prepared to do battle. "On . . . Monday there are carnations in the button-holes of Wall Street," says Carman in *The Kinship of Nature*, and "every hansom on the Avenue is freighted with the destruction of another Troy" (54). When armed with the sword of strenuousness and the shield of rejuvenated sanity, the vagabond poets cheeringly imply, the businessmen battling on Wall Street are the modern equivalents of the Saxon and Greek warriors fighting "to the death" for the walled cities of more authentic times.[52] *Plus ça change, plus c'est la même chose* in the realm of male activity is one of the therapeutically bracing illusions[53] conveyed by many poems in the three *Vagabondia* volumes of the period (c. 1892–1908) when Carman's enthusiasm for mind cure was apparently at its height.

Very likely because the Canadian poet harboured almost as much distaste for militarism as he did for the "business code" (*PL*, 199; and, in fact, saw the two as dismayingly rather than heateningly similar),[54] he wrote several poems in which the therapeutic gestalt of virility, male bonding, and a natural environment is projected onto characters and situations with a minimal military or economic component. Two such poems are the quite early "Arnold, Master of the Scud" (1893) and the much later "David Thompson" (1922),[55] both of which focus on "doer[s] of deeds" who perform heroic acts outside the "boundaries of modern safety and routine,"[56] the sailor in the life-threatening (and therefore invigorating) seas off Nova Scotia and the explorer in the "Untrailed, unmapped, unguessed" (and therefore expansive) "hin-terrains" of the Canadian Northwest. Both Arnold and Thompson are youths (a "youngster" and a "lad") but both are also men "full-sized," "master[s]" of their destinies, because they "will to dare" "without heed of self" or "greed of pelf," the latter in his explorations and the former in an act of bravery that is clearly presented as a *rite de passage*. There is not room here to analyze either poem in detail, but the following stanzas from "Arnold, Master of the Scud" may serve to illustrate the manner in which Carman, already in 1893 convinced of the debilitating effeminacy of modern civilization, accords special, even therapeutic, status to male potency, male "bonding," and strenuous activity:

> How the tough wind springs to wrestle,
> When the tide is on the flood!
> And between them stands young daring—
> Arnold, master of the scud.

> * * *

> Legs astraddle, grips the tiller
> This young waif of the old sea;
> When the wind comes harder, only
> Laughs "Hurrah!" and holds her free.

> Little wonder, as you watch him
> With the dash in his blue eye,
> Long ago his father called him
> "Arnold, Master," on the sly,

> While his mother's heart foreboded
> Reckless father makes rash son.
> So to-day the schooner carries
> Just these two whose will is one.

In ballad stanzas suggestive of a "primitive" and pre-Modern authenticity,[57] the poem goes on to relate the heroic incident—Arnold's return of the scud to safety after the violent death of his father—that leaves him the Emersonian master, not merely of his own ship, but also of his own soul. There can be little doubt that this is the sort of "poetry of life" that Carman regarded as a "tonic" for its ability to "stimulate . . . the spirit [and] renew . . . its zest, its strength, its fortitude" (*PL*, 11).

At the risk of oversimplifying Carman's approach to mind cure and going against the grain of his unitrinian program, it is worth exploring the possibility, based on a hint in *The Making of Personality*, that he planned (or at least came to consider) some of his therapeutic books and poems primarily as "tonics" and others primarily as "sedatives." "Much has been written of bedside books," runs the suggestive passage in the book that Carman co-authored with Mary Perry King, "—books of solace and peace suitable to induce rest and invite sleep to uneasy brains. But there should be morning books on the same shelves, volumes of inspiration and tonic cheer for our waking hours, when the spirit is unstrung and the mind unattuned. A brave, courageous thought or a happy inspired fancy when we first open our eyes, strikes a fine key-note for the soul to vibrate to, and helps us to set out upon the old road again to a quickstep" (*MP*, 239–240). Assuming for a moment for heuristic purposes that, like an Emerson essay, a Wordsworth lyric, or a passage from Whitman's *Leaves of Grass* (three of the tonics that Carman and Mrs. King mention specifically), *Songs from Vagabondia* and "Arnold, Master of the Scud" were intended primarily as "morning" works, then how do they strike the "key-note" that enables the soul to vibrate in sympathy and prompts the body to fare forth in "quickstep"? The answer, of course, is through rhythm and form—through the tripping trochaic and anapestic rhythms that account for much of the boisterousness of the *Vagabondia* poems and through the buoyant and tuneful ballad[58] and ballad-like stanzas of "Arnold, Master of the Scud" (and "Spring Song") that have the added advantage for Carman's unitrinian program of bringing with them suggestions of both primitive authenticity (emotion) and careful organization (mind).

To ascribe meaning to form and rhythm in this way would be extremely far-fetched if it were not for the fact that both Hovey and Carman explicitly did so themselves. In three extraordinary essays that were published and known to Carman in the early 1890s (in fact, the Canadian poet contributed the term "*Colliteration*"[59] to the third of them, "The Technic of Rhyme," printed in the *Independent* in October 1893), Hovey articulated a detailed unitrinian poetic based primarily on the ideas of Delsarte as mediated by his future wife, Henrietta Russell, but drawing also on Herbert Spencer (in the area of rhythm), Sidney Lanier (in the area of verse form) and J. J. Sylvester, an English mathematician who "use[s] . . . Delsartean methods in his analysis [of poetry] . . . probably by right of his own discovery."[60] In the first of these essays, "Delsarte and Poetry," to which Carman responded with great enthusiasm when he read it in late July or early August 1891 (*L*, 41), Hovey argues that "feet like the trochee, which are accented on the first syllable, are emotional in expression and feet like the English pseudo-anapest, which are accented on the final syllable, are physical." Since "meter is itself the physical part of poetry," he suggests, "to use a physical meter is to express one's self by very primitive and undifferentiated means." To "the iambus," a foot that Hovey claims to be "accented on the middle syllable, which . . . usually absorbs the final [one]," falls the honour of being less emotional or physical than "mental in expression."[61]

In a slightly modified and elaborated form, Hovey's Delsartean equivalences resurface in "Personal Rhythm," Carman's essay in *The Friendship of Art* on the similarities of "charm and power" between the rhythms of "poetry" and "people." "Dons and dowagers and policemen are always iambic in their rhythm" because they are "ponderous character[s]" who move "step after step, word after word, with the emphasis always delayed until the second thought, the second look, the second movement, the second word." Worse off than these cautious iambic types (who can at least aspire to the "settled . . . prosperous . . . conservative . . . aristocratic and assured" qualities of blank verse) are those "large," "[u]ndecided people of . . . [the] dactyllic measure" who are doomed to "the slow, uncertain, meandering rhythm" of hexameters. Most blessed are the "sprightly, tripping, gay, and emotional" people who move to such "excellent" trochaic rhythms as those of Tennyson's " 'In the spring a young man's fancy turns to love' " (*FA*, 183–184). Carman's explicit point in "Personal Rhythm" is that "[t]o live according to one's rhythm is the law of common sense and common honesty. It is the first requisite of sanity, too. And it is one of the great evils of modern life that it tends to throw us out of rhythm. We are nearly all hurried to a point of hysteria. It is not so much that we have more than we can do, as that we allow the haste to get on our nerves" (*FA*, 186–187). Yet implicit in the essay, not least in the observation that, "[i]f we are naturally iambic," we should "be careful how we *break into* trochees" and, "if we are naturally trochaic, we must be *wary of lapsing into* iambics" (*FA*, 185; emphasis added), is surely the implication that the emotional trochee is more admirable than the mental iambus (let alone the poor, bloated dactyl) and that a good trochaic tonic such as that found in *Songs from Vagabondia* would do both the overmentalized blank verse types and the physically inactive hexameters a power of good. It is perhaps as difficult for us to take all this seriously as it doubtless would be for a Masai tribesman to contemplate without mirth our own obsessions with balanced diet and physical fitness.

As detailed as and, if anything, more serious than Carman's theories of the correspondence between the rhythms of poetry and people are his explanations of the way in which various poetic techniques, particularly those related to rhythm, serve the therapeutic purpose of allowing the physical and the spiritual elements of the Delsartean triad to gain power and achieve balance in an "overmentalized" reader. Drawing on a major and controversial component of several mind-cure therapies of the time, mesmerism or, as it was becoming more frequently called, hypnotism,[62] Carman argues in *The Kinship of Nature, The Making of Personality*, and elsewhere that in certain forms of poetry—his "bedside books" and sedative poems are obvious candidates for this class—the "constant reiteration" that is present in "rhythm . . . metre . . . rhyme and alliteration" serves as a "mesmeric or hypnotic agent," lulling the conscious mind into what the Rev. Evans in *Mental Medicine* calls "the *impressible . . . state.*"[63] The advantage of such a state, argues Carman, is that it allows the spiritual message of the poet-hypnotist—indeed, his spiritual energy as it is incarnated in the poem—to pass relatively unimpeded across the "threshold of the outer mind" ("the rational waking objective self, the self which is clever and intentional and inductive") and to "sway" directly "the mysterious subconscious person who inhabits us," "the deeper unreasoning self" (*KN*, 148–149). (A host of writers, including Wordsworth, Swedenborg, and Emerson doubtless contributed to Carman's conception of the "outer" and "inner" mind, but the Arnold of "The Buried Life," with its accounts of "Our hidden self" and "the soul's subterranean depth," seems especially pertinent here.)[64] In order "to elude the too vigilant reason of his fellows and gain instant access to their spirit," Carman explains in "Subconscious Art," the poet must employ his "whole being,—mind, body, and spirit"; more precisely, he must place at the service of his "intuitive," "submerged, unsleeping self" the full "alphabet or medium of his art"— that is, all the poetic skills and techniques "which training and study" have given him (*KN*, 150, 153). As Carman's subsequent discussion of a stanza from Tennyson's "Crossing the Bar" in "Subconscious Art" reveals, his argument is essentially a metre-making one: it is "metre" or "cadence" in its various manifestations that enables poetry to appeal, not merely to our "intelligence," but also to our "sense and soul." It is the "monotonous music of . . . verse" that gains poetry and the poet "access" to the "soul" and secures "egress for it [the soul]" from the constraints of the rational mind (*KN*, 151–154).

An obvious place to look for the "alphabet" of Carman's hypnotic art is in Hovey's three essays of the early 1890s, "Delsarte and Poetry," "The Technic of Poetry," and "The Technic of Rhyme." That this is also the right place to look is quickly confirmed by Hovey's assertion that "*[c]olliteration*," the term invented by Carman to describe "[r]epetitions that fall indiscriminately on accented and unaccented places in sufficient number to give unity to a passage by subtly filling the ear with the insistence of a dominant tone colour," serves in Tennyson's poems especially "to unconsciously impress the mind with a sense of a prevailing"[65] mood or emotion ("colour").[66] While all of Hovey's Delsartean equivalences between poetic techniques and human faculties do not accord precisely with Carman's theory and practice, most of them—as already intimated in the earlier discussion of correspondences between the rhythms of poetry and people—do appear to be crisply reflected in the Canadian poet's thinking and work. For example, Hovey's associa- tion of rhyme with reason[67] and of alliteration with physicality[68] prob- ably accounts for the presence or absence of these techniques in many of Carman's therapeutic poems, as does his association of "*[c]olliteration*" with the emotional (or spiritual). (These correspondences might also, incidentally, prompt a re-reading of Hovey's "Vagabondia" as a poem that, by virtue of its "mentalizing"[69] rhymes alone, was probably intended to be more balanced and less boisterous than it first appears.) In a few moments, a reading of one Carman poem on Delsartean prin- ciples will be attempted. In the meantime, and partly to provide the last tool necessary for that analysis, one more element of Carman's uni- trinian and therapeutic program must be placed briefly on view: his Swedenborgian conception of landscape and colour.

Whether visited at the weekend or represented in a poem, the external world was for Carman a *paysage moralisé* of precise correspond- ences between landscape "zones" and personality traits. As he explains in "Seaboard and Hillward" in *The Kinship of Nature*, the ocean- and sea-side zone corresponds to the "emotional" and "spiritual" realm in man, the hill or mountain zone to the "mental," and, less certainly, the "plain and level" to the "physical" (*KN*, 157–158). "[T]he sea is the great nourisher of imagination, the stimulator of romance," the inspiration of "creative artists," he suggests, and heights are condu- cive to "moods [rather] than passions . . . elemental sorrow . . . [and] the overweight of thought" characteristic of the "critic" (*KN*, 158–159). Clearly, the bookish don who figured earlier in this discussion would benefit from a seaside holiday and, to an extent (was this Carman's reason for settling into a cottage in the Catskills?), an emotional or creative person would be better balanced for a sojourn in the hills. In "The Scarlet of the Year" (also in *The Kinship of Nature*) Carman advances a similar series of correspondences for a " 'trinity' " of primary colours: "warm," "burly" red is physical, "ethereal tremulous" yellow is spiritual and emotional, and the "cerulean" blue that "overarches" and compre- hends the whole scene and scheme is mental (*KN*, 259–260). "If you think of . . . elementary colours as symbols of certain qualities," asserts Carman, "you will see something more than a mere wayward fancy in such a title as [Andrew Lang's] 'The Red Fairy Book,' or 'The Blue Fairy Book' " (*KN*, 260). *To see something more* in the colour, the land- scape, the metre, the "technic" of a poem—this is the key to a proper hermeneutic of Carman, a hermeneutic that accords mind, body, and emotion a balanced role in the appreciation of his poetry and—

100

therapeutics aside—discovers in even the most rollicking and superfi-
cially mindless lines such as the following much more than meets the eye:

> There is something in the autumn that is native to my
>   blood—
> Touch of manner, hint of mood;
> And my heart is like a rhyme,
> With the yellow and the purple and the crimson
>   keeping time.
>
> (*MSV*, 39)

In Carman there is no more rhyme without reason than there is rhythm
without sense, yellow without spirit, or crimson without body. Affective, reasoned, and spirited, even "A Vagabond Song" suggests that,
after all, Carman may just have been his own ideal Delsartean poet.

Nor is this assessment contradicted by the poem chosen for close,
Delsartean analysis. The volume from which it is taken, *Sappho: One
Hundred Lyrics*, could be classified as a "bedside book"; quietistic in mood,
it certainly generates at many points the kind of "solace and peace
suitable to induce rest and invite sleep to uneasy brains." Nevertheless, the *Sappho* volume contains a great deal of "intelligent significance"
(*L*, 150). Permeated with unitrinianism and, as argued elsewhere,[70]
hermeticism, it consists of some of Carman's most affectively beautiful
lyrics (physical), and offers the reader a chance to contemplate (mental)
the possibility that human life and love may persist beyond death (spiritual). Moreover, Sappho's love for Atthis, Phaon, and others is itself
by turns physical, mental, and spiritual (emotional), and quite
frequently—as in our chosen poem, Lyric XXIII ("I loved thee, Atthis,
in the long ago . . .")[71]—a combination of all three.

A preliminary reading of Lyric XXIII in the light of Carman's
therapeutic theory and Delsartean correspondences not only confirms
its sedative qualities but also raises some distinct symbolic possibilities—
the "broad . . . meadows" "by the sea" as a physical zone with
emotional–spiritual associations, for instance, and the "purple" of the
"grass" as a combination of red (physical) and blue (mental), a blen-
ding reflected in the "wet[ness]" of the "grass-*heads*" (emphasis added).
And notice also the coming together of the physical and spiritual in "the
unutterable glad release / Within the temple of the holy night" that
climaxes the poem:

> I loved thee, Atthis, in the long ago,
> When the great oleanders were in flower
> In the broad herded meadows full of sun.

> And we would often at the fall of dusk
> Wander together by the silver stream,
> When the soft grass-heads were all wet with dew
> And purple-misted in the fading light.
> And joy I knew and sorrow at thy voice,
> And the superb magnificence of love,—
> The loneliness that saddens solitude,
> And the sweet speech that makes it durable,—
> The bitter longing and the keen desire,
> The sweet companionship through quiet days
> In the slow ample beauty of the world,
> And the unutterable glad release
> Within the temple of the holy night.
> O Atthis, how I loved thee long ago
> In that fair perished summer by the sea!

Much of the soporific or hypnotic power of this lyric unquestionably derives from its rhythm, which is rendered all the more coercive (in Delsartean terms, physical) by alliteration and by parallel metrical and syntactical structures:

> And we would often at the fall of dusk
> Wander together by the silver stream,
> When the soft grass-heads were all wet with dew
> *And* purple-misted in the fading light.
> *And* joy I knew *and* sorrow . . .
> *And* . . .

Playing across the iambic norm of these and other lines are various effects that recall Hovey's association of trochees with emotion ("fading," "sorrow," "longing," "perished summer") and anapests with physicality ("and the keen desire," "unutterable glad release," "of the holy night"). These last quotations also employ terminal iambic or rising rhythms—"desire," "release," "holy night"—to emphasize moments of achievement in a love whose "superb magnificence" resides in its rhythmic alternations and ultimate fusion of mind, body, and spirit.

Perhaps most metrically notable of all in Lyric XXIII is Carman's use of ionic feet at the beginning of several lines ("When the great oleanders," "In the broad herded meadows," "When the soft grass-heads," and so on) for what appears to be two purposes: first, to assist the lyric in working its hypnotic effect on the reader by lulling the reason and speaking directly to the spirit; and, second, to associate the poem even at the technical level with the pre-Modern and, in that sense alone, therapeutic world of ancient Greece. The reader who both experiences the rhythms of the poem and then analyzes them for their qualities and associations should benefit intellectually as well as physically from the product of what Carman calls in "Subconscious Art" "the achievement" of "both the personalities of the artist"—"intentional mind" and "subconscious spirit" (*KN*, 150). To what extent the techniques present in a poem such as Lyric XXIII are employed deliberately is in many instances difficult, if not impossible, to determine. A case in point—and one which will probably stretch the credence of more readers than it convinces—is the possible Delsartean significance of the word "long" in the opening line of "I loved thee, Atthis, in the long ago . . . ."

According to Hovey in "Delsarte and Poetry," "every syllable contains one vowel (or diphthong), and . . . most syllables are made up of three parts—an initial consonant, or consonant-group, a vowel or diphthong, and a final consonant or consonant-group." "[I]n pronouncing words by dwelling on the final consonants," he argues, "we make our expression passionate and physical, by dwelling on the initial consonants emotional, and by dwelling on the vowels we exaggerate the ideas of the words we use. If any one will take the word 'long,' for instance, and pronounce it in these three ways, he will see in an instant the truth of this statement."[72] As bizarre as Hovey's example may appear, it does seem to work for the opening line of Lyric XXIII where each of the "three parts" of the word "long"—the emotional "l," the intellectual "o," and the physical "ng"—could be said to be highlighted by different features of the line: the first by alliteration ("I lóved thee, Atthis, in the lóng ago . . . "), the second by assonance or "colliteration" ("I lōved thee, Atthis, in the lōng agō . . . "), and the third by the alliterative pattern that it initiates ("I loved thee, Atthis, in the lon̆g ăgo, / When the ğreat oleanders were in flower . . ."). Taken to its logical conclusion, this line of analysis suggests that in the penultimate line of the poem, "O Atthis, how I loved thee long ago . . . ," where the metre and the assonance conspire to place emphasis particularly on the "o" of "how" and "love," Sappho has reached an intellectual understanding of the (unitrinian) nature of her great love for Atthis.[73] While such directions and possibilities may strain the credibility of many readers, they at least have the advantage of locating Carman's poems in a context that emphasizes their possible meaning rather than, as all too often in the past, ignoring or denying it.

If Carman was alone among the Confederation poets in adopting a Delsartean program, he was not alone in assigning a therapeutic function to literature. "I confess that my design for instance in writing 'Among the Timothy' was not in the first place to describe a landscape,"

Lampman told Hamlin Garland in 1889, "but to describe the effect of a few hours spent among the summer fields on a mind in a troubled and despondent condition,"[74] a condition described in the poem itself as an "aching mood" of weariness and lifelessness born of "the drifting hours / The echoing city towers, / The blind gray streets, the jingle of the throng. . . ."[75] Central to Lampman's canon, as to the *Vagabondia* poems, is a therapeutic rhythm of excursion to nature and return to the city which the poems enact in order that—to quote the final lines of "April"—"we toil, brothers, without distress / In calm-eyed peace and godlike blamelessness."[76] It would be a mistake, of course, to overestimate the similarities between Lampman and Carman in their conceptions of the social and psychological purposes of poetry; both owe debts to Wordsworth, Arnold, and Emerson in these regards, but they develop these influences in quite different directions. Nevertheless, the point may be made that, in the 1890s, most obviously in "To Chicago" and "The City of the End of Things" (published respectively in the *Arena* and the *Atlantic Monthly*, two Boston periodicals), Lampman addressed himself directly to the problems attendant upon urbanization in the American Northeast,[77] and, if only in this concern, came to resemble his expatriate "friend."[78]

A greater resemblance, not least in the realm of book therapy, can be discerned between Carman and his fellow expatriate Roberts. In his seminal "Pipes of Pan," Carman's cousin depicts "the outworn pipes" of the goat-god, which have been "scattered" "Over the whole green earth and globe of sea" by the waters of the Arcadian river into which he threw them, as the source of a "secret madness . . . ,—a charm-struck / Passion for woods and wild life, the solitude of the hills."[79] All who have experienced the effect of the pipes, Roberts claims, will forever wish to "fly the heedless throngs and traffic of the cities," and to "Haunt mossed caverns, and wells bubbling ice-cool" where "their souls / Gather a magical gleam of the secret of life, and the god's voice / Calls to them, not from afar, teaching them wonderful things." Roberts' explanation of the liberating and rejuvenating effects of the animal story in his Introduction to *The Kindred of the Wild* is a lucid and explicit statement of the therapeutic function of the literature of "woods and wild life": "It frees us for a little from the world of shop-worn utilities and from the mean tenement of self. . . . It helps us to return to nature. . . . It leads us back to the old kinship of earth. . . . It has ever the more significance, it has ever the richer gift of refreshment and renewal, the more humane the heart and spiritual the understanding which we bring to the intimacy of it."[80] A full understanding of Roberts' poetry from around the turn of the century especially—*Songs of the Common Day, The Book of the Native,*

New York Nocturnes and *The Book of the Rose* are, of course, the pertinent volumes—would take into account the context of the New England mind-cure movement.

Carman's concern with modern civilization and its discontents links him to his fellow poets of the Confederation (and both Scott and Campbell could also be mentioned in this respect, as could a host of lesser-known figures such as Tom MacInnes and Marjorie Pickthall) because it is a fundamental component of the modernity—the reaction to modern life—that they all share. Needless to say, the Confederation poets and their Canadian successors differ radically in their philosophical ideas and literary techniques from the great Anglo-American Modernists, but they do not differ in perceiving the psychological and psychosomatic diseases of modern civilization or in practicing an art dedicated to diagnosing and curing those diseases. Pound, Eliot, Lewis, Lawrence, Auden, and others were much less interested than the Confederation poets (or, indeed, some of their fellow Modernists)[81] in soothing, rejuvenating, and appeasing the neurasthenic middle classes, but in addressing themselves to what Arnold had called the "strange disease of modern life" they were anticipated by many writers, not least Bliss Carman.

NOTES

As always, I am grateful to various people at the University of Western Ontario and elsewhere, particularly H. Pearson Gundy, Heather Nolan, R. M. Stingle, Leon Surette, and Michael Williams, for valuable discussions of ideas and information contained in this essay. My thanks to Launa Fuller for transforming the essay from scrawl to print.

1. *The Poetry of Life* (Toronto: Copp, Clark, 1905), pp. 122–123; hereafter cited as *PL*.
2. See, however, James Cappon, *Bliss Carman and the Literary Currents and Influences of his Time* (Toronto: Ryerson, 1930), pp. 130–131, 210ff., 224–227 and elsewhere, and Terry Whalen, "Bliss Carman," in Robert Lecker, Jack David, and Ellen Quigley, eds., *Canadian Writers and their Works*, Poetry Series, Vol. 2 (Downsview: ECW Press, 1983), pp. 93–121.
3. See *PL*, p. 51, where Carman argues that, once the "vital importance of art to a nation is recognized" and emphasis properly placed on "beauty and kindliness," the "specific development [or 'technic'] of poetry may safely be left to take care of itself." Form follows function.
4. See Gail Thain Parker, *Mind Cure in New England from the Civil War to World War I* (Hanover, NH: University Press of New England, 1973), *passim*, Donald Meyer, *The Positive Thinkers: Religion as Pop Psychology from Mary Baker Eddy* (1965; rpt. [with a new Preface and Conclusion] New York: Pantheon, 1980), the early chapters especially, and T. J. Jackson Lears, *No Place of Grace: Antimodernism and*

the Transformation of American Culture, 1880–1920 (New York: Pantheon, 1981), *passim*, but particularly pp. xiii–58. Also useful, though lacking in the perspective of Parker, Meyer, Lears, and others (it is not the present purpose to provide a bibliography of the mind-cure movement), is Horatio W. Dresser's *A History of the New Thought Movement* (New York: Thomas Y. Crowell, 1919). Parker defines "mind cure" as "a faith (and the practices growing out of it) in the power of mind over body, and, more specifically, in the power to heal oneself through right thinking" (p. ix), a definition that, for the present purposes, has been extrapolated in the direction of a Delsartean interdependence of mind, body, and spirit.
5.   Meyer, p. 124.
6.   Lears, whose formulation of the "therapeutic world view" (see pp. 47–58) has been especially helpful in the development of this essay, mentions Carman at various points in *No Place of Grace*. In his chapter entitled "Songs from Vagabondia" (pp. 59–80), Cappon recognizes the renovating role of nature in the work of Carman and Hovey, and Whalen observes that for the Canadian poet "[p]oetry should struggle towards spiritual health" and that "Nature is therapeutic" in such poems as "A Vagabond Song" (pp. 99, 114).
7.   In *The Kinship of Nature* (Boston: L. C. Page, 1903), p. 58; hereafter cited as *KN*.
8.   *Poetry and Criticism*, ed. A. Dwight Culler, Riverside Editions (Boston: Houghton Mifflin, 1961), p. 152. Carman quotes this phrase from "The Scholar-Gipsy," (l. 203) in *PL*, 193.
9.   Arnold, p. 108 ("Memorial Verses," l. 17).
10.   See Parker, pp. 57–79 and *passim*, and Meyer, pp. 75–81.
11.   See *No Place of Grace*, pp. 55–58 especially.
12.   *American Nervousness, its Causes and Consequences: a Supplement to Nervous Exhaustion (Neurasthenia)* (New York: G. P. Putnam's Sons, 1881), pp. 98–99, also cited in Meyer, p. 27.
13.   See Beard, p. 10, Meyer, p. 24, and Lears, pp. 49–51.
14.   *The Friendship of Art* (1904; London: John Murray, 1905), pp. 186–187; hereafter cited as *FA*.
15.   *The Making of Personality* (1906; Boston: L. C. Page, 1908), p. 258; hereafter cited as *MP*.
16.   *No Place of Grace*, p. 51.
17.   *Letters of Bliss Carman*, ed. H. Pearson Gundy (Kingston and Montreal: McGill-Queen's University Press, 1981), p. 130; hereafter cited as *L*.
18.   *American Nervousness*, p. 10.
19.   No connection between Hall and the mind-cure movement has yet been discovered; he is not mentioned by Dresser. Before her death in 1896, Carman had in Gertrude Burton a friend and correspondent who was clearly knowledgeable about the causes and cures of neurasthenia; see the letter of December 1892, quoted by Muriel Miller, *Bliss Carman: Quest and Revolt* (St. John's: Jesperson, 1985), p. 94, in which Burton warns Carman of the dangers of nervous "dyspepsia" for those of "artistic temperament." For Carman's various bouts of " 'gloom,' " see *ibid.*, pp. 146–148 and, of course, Mrs. King had more than one stay in a sanatorium for the purpose of "rest" (see *ibid.*, p. 199 and *L*, p. 140).
20.   See *FN*, p. 141: "Is not our love of Nature only the sentiment of abounding vitality and rugged self-reliance?" and Ralph Waldo Emerson, "Nature," *Complete Works*, Century Edition (Boston: Houghton Mifflin, 1903), I, 10. As both Parker (p. 58) and Meyer (p. 81) point out, mind-cure therapies frequently combined (or confused) tendencies towards selflessness ("love of Nature," self-transcendence in the Over Soul, and so on) with those tending towards—in the title of the famous

Emerson essay quoted by Carman—"Self Reliance" (character development,
invigorating activity, and so forth). See also Lears, pp. 52-54.
21.   See *MP*, pp. 120-121: "As much time as possible in the great fresh out-of-
doors, where our natures are at home, is medicine for many ills and brings
unguessed reinforcements of vitality to the thwarted spirit. Perplexities will often
vanish like a pallid sickness in open sunshine. And, be it soberly said, tired nerves
may be wonderfully refreshed by resting or sleeping on the naked ground, where
all their jangling rhythms may be reattuned and their discordant pain absorbed by
the great unseen magnetic currents of the earth." Here, as in countless other passages (see also *MP*, pp. 227 and 246) and poems, the abnormality and dissonance
("jangling") created in individuals by their artificial and cacophonous civilization
are cured by the spirituality and harmony of nature (or poetry). For music and
the music of poetry as agents of personal harmony, see, for example, *MP*, pp. 77
and 238 and *PL*, p. 61.
22.   Meyer, p. 28.
23.   *Ibid.*, p. 26 and *American Nervousness*, pp. 98-99. See also Lears, pp. 53-54
for the argument that "by the turn of the century . . . [there began to emerge] a
new type of therapy based not on the assumption of psychic scarcity but on a new
faith in psychic abundance"—a reservoir of energy within the individual that
could be released by certain activities. In *The Making of Personality*, the two therapies appear to rub elbows, as it were; see, for example, pp. 102 and 223 (and see
also *FA*, pp. 25-27).
24.   See especially "Of Vigour" in *The Friendship of Art*, where Carman asserts
that art that lacks "vigour"—the energy of the artist's "whole personality, body,
mind, and spirit!"—"has not that electric power of impressing itself upon one"
(pp. 25-26).
25.   Or serene; see *KN*, p. 187, *FA*, p. 17 and elsewhere.
26.   This point is, of course, merely a localization of the arguments of Meyer,
Lears, and other social and intellectual historians of a Marxist and Tory bent.
27.   Arnold, pp. 113 ("The Buried Life," l. 8) and 152 ("The Scholar-Gipsy,"
l. 190).
28.   In a speech delivered to businessmen in New York in 1882 and quoted by
Lears (p. 52), Herbert Spencer concluded: "I may say that we have had somewhat too much of the 'gospel of work.' It is time to preach the gospel of relaxation." As observed later in the present paper, Carman's notion of the large and
small rhythms governing life and poetry has roots in Spencer, a thinker whose
impact on the Canadian poet deserves to be studied in more detail than is possible
here.
29.   Cappon, p. 65.
30.   See *MP*, pp. 314-316: "One need not be a detractor of our own time to
praise justly the more primitive life of the open. . . . In our sanitation, our philan-
thropy, and our multifold conveniences, we have outstripped [past ages] beyond
. . . measure; and yet there remain the elemental needs to be remembered and
respected . . . . We go back to nature every time we take a deep breath and stop
worrying, every time we allow instinct to save us from some foolish indiscretion of
greed or heedlessness or bad habit. A tiled bath-room is not essentially a menace
to health; neither is a roll-top desk, nor a convenient electric light, nor any one of
the hundred luxuries we have become habited to."
31.   For the "cult of strenuosity" in the United States around the turn of the
century, see Lears, pp. 98-139; for the tendencies that it supposedly counteracted,
see Ann Douglas, *The Feminization of American Culture* (New York: Knopf, 1977),
passim. Carman frequently associates weakness in life and art with the feminine

(see, for example, Lears, p. 106), and he was drawn to the character and work of at least one "masculine woman," Louise Imogen Guiney, whom he salutes in his letters as "sir," "chum," "my brother," and so on (see *L*, pp. 35ff.) and regarded as "the best of our day" (*L*, 207), perhaps in part because "her swaggering activism [and] . . . martial motifs" (Lears, p. 127) seemed to him to be an antidote to the "effeminacy" of certain aspects of modern culture such as domestic drama. Lears notes that Guiney "[s]uffered from insomnia and neurasthenia, . . . [and] worried about the diminution of individual potency in a determined universe."

32.   Carman also offers the "captains of humanity" the consolation of other lives than their present ones: "the vast cisterns of repose may be opened to you in another incarnation; indeed they were possibly yours long since and from them you have derived this burning energy" (*KN*, p. 20).

33.   See John R. Sorfleet, "Transcendentalist, Mystic, Evolutionary Idealist: Bliss Carman, 1886-1894," in George Woodcock, ed., *Colony and Confederation: Early Canadian Poets and their Background* (Vancouver: University of British Columbia Press, 1974), pp. 189-210 and Whalen, pp. 99 and 119-120 for discussions of Carman's melioristic views of civilization. See also *PL*, p. 16 for his notions of the stages of civilization and the role of "leisure" in social progress.

34.   See *FA*, pp. 54-59 and *PL*, pp. 90-91.

35.   See *FA*, p. 205 and *L*, p. 74.

36.   See *PL*, pp. 72-77 for some very Ruskinian and Morrissian ideas about the relationships among art, manual labour, and industrial society.

37.   See *L*, p. 70 for Carman's account of his visit to Norton ("[t]he chief American precursor of Arts and Crafts ideology . . . , a close friend of Ruskin [and D. G. Rossetti] and first Professor of Fine Arts at Harvard" [Lears, p. 66]) in July 1894: "We sat in his study and talked—or rather he talked—all subjects, but chiefly art and poetry and the ugliness of modern life. . . . How princely of him! [Norton had offered Carman a house in the area 'for the rest of the summer, if I care to spend it there near him.'] I am now thoroughly Nortonized." Lears, pp. 245-246, observes that "Norton's escape from the achievement ethos was accompanied by neurasthenia. . . . But on the whole he adjusted to modern ego ideals, sublimating his 'feminine' impulses in socially acceptable forms." See also Miller, p. 45 and ff.

38.   Cf. *FA*, p. 106 for Carman's suggestion that if "modern art [is] frivolous, vapid, [and] unmanly," it is so because it is a reflection of its age, which can be put to rights by the eradication of "falsehood and greed."

39.   See, for example, *PL*, pp. 38-39, 76-77, 92-94, and 199.

40.   See "The Crime of Ugliness" in *KN*, pp. 25-34, where Carman plays with the notion of ugliness as crime *en route* to treating it as a "disease" whose "cure . . . lies in securing freedom for the workman."

41.   Many examples of Carman's use of these terms could be cited; see, for example, *PL*, pp. 61 and 72 and *FA*, pp. 172 and 187.

42.   See *PL*, pp. 2-4.

43.   See *PL*, pp. 59-60 and cf. p. 140.

44.   See *PL*, pp. 95-97.

45.   Cappon, p. 71.

46.   On the inside front-cover and first page of *Songs from Vagabondia* is an illustration of a twilit (?) harbour deserted of people (who have presumably left the town, for either the country or the open sea) and on the final page and inside back-cover is a view through pine trees out to sea. The cover depicts Hovey, Carman, and Tom B. Meteyard (the book's illustrator) within a moon-like circle,

an image that suggests male companionship in a context of mystery and natural rhythm. This iconic image appears on the covers of the later *Vagabondia* books, which, however, carry different internal illustrations, including, most tellingly for the present discussion, depictions of male figures smoking and reading in relaxed postures and among natural surroundings (*More Songs from Vagabondia*).

47.   *Songs from Vagabondia* (Boston: Small, Maynard, 1894), p. 2; hereafter cited as *SV*.

48.   *MP*, p. 102. See Parker, pp. 42, 53 and elsewhere for the Swedenborgian associations of this term.

49.   See *FA*, pp. 25, 30, and 106 and *MP*, p. 56 for instances of Carman discussing instinct and its role in mind cure.

50.   The opening and closing poems in *More Songs from Vagabondia* (Boston: Small, Maynard, 1896) (hereafter *MSV*) convey a similar rhythm of release from work (''Lay down your ledgers, your picks and your shovels, / Your trowels and bricks . . . '' [p. 1]) and return to battle (''Here's to a dark tomorrow, / And here's to a brave to-day!'' [72]). In *Last Songs from Vagabondia* (Boston: Small, Maynard, 1900), the rhythm has become structurally weaker but not the book's therapeutic thrust, as witness the equation in Carman's ''Holiday'' between the movement out of ''the sweltering city,'' ''the blaring streets,'' and ''the narrow houses of men'' with a rejection of ''despondency, fear, / Ambition, . . . pitiless greed, / And sordid unlovely regrets!'' in favour of a spiritually renovative sojourn among the ''elms'' and ''daisies'' in ''the country to the North'' (p. 22).

51.   See *L*, p. 129 and ''To 'Moonshine,' '' the opening piece in *The Friendship of Art*. ''[T]he habit of a country holiday [is growing] more universal,'' Carman accurately asserts in ''The Migrating Mood,'' taking people, not to ''huge, hideous hotels,'' but to ''some sleepy farmhouse in a nest of hills'' (*FA*, p. 172).

52.   See Lears, pp. 117–124.

53.   That literature should be touched with romance and idealism was a tenet of Carman's aesthetic, and one reason for his dislike of Realism and Naturalism (see, for example, *PL*, p. 9 and *FA*, p. 116).

54.   See also *MP*, p. 8 for Carman's conviction that the ''persistent punchings and pommelings of some forms of exercise strengthen not only the habits of physical violence, but deeper lying habits of aggression and pugnacity as well. . . . [T]hese manly arts must require and inculcate a code of manly honour and fair play, in order to maintain our respect.'' In ''Of Vigour'' (*The Friendship of Art*) and elsewhere Carman differentiates between sports that ''dissipate . . . energy'' and those that, by giving ''vigour to the personality through the body,'' help to ''counteract the bad physical effects of overmentalization'' (27).

55.   These poems are dated on the authority of John R. Sorfleet's edition of *The Poems of Bliss Carman*, *NCL*, 9 (Toronto: McClelland and Stewart, 1976), pp. 165 and 169. For convenience, quotations from the two poems are also taken from the texts in Sorfleet's edition, pp. 41–44 and 149–151.

56.   Lears, pp. 137–138.

57.   See Paul Fussell, Jr., *Poetic Metre and Poetic Form*, Studies in Language and Literature (New York: Random House, 1965), pp. 142–143. Francis James Child, the editor of *English and Scottish Popular Ballads*, published in five volumes between 1883 and 1898, was the English Professor from whom Carman ''got most'' (*L*, 190) at Harvard in 1886.

58.   See the entry under ''Ballad Meter'' in the enlarged edition of the *Princeton Encyclopedia of Poetry and Poetics*, ed. Alex Preminger (Princeton: Princeton University Press, 1974).

59.   ''The Technic of Rhyme,'' *Independent*, October 19, 1893, p. 3.

60.   See "Delsarte and Poetry," *Independent*, August 27, 1891, pp. 3–4, and Herbert Spencer, *First Principles*, 6th. ed. (New York and London: D. Appleton, 1900), pp. 228–235 especially; Sidney Lanier, *The Science of English Verse* (New York: Charles Scribner's Sons, 1893), *passim*; and J. J. Sylvester, *The Laws of English Verse*, or *Principles of Versification Exemplified in Metrical Translations* (London: Longmans, Green, 1870), pp. 9–19 and 30–49 especially. See also *L*, p. 41 ("I was amused at the idea of poets being mathematicians . . .") and *PL*, p. 61: "The kingdom of poetry is bordered on the north by mathematics [i.e., thought], and on the south by music [i.e., emotion], partaking of the character of each."
61.   *Independent*, August 27, 1891, pp. 3–4.
62.   See Parker, pp. 3–4, 122–123, and 131–133. Meyer makes the important point that hypnosis (and this applies also to hypnotic poetry) is "the surrender of conscious control in favor of external authority," and thus locates itself at the other- rather than self-reliant end of the mind-cure spectrum.
63.   *Mental Medicine: a Theoretical and Practical Treatise on Medical Psychology*, 3rd. ed. (Boston: Carter and Pettee, 1874), p. 42. Evans' approach to "the diseases of the present age" (p. 18) emphasizes the achievement of health and harmony through a combination of the physical, spiritual, and mental, and therefore offers many parallels with the Delsartean program of Carman, Hovey, and Mary Perry King. Moreover, Evans relies heavily on Swedenborg and places emphasis on "educating humanity to a higher range of life and activity" (p. 17). Most interesting of all, he intersperses his chapters and discussions with poems by himself and others, those in the former category under such titles as "The Unseen," "Ever Present," "Rest," and "There is No Death." It is certainly possible that Evans' implicitly therapeutic use of poetry, like his conviction that "an all-pervading, ever-present spiritual life . . . is . . . the unseen cause of all . . . visible phenomena" in "nature, the world, the universe" (p. 135), lies in Carman's background. Evans' approach to mind cure is discussed in Parker, pp. 48–56 and elsewhere.
64.   Arnold, p. 114; and cf. *KN*, pp. 53–59.
65.   *Independent*, October 19, 1893, p. 3.
66.   See "Delsarte and Poetry," *Independent*, August 27, 1891, p. 4.
67.   See "The Technic of Rhyme," *Independent*, October 19, 1893, pp. 3–4.
68.   See *ibid.*, p. 3.
69.   *Ibid.*, p. 4.
70.   See D.M.R. Bentley, "Threefold in Wonder: Bliss Carman's *Sappho: One Hundred Lyrics*," *Canadian Poetry: Studies, Documents, Reviews* 17 (Fall/Winter 1985), pp. 29–58.
71.   The text of the poem used here is quoted from *Sappho: One Hundred Lyrics* (1903; rpt. London: Chatto and Windus, 1930), p. 27.
72.   "Delsarte and Poetry," p. 4.
73.   Although, for obvious reasons, the focus of analysis here has fallen on the word "long" in the opening line of Lyric XXIII, similar arguments could be made on behalf of "love," a word whose referent Carman inevitably believed could comprehend mind, body, and spirit (see *L*, p. 190 and my "Threefold in Wonder," p. 34 and ff.).
74.   Quoted in James Doyle, "Archibald Lampman and Hamlin Garland," *Canadian Poetry: Studies, Documents, Reviews* 16 (Spring/Summer 1985), p. 42.
75.   *The Poems of Archibald Lampman*, ed. Duncan Campbell Scott (Toronto: George N. Morang, 1900), p. 14.
76.   *Ibid.*, p. 6.
77.   The case for this is argued in my forthcoming article " 'The City of the End of Things,' and an Approach to Influence in Canadian Poetry."

78. This is Lampman's term in his "At the Mermaid Inn" column for October 1, 1892, *At the Mermaid Inn: Wilfred Campbell, Archibald Lampman, Duncan Campbell Scott in* The Globe *1892-93,* ed. Barrie Davies, Literature of Canada: Poetry and Prose in Reprint (Toronto: University of Toronto Press, 1979), p. 159.

79. *Poems,* New Complete Ed. (Toronto: Copp, Clark, 1907), pp. 26-27.

80. "Introductory: The Animal Story," *Kindred of the Wild* (1902; rpt. Boston: L. C. Page, 1935), p. 29.

81. Lears, p. 191, quotes and translates as follows a passage from *Notes d'un peintre* (1908) in which Henri Matisse hopes for "an art which will be for every mental worker, be he businessman or writer, like an appeasing influence, like a mental soother, something like a good armchair in which to rest from physical fatigue." A point worth making by way of postscript is that Canada's northern hinterlands have in Modern Canadian art and literature—Lawren Harris comes particularly to mind, as does the A.J.M. Smith of "The Lonely Land"—tonic qualities that minister therapeutically to the mind and spirit of the "overmentalized" reader. In *The Sense of Power: Studies in the Ideas of Canadian Imperialism, 1867-1914* (Toronto: University of Toronto Press, 1970), pp. 128-133, Carl Berger places on view the long tradition that the Canadian climate is healthy and health-giving. This tradition, inherited perhaps from his "Teacher and Friend George . . . Parkin" (*FN,* p. v), may well have contributed to Carman's therapeutic conception of nature, particularly northern nature, which he regarded as especially imbued with intimations of rebirth on account of the importance of spring in northern latitudes (see, for example, "The Vernal Ides," "Easter Eve," "Rhythm," and "April in Town" in *FN* and "Saint Valentine" and "The March Hare's Madness" in *FA,* not to mention numerous "Aprilian" poems in the *Vagabondia* volumes and elsewhere).

Bringing "Gladness out of Sorrow": *By the Aurelian Wall*

TRACY WARE

When poetry, poetry that is highly esteemed and widely valued, refers to death, it seeks and celebrates some trace of survival, some hint of immortality. It strives to minimize the depressing aspect of death, and bring gladness out of sorrow. [1]

BLISS CARMAN

The tomb of the poet is built by other poets; their verses take him in. [2]

LAWRENCE LIPKING

In 1898 Bliss Carman collected his elegiac and commemorative verse in *By the Aurelian Wall and Other Elegies*, carefully arranging the book so that its first and title poem is about Keats, its longest poem is about Shelley, its first three poems are for English Romantics, and its concluding poem is for Carman himself. One of the reasons why this book should be better known is that it provides a corrective to some influential generalizations about Carman. It is regrettably and notoriously true that the later Carman was fond of rhyming "God" and "sod," but at his best he was not a poet of facile Romanticism. A poet whose ideas, according to Roy Daniells, involve a sufficiency within nature which "could only be plausible in a new country where the terrain carried few memories or associations," [3] could never have written these poems. They reveal that Carman is not naive precisely because his understanding of Romanticism is not naive. There is a profound sadness in these poems and elsewhere in Carman, a sadness that A.J.M. Smith held in 1946 to have been inadequately recognized. Actually, in 1896 Harry W. Brown noted Carman's sadness and realized its significance:

> The feeling of discontent is properly one with which we should all be imbued in order that the resultant dissatisfaction should inspire us to increased effort and power, and provide us with the satisfaction of knowing we have a latent force to open out before us a wider world. [4]

In addition to its intrinsic merit, the importance of *By the Aurelian Wall* is that it is an acknowledgement of influence, an admission that both

Carman's sadness and his idealism derive at least in part from Romanticism. Like the Romantics, Carman sees the alienation of the human condition: "Once given the perilous gift of self-consciousness," he writes elsewhere, "the large slow contentment of nature is no longer possible."[5] The Romantics are exemplary because, refusing to accept this alienation as irremediable, they make their dissatisfaction inspire "increased effort and power," thereby bringing "gladness out of sorrow."

An exact contemporary of Charles G. D. Roberts' *Ave*, "The White Gull" is generally recognized as Carman's most ambitious and successful commemorative poem.[6] As the title implies, Carman's technique involves the transformation of natural images into suggestive tropes. In the opening section of "The White Gull," the powers of the sea are addressed and personified, and we are placed beneath their influence:

> For we are his [the sea's], bone of his bone,
> Breath of his breath;
> The doom tides sway us at their will;
> The sky of being rounds us still;
> And over us at last is blown
> The wind of death.[7]

As in *Ave*, the tides have a figurative meaning, but here that meaning is explicitly allegorical: they are the "doom tides," moving beneath the "sky of being" and the "wind of death." The whole scene is suffused with melancholia, and the dying fall in the shorter second and sixth lines, short clauses, and simple diction combine to enhance Carman's lament for mutability, a specific example of which is the death of Shelley.

Developing the poetic possibilities of the setting in the next section, Carman makes the sea gull into an analogue of Shelley:

> And something, Shelley, like thy fame
> Dares the wide morn
> In that sea-rover's glimmering flight,
> As if the Northland and the night
> Should hear thy splendid valiant name
> Put scorn to scorn.   (p. 18)

As the speaker turns from nature to Shelley, his diction and sentence structure become more complex. Carman's gull appropriately echoes, but does not simply repeat, Shelley's identification of the poet and the skylark. As a metaphor the gull also suggests the ideal of freedom that Carman often expresses in terms of the concept of "vagabondia," a prominent motif in *By the Aurelian Wall*, where Robert Louis Stevenson, Paul Verlaine, Goodridge Roberts, Andrew Straton, and finally Carman himself are depicted as types of this ideal. The pilgrimage of the vagabond symbolizes the spiritual life, which Carman regards as an "endless quest" (p. 110). Believing that, as he writes elsewhere, "to cease to strive is to begin to degenerate,"[8] Carman exhorts his audience to continue the quests of the elegiac subjects. Moreover, in "The White Gull" the elements of nature are themselves figurative vagabonds: the "pale Summer" speaks of her "wayward journeyings," the "great cloud-navies" leave port for "havens of the sun," "The gray sea-horses troop and roam," and, most important, "A white gull searches the blue dome / With keening cry" (pp. 17–18). Shelley emerges as a model of heroic defiance, daring the morn as if he could "Put scorn to scorn" and banish darkness.

In the third section, Carman makes the crucial elegiac transition from lamentation to praise. Addressing Shelley as the "heart of all the hearts of men, / Tameless and free" (p. 19)—this last phrase an allusion to "Ode to the West Wind" (l. 56)—Carman emphasizes the difficulties besetting Shelley's quest. When Shelley tried "to rouse / His comrades from their heavy drowse" (p. 19), he received an indifferent reaction: "the dim world will dream and sleep / Beneath thy hand" (p. 20). James Cappon argues that Carman presents Shelley as

> a Knight of the Holy Ghost spending his life in a struggle with the powers of darkness. Not that he won the battle or even made the victory sure, for Carman's idea is naturally that of a Promethean revolt ages long and even doubtful in its issue.[9]

The reference to "Promethean revolt" is pertinent, but not the reference to "the Holy Ghost." Not only does Carman show little interest in Christian orthodoxy throughout *By the Aurelian Wall*, he also adapts Shelley's Romantic Satanism. His account of Shelley as "vague as that marsh-wandering fire" (p. 19) is a probable allusion to Milton's Satan (see *Paradise Lost*, IX, 634–42), a probability that increases when Shelley is called the "captain of the rebel host" (p. 20). Unlike Roberts, Carman does not try to reconcile Shelley's idealism with Christianity. As he does also in the commemorative poems to Verlaine and Raphael in this volume, Carman argues that if the rebelliousness of the artist upsets an orthodox morality, then so much the worse for that morality. He is on the side of Shelley, the rebel-artist:

> Thy toiling troopers of the night
> Press on the unavailing fight;
> The sombre field is not yet lost,
> With thee for star.   (p. 20)

Like Lucifer, Shelley becomes a star, glorious even though his fight is "unavailing."

Continuing Shelley's revolt, Carman falls heir to its discontents, and hence the sadness that Brown and Smith find pervading Carman's work. In the following stanza, Carman joins Shelley's "unavailing fight":

> Thy lips have set the hail and haste
> Of clarions free
> To bugle down the wintry verge
> Of time forever, where the surge
> Thunders and crumbles on a waste
> And open sea.   (p. 21)

Here the sombre seascape is that of Carman's beloved Maritimes, while the "lips" and the "clarions" are those of the Shelleyan poet, "forever" at strife with the indifferent elements. The stanza concisely and appropriately alludes to Spring's regenerative "clarion" in "Ode to the West Wind" (l. 10), and to the description of poets as "the trumpets which sing to battle and feel not what they inspire" in *A Defence of Poetry*.[10]

Although the sombre mood of "The White Gull" contrasts with the exuberance of Roberts' *Ave*, there are resemblances in style and content in the two poems. Both poets provide an abundance of images and similes for Shelley, paying him the homage of stylistic imitation. Carman compares Shelley to a gull, a captain, a trumpeter, the *ignis fatuus*, a wanderer in nature, a blessed son of the Great Mother, and an outcast. Like Roberts and Shelley, Carman "undermines the authority of any one figure by the sheer profusion" of his images.[11] Collectively, Carman's images call attention to the many dimensions of Shelley's personality and to his vital influence. Following Shelley's depiction of the poet in *Alastor*, both Roberts and Carman regard Shelley as favoured by, yet ultimately unsatisfied in, nature. That is to say, both are aware of what Harold Bloom has called "the dialectic of nature and the imagination" in Romanticism: because the home of the imagination is with infinitude, nature is inadequate to meet its demands.[12]

Carman suggests that the transmission of Shelley's quest is a consolation for his death, and for the inadequacy of nature. He asks, and, in raising the question, implies an affirmative answer to it, whether "the cold Norns who pattern life"

Set their last kiss upon thy face,
And let thee go
To tell the haunted whisperings
Of unimaginable things,
Which plague thy fellows with a trace
They cannot know?   (pp. 21–22)

Carman's idea, that the true poet is able to communicate what others dimly feel, accords with Shelley, who argues that poetry bears "sweet news of kindred joy" to those who have "no portal of expression from the caverns of the spirit which they inhabit into the universe of things."[13] But Carman also adapts Scandinavian mythology: the Norns (goddesses of Fate) bless Shelley, who becomes "A resonant meteor of the North," a symbol of the supernatural, in "the pale splendor of the night" (p. 22), that is, in the lesser realm of the merely natural. To accentuate that contrast, Carman juxtaposes the lassitude of nature, whose hills, in summer, "Muttered of freedom in their sleep / And slept again" (p. 23), with the ardent courage of Shelley, bade to "follow without fear / The endless trail" (p. 24).

Like so many writers in the Western tradition, Carman is constructively dualistic: he recognizes that "At his best [man] is well poised between two realms,"[14] the natural and the supernatural, but he demands that we ceaselessly try to improve ourselves. Essentially the same philosophy is held in common by the Confederation poets, and given its definitive expression by Lampman, who states that "human nature may be represented by the ancient Pan—half human and half beast—but the human is the mightier part, and the whole is ever striving to be divine."[15] For Roberts and Carman, Shelley is exemplary for similar reasons:

And yet within thee flamed and sang
The dauntless heart,
Knowing all passion and the pain
Of man's imperious disdain,
Since God's great part in thee gave pang
To earth's frail part.   (p. 26)

Like Keats and others before him, Carman hopes to redeem suffering by regarding it as formative, by seeing pain as an inevitable consequence of our endless need for change. Such is the theodicy implicit in these lines, and its value is not diminished because it has Romantic antecedents: as Peter M. Sacks argues, "More than other poems, elegies are indeed condemned to repeat themselves and their predecessors."[16]

In the first five stanzas of the seventh and penultimate section, the speaker holds that Shelley's "sleep" would be gentler in "this far western headland" (pp. 27–28). As he soon realizes, however, the point is moot, for Shelley does not sleep at all. In a dignified understatement of the ultimate consolation, the speaker describes the completion of Shelley's quest in another and better world:

> For thou hast overcome at last;
> And fate and fear
> And strife and rumor now no more
> Vex thee by any wind-vexed shore,
> Down the strewn ways thy feet have passed
> Far, far from here. (p. 30)

Carman's sense of elegiac decorum allows only a restrained assertion of faith. Carman thought that an elegy should "bring gladness out of sorrow," but he stressed that this should be done through "some trace of survival, some hint of immortality."[17] As Eric Smith argues, if the consolation is not understated, "human life is liable to be diminished." Hence the conclusion of "The White Gull" merely suggests a religious perspective that would allow one to look through death with a "philosophic mind." Partly for closural purposes, this conclusion is a coda of two stanzas repeated from the opening two sections. The "many things" that the wind has to tell, the "many a tale" that the sea has to offer (p. 30), have been symbolically stated in the body of the poem. Therefore "the restless heart" (p. 30) can now return to the present scene and, thankful for its restlessness, perceive in the gull a symbol of its own infinite aspirations. In Malcolm Ross's words, the purpose of such a symbol is "the reason for song—the resurrection of beauty out of loss by the rejection of final affinity with the individual."[18] "The White Gull" neither denies nor devalues human suffering, but it expresses Carman's belief that it can be transcended.

Elsewhere in *By the Aurelian Wall*, in "Phillips Brooks" and "Henry George," Carman expresses his ideas in Christian imagery and diction. Like Roberts, he is not opposed to Christianity, but to its narrow adherents. In "Phillips Brooks," Carman adopts a homiletic manner that suits his subject: Brooks was a liberal clergyman who had been charged with heresy; his most famous sermon, on "the spirit of man is the candle of the Lord," indicates his affinities with the latitudinarian Cambridge Platonists of the seventeenth century, who repeatedly stated that theme.[19] Carman succinctly combines his approval of Brooks's teaching with a subtle admonition of its opponents in the line, "Churches are narrow to hold such as he" (p. 59). After praising Brooks as the "hero," not of the Church, but of Harvard (p. 61), he concludes by exhorting his audience that there is "One Way till strife be done, strive each his most," for such is the true *imitatio Christi*:

> Take the last vesture of beauty upon thee,
> Thou doubting world; and with not an eye dim
> Say, when they ask if thou knowest a Saviour,
> "Brooks was His brother, and we have known him."
>
> (p. 63)

"By the Aurelian Wall, In Memory of John Keats," the first poem in the volume, opens with a description of Keats's Roman grave:

> By the Aurelian Wall,
> Where the long shadows of the centuries fall
> From Caius Cestius' tomb,
> A weary mortal seeking rest found room
> For quiet burial,
>
> Leaving among his friends
> A book of lyrics.   (p. 9)

As these lines indicate, Carman's simple stanzas and sparse lines have none of the sensuous intensity and rich pictorial vividness so characteristic of Keats and his nineteenth-century followers. Its initiative position in the book, however, and its subordination of other elements to its parable, suggest that through the parable of a child who learns to play a flute given him by a traveller, Carman is making a point of overriding importance: that the real Pan, the true pied piper, of the nineteenth century is Keats. Carman makes the connection in the fourteenth stanza, where he compares Keats's rise to fame with the universal popularity of the child-flutist:

> And so his splendid name,
> Who left the book of lyrics and small fame
> Among his fellows then,
> Spreads through the world like autumn—who knows
>   when?—
> Till all the hillsides flame.   (p. 13)

Despite its lightly sketched quality, this account of Keats's reputation is accurate. As George H. Ford demonstrates, Keats's fame was so slight at his death that a reprint of his poetry did not appear for nineteen years;

after 1850, however, Keats rapidly gained prominence, and his grave had been a popular "pilgrimage point" for some three decades before "By the Aurelian Wall" was first published in the February 1893 issue of the *Independent*.[20] In his parable, Carman uses the metaphor of a universal "weird enchantment" (p. 13) to describe Keats's immense influence. In a stanza similar to the conclusion of "The Green Book of the Bards," where he calls "Low Tide on Grand Pré" a "footnote" to the world's great literature,[21] Carman adds his own name to the roll of Keats's followers:

> Grand Pré and Margaree
> Hear it upbruited from the unresting sea;
> And the small Gaspereau,
> Whose yellow leaves repeat it, seems to know
> A new felicity.   (p. 14)

The voice of Keats comes to be heard through nature, and in the nature poetry of Bliss Carman, in which the regions named here are featured. "By the Aurelian Wall" is Carman's figurative pilgrimage to Rome and his acknowledgement that the pervasive influence of English Romanticism extends to Canada.

In "The Country of Har," Carman commemorates William Blake, then a much less influential poet. Published in the *Athenaeum* in 1890, "The Country of Har" precedes the landmark Yeats–Ellis edition of Blake by three years. We have Arthur Symons's word that Carman's poem "caused considerable enthusiasm over here."[22] The subtitle, "For the Centenary of Blake's *Songs of Innocence*," alerts us that Carman is unaware of some of the ironies that critics after *Fearful Symmetry* take for granted. Believing that, as Frye has it, Innocence and Experience satirize each other,[23] we would not refer, as Carman does, exclusively to one of these contrary states. Furthermore, we might also be troubled by Carman's celebration of Blake as a pastoral poet. Until Frye, however, there was little or no awareness of any irony in Blake's use of pastoral. Some historical sympathy, therefore, should be extended to "The Country of Har," in which Carman at least recognizes a connection between the *Songs of Innocence* and *The Book of Thel*. To be sure, Carman does not regard Blake "steadily and whole," as Frye does, but he was perceptive enough to recognize Blake's influence on Yeats, calling the latter "the William Blake of this smaller generation" in an 1896 letter.[24]

Har is the ideal of England that Blake imagines as a contrast to "the crying chords of night" (p. 32) in contemporary London: Blake's "soul was a-wonder / At the calling vales of Har" (p. 33). Using the imagery and diction of "Ah! Sun-flower" (actually a song of Experience), Carman praises Blake for the boundlessness of his "desire":

> He, a traveller by day
> And a pilgrim of the sun,
> Took his uncompanioned way
> Where the journey is not done.
>
> Where no mortal might aspire
> His clear heart was set to climb,
> To the uplands of desire
> And the river wells of time.   (p. 33)

In Blake's poem—a formal model for "The Country of Har" and other Carman lyrics—the sun-flower is a symbol of futile aspiration, bound to the earth while yearning for the sun:

> Ah! Sun-flower, weary of time,
> Who countest the steps of the Sun:
> Seeking after that sweet golden clime
> Where the traveller's journey is done.
>
> Where the Youth pined away with desire,
> And the pale Virgin shrouded in snow
> Arise from their graves and aspire
> Where my Sun-flower wishes to go.[25]

Carman's indebtedness to Blake is obviously extensive, but he uses "Ah! Sun-flower" in order to build his own poem: all his allusions eliminate the demonic aspects of Blake's poem. Blake's sun-flower yearns for a paradise "Where the traveller's journey is done"; Carman's Blake is an eternal "pilgrim of the sun," a brave vagabond whose "journey is not done" because it is endless. Blake's youth has "pined away with desire"; Carman's Blake aims for "the uplands of desire," a goal to which "no mortal might aspire" (in the sense of "mount up"), but where the immortal belong. Once again the elegist imitates the precursor's style, thereby implying his praise through the compliment of imitation, and his consolation through an acknowledgement of an influence that transcends death.

Carman's references to "manna in the rain" (an allusion to *Thel*, Plate 1, l. 23) and a voice "above the rills" (p. 35) prepare for a divine voice that assigns Blake his prophetic vocation:

> "Thou shalt be a child to men,
> With confusion on thy speech;
> And the worlds within thy ken
> Shall not lie within thy reach." (p. 35)

Blake is seen as a mystic who has insight into a divine splendour that he can apprehend but not comprehend.[26] His Har is a pastoral ideal free from mutability:

> "April rain and iron frost
> Shall make flowers to thy hand;
> Every field thy feet have crossed
> Shall revive from death's command." (p. 36)

Har represents the world of our desire, the function of which is to keep the imagination alive in the world of Experience:

> "For the lone child-heart is dying
> Of a love no time can mar,
> Hearing not a voice replying
> From the gladder vales of Har." (p. 37)

In Experience, the "child-heart," signifying the aspirations of youth, becomes cut off from the objects of its desire, much as the figures in "Ah! Sun-flower" are confined to the graves of repression. Presenting the contemporary world as a wintry iron age, Carman adapts the imagery of such songs of Experience as "The Chimney Sweeper" and "London":

> Centuries of soiled renown
> To the roaring dark have gone:
> There is woe in London town,
> And a crying for the dawn. (p. 38)

"In derision," the world mocks the visionary, not sensing the imaginative truths in his "delirium of vision" (p. 39). And the elegist can gain no hope from nature, for the spring that follows winter is equally demonic:

> April frost and iron rain
> Ripen the dead fruit of lust,
> And the sons of God remain
> The dream children of the dust. (p. 38)

A grotesquely industrialized society sees the natural in terms of the mechanical ("iron rain")—as Blake might have said, all that it sees is owing to its metaphysics. The imaginative "sons of God," alienated from this society, remain mere dreamers, helpless to effect change in a world that will not heed them. The phrase "April frost and iron rain" neatly inverts the "April rain and iron frost" of the divine voice's speech, thereby giving force to the lamentation over an unnaturally prolonged winter.

In the last six stanzas of "The Country of Har," Carman describes his own vision or regeneration. The dream occurs in autumn, when "The white Herald of the North," the harbinger of the imminent winter, visits him while "Faring West" (p. 39), a direction that evokes associations of death and rebirth. The Herald reveals what at first appears to be an endless winter in a desecrated Har:

> Then I saw the warder lifting
> From its berg the Northern bar,
> And eternal snows were drifting
> On the wind-bleak plains of Har. (p. 40)

Carman alludes to the "Holy Thursday" of Experience, with its "eternal winter," and to Thel's visit to the world of Experience: "The eternal gates terrific porter lifted the northern bar: / Thel enter'd in & saw the secrets of the land unknown" (Blake, Plate 6, ll. 1–2). Bloom explains that "the symbolism of the eternal gates is derived from *The Odyssey*, Book XIII . . .":

> The northern gate is the passage from lower innocence to experience, and so a gate for men, because this passage is necessary for human existence. The southern gate is the passage from experience to a higher, imaginatively organized innocence, and so more akin to the gate of the gods. Thel flees back through the northern gate, and so returns to the unorganized innocence or ignorance of the lower paradise. (In "Blake," pp. 808–809)

Instead of fleeing, however, Carman in his dream perseveres to find that there are forces transcending death:

> "Listen humbly," said my guide.
> "I am drear, for I am death,"
> Whispered Snow; but Wind replied,
> "I outlive thee by a breath,
>
> "I am Time." (p. 40)

Carman's symbolism derives from Romanticism's "correspondent breeze,'' which M. H. Abrams has shown to be linked with an ''outer transition from winter to spring'' and an inner transition from ''a death-like torpor'' to a renewal of ''emotional vigor'' and ''creative power.''[27] As ''The Country of Har'' concludes, the regeneration of the outer world remains in the future:

> Spring, the angel of our sorrow,
> Tarrying so seeming far,
> Should return with some long morrow
> In the calling vales of Har. (p. 41)

The regeneration of the speaker, however, is complete. His return to creativity may be measured by his imaginative perception of the ''immense world of delight''[28] of ''One gray golden-shafted bird'' (p. 40)—a portent of the apocalyptic restoration of the world. The bird hails ''the uplands'' (p. 40), and the word ''uplands'' echoes the poem's earlier reference to the ''uplands of desire'' (p. 33). As time transcends death, so Har, like heaven, transcends the things of this world.

In a fitting conclusion to *By the Aurelian Wall*, Carman writes his own elegy, ''The Grave-Tree,'' which repeats and unites many of the book's recurring themes and images.[29] One of Carman's ancestors, Emerson, wrote that ''every man is a quotation from all his ancestors.''[30] Having delineated his literary ancestry in previous poems, Carman concludes by revealing something of the man behind the quotations. ''The Grave-Tree'' has a deserved place in the post-Romantic tradition that includes Tennyson's ''My Life is Full of Weary Days,'' Christina Rossetti's ''Song'' (''When I am dead, my dearest''), and Yeats's ''Under Ben Bulben.''

''The Grave-Tree'' is set in Carman's native New Brunswick, where he eventually received the commemorative scarlet maple that he desired. For his titular symbol, Carman is probably indebted to Matthew Arnold's ''Thyrsis,'' with its ''signal-elm'' that symbolizes the enduring merit of Clough's quest.[31] The pagan associations of the tree are also relevant, for the maple symbolizes the beauties of nature with which Carman, when dead, will continue to identify himself:

> Let me have it for a signal,
> Where the long winds stream and stream,
> Clear across the dim blue distance,
> Like a horn blown in a dream. (p. 127)

I interpret the sounding of the horn to be a metaphor of the survival of the spirit beyond the grave, where the spirit keeps its integrity against the "long winds" and "the dim blue distance." Carman's idea is that the soul enters into a period of rest after death:

> I would sleep, but not too soundly,
> Where the sunning partridge drums,
> Till the crickets hush before him
> When the Scarlet Hunter comes. (p. 130)

Viewed as a finality, death confirms our identity with the natural world:

> It will be my leafy cabin,
> Large enough when June returns
> And I hear the golden thrushes
> Flute and hesitate by turns. (p. 128)

Although Carman asserts, in the eighth stanza, that he will be content in "the Great Lone Country" of nature (p. 129), he also desires to be reborn from the seasonal cycle. His pantheism bears striking resemblance to one form of Christian eschatology, because his period of rest after death is finite, not final, and it precedes a sort of resurrection. Carman "would sleep, but not too soundly," so as not to miss the coming of the "Scarlet Hunter":

> That will be in warm September
> In the stillness of the year,
> When the river-blue is deepest
> And the other world is near. (p. 130)

Instead of repudiating the natural for the supernatural, he looks for a moment when "the other world is near," when he can move from cyclical time into eternity.

The "Scarlet Hunter" stands for forces beyond the natural world:

> It will be the Scarlet Hunter
> Come to tell me time is done;
> On the idle hills forever
> There will stand the idle sun. (p. 131)

Just as Carman's rest in the grave corresponds to the millenarian doctrine of "psychopannychism," the sleep between death and the day of judgement, so the coming of the Scarlet Hunter corresponds to the Second Coming and the Last Day.[32] When "time is done" so is the temporal world, as well as Carman's sleep. Carman quietly states his faith in deliverance from the world of death in the lines, "I shall not fear to follow / Where my Scarlet Hunter leads" (p. 131). The Scarlet Hunter is a daimonic intermediary between the supernatural and the natural: Carman expects to greet him "Stooping down to summon me" (p. 132), in a gesture of divine condescension. The poet's grave, it is now clear, is not a permanent abode at all, but a place of temporary rest, from which he and his saviour will venture forth to a trail that is "endless" because it is eternal:

> Leave me by the scarlet maple,
> When the journeying shadows fail,
> Waiting till the Scarlet Hunter
> Pass upon the endless trail.   (p. 132)

Two general observations will conclude this paper. The first is simply that the well-wrought volume of poetry, of which *By the Aurelian Wall* is an example, is one of the major achievements of Confederation poetry. The second is that, at their best, Carman and his Canadian peers are remarkably aware of their place in literary history. In 1898, as one can see from "By the Aurelian Wall," the influence of Keats is at its zenith. By 1921, as one can see from Duncan Campbell Scott's "Ode for the Keats Centenary," the literary climate has changed dramatically. That Confederation poetry can serve as a gauge to international literary trends should surprise no one who has given it a careful study. As A.J.M. Smith came increasingly to realize, the Confederation poets had a balanced awareness of their position in space and in time. More than some subsequent poets and critics, they knew the truth of Smith's assertion: "to be aware of our temporal setting as well as of our environment, and in no obvious and shallow way, is the nearest we can come to being traditional."[33] In their elegiac poems, the Confederation poets show a keen awareness and intelligent adaptation of tradition. That these poems were rarely considered by Canada's Modernist critics reveals some of the limitations of Modernism. As Malcolm Ross states, "our best writers today have much more in common with Roberts and the others than they would care to admit."[34]

NOTES

I am grateful to D.M.R. Bentley and R. M. Stingle for their comments on an earlier version of this paper.

1.   *The Poetry of Life* (Boston: L. C. Page, 1905), p. 9.
2.   *The Life of the Poet: Beginning and Ending Poetic Careers* (Chicago and London: University of Chicago Press, 1981), p. 139.
3.   "Crawford, Carman, and Scott," in *Literary History of Canada: Canadian Literature in English*, ed. Carl F. Klinck et al. (Toronto: University of Toronto Press, 1965), p. 415.
4.   "Bliss Carman's Latest Book of Poems," rev. of *Behind the Arras: A Book of the Unseen*, the *Canadian Magazine* VI, No. 5 (March 1896), 478. Smith's observation is in "The Fredericton Poets," a 1946 speech available in *Twentieth-Century Essays on Confederation Literature*, ed. and introd. Lorraine McMullen (Ottawa: Tecumseh Press, 1976), p. 137.
5.   *The Friendship of Art* (Boston: L. C. Page, 1904), p. 119.
6.   See James Cappon, *Bliss Carman and the Literary Currents and Influences of His Time* (Toronto: Ryerson, 1930), p. 87; Muriel Miller, *Bliss Carman: A Portrait* (Toronto: Ryerson, 1935), p. 55. Carman worked on "The White Gull" for many years. According to Gundy, the Shelley verses that Carman refers to in "To Muriel Carman," January 25, 1887, Letter 15 (*Letters of Bliss Carman*, ed. and introd. H. Pearson Gundy [Kingston and Montreal: McGill-Queen's University Press, 1981], p. 14n), are an early version. "The White Gull" was first published in the *Independent*, August 4, 1892. Susan Glickman has recently identified and reprinted the Shelley verses; see "Carman's 'Shelley' and Roberts' 'Ave,' " *Canadian Poetry: Studies, Documents, Reviews* 24 (Spring/Summer 1989), pp. 20–28.
7.   *By the Aurelian Wall and Other Elegies* (Boston, New York, and London: Lamson, Wolffe, 1898), p. 16. Subsequent citations will be given in parentheses.
8.   *The Kinship of Nature* (1903; rpt. Toronto: Copp Clark, 1904), p. 15.
9.   Cappon, p. 89.
10.   In *Shelley's Prose, or the Trumpet of a Prophecy*, ed. David Lee Clark (1954; rpt. Albuquerque: University of New Mexico Press, 1956), p. 297.
11.   See my discussion in "Charles G. D. Roberts and the Elegiac Tradition," *The Sir Charles G. D. Roberts Symposium*, ed. and introd. Glenn Clever (Ottawa: University of Ottawa Press, 1984), p. 49.
12.   *The Visionary Company: A Reading of English Romantic Poetry* (1961; rev. ed., Ithaca and London: Cornell University Press, 1971), pp. vii, 286–87.
13.   *Shelley's Prose*, pp. 294–95.
14.   *The Making of Personality* (Boston: L. C. Page, 1908), p. 96. Though only Carman's name appears, Mary Perry King is in fact the co-author of this book.
15.   "The Modern School of Poetry in England," in *Archibald Lampman: Selected Prose*, ed. and introd. Barrie Davies (Ottawa: Tecumseh Press, 1975), p. 93. See D.M.R. Bentley, "Pan and the Confederation Poets," *Canadian Literature* 81 (Summer 1979), pp. 59–71.
16.   *The English Elegy: Studies in the Genre from Spenser to Yeats* (Baltimore and London: Johns Hopkins University Press, 1985), p. 327.
17.   See note 1. Smith's comment is from *By Mourning Tounges: Studies in English Elegy* (Ipswich: Boydell Press, 1977), p. 2.
18.   "A Symbolic Approach to Carman," *Canadian Bookman* XIV, No. 11 (December 1932), 142.
19.   Brooks used this theme from Proverbs 20:27 as the title of his second volume of sermons, *The Candle of the Lord, and Other Sermons*; see Alexander V. G. Allen, *Life and Letters of Phillips Brooks* (New York: E. P. Dutton, 1900), II, p. 319. Ernst Cassirer argues that this theme is "the motto of the Cambridge movement"; see his *The Platonic Renaissance in England* (1932), trans. James P. Pettegrove

(New York: Thomas Nelson and Sons, 1953), p. 40.

20. *Keats and the Victorians: A Study of His Influences and Rise to Fame 1821–1895* (1944; rpt. Hamden and London: Archon Books, 1962), pp. 2, 70. For information on the publication of ''By the Aurelian Wall,'' see Gundy, *Letters of Bliss Carman*, p. 102n.

21. In *From the Green Book of the Bards* (1903), rpt. in *Pipes of Pan: Definitive Edition* (Boston: The Page Company, 1906), Section II, p. 8.

22. Letter to Bliss Carman, July 4, 1890, Bliss Carman Papers, Smith College Library, Northampton, Massachusetts. I am grateful to Ruth Mortimer and her staff for help with this material. ''The Country of Har'' appeared in the *Athenaeum* 3251 (February 15, 1890), 213.

23. *Fearful Symmetry: A Study of William Blake* (1947; rpt. Princeton: Princeton University Press, 1974), p. 237. I am indebted to David Clark for my awareness of historical developments in Blake criticism.

24. ''To Louise Imogen Guiney,'' September 2, 1896, Letter 157, *Letters of Bliss Carman*, pp. 109–10.

25. In *The Poetry and Prose of William Blake*, ed. David V. Erdman, commentary by Harold Bloom (1965; rpt. New York: Doubleday, 1970), p. 25. Subsequent citations will be given in parentheses after the designation ''Blake.''

26. Carman remarks that ''Blake and Shelley and many another mystic were mad as March hares, by reason of the too great stress of inspiration laid upon them'' (*Friendship*, p. 293).

27. ''The Correspondent Breeze: A Romantic Metaphor,'' rpt. from *The Kenyon Review* (1957) in *English Romantic Poets: Modern Essays in Criticism*, ed. M. H. Abrams (New York: Oxford University Press, 1960), pp. 37–38.

28. My allusion is to *The Marriage of Heaven and Hell*, Plate 6.

29. Like the whole volume, ''The Grave-Tree'' has not been closely examined, although such criticism as there is accords it some degree of merit. Writing in 1906, Archibald MacMurchy finds it to be an instance of Carman's best work; see *Handbook of Canadian Literature (English)* (Toronto: William Briggs, 1906), p. 206. Desmond Pacey finds it to be one of the two poems in the volume of ''any originality''; see *Ten Canadian Poets: A Group of Biographical and Critical Essays* (1958; rpt. Toronto: Ryerson, 1969), p. 106. Donald Stephens argues that ''Carman reaches the widest dimensions of his work as an elegist'' in ''The Grave-Tree,'' ''A Norse-Child's Requiem,'' and ''In the Heart of the Hills''; see *Bliss Carman* (New York: Twayne, 1966), p. 58.

30. *Representative Men: Seven Lectures* (1849; rpt. New York: A. L. Burt, n.d.), p. 36.

31. As Eric Smith argues, *By Mourning Tounges*, p. 95, the ''signal-elm'' has a rich elegiac ancestry: ''It recalls to us the 'favourite tree' of Gray's 'Elegy' and the 'familiar elm' of Milton's 'Epitaphium Damonis'—symbols of identity with nature whose origin is lost in the tree-worship of antiquity.''

32. According to Jerome J. McGann, the doctrine of psychopannychism or ''Soul Sleep'' ''means to deal with the problem of the so-called waiting time, that is, the period between a person's death and the Great Advent (or Second Coming) . . . . According to Adventist doctrine of Soul Sleep . . . death initiates the period during which the soul is placed in a state of 'sleeping' or suspension''; see ''The Religious Poetry of Christina Rossetti,'' *Critical Inquiry* 10, No. 1 (September 1983), 134–35. McGann notes Rossetti's use of this doctrine in several poems, including ''Song'' (''When I am dead, my dearest''), a poem to which Carman is particularly indebted.

33.   "Wanted—Canadian Criticism," the *Canadian Forum* VIII (April 1928), 601. This article is hardly complimentary to the Confederation poets, but Smith later admitted that his knowledge of them was then superficial: "Bliss Carman was the only Canadian poet that we had heard of and what we heard, we didn't care for much. It was only later, when I began to compile books on Canadian poetry, that I found that Lampman, Roberts and Carman had written some very fine poetry"; cited from "The Fortnightly's Forthright Four," the *McGill News* (1963) in "Some Annotated Letters of A.J.M. Smith and Raymond Knister," *Canadian Poetry: Studies, Documents, Reviews* 11 (Fall/Winter 1982), p. 99.
34.   Introd., *Poets of the Confederation*, ed. Malcolm Ross (Toronto: McClelland and Stewart, 1960), p. xi.

Grues and Gaunts: Carman's Gothic

LOUIS K. MacKENDRICK

Beginning at least as early as James Cappon's *Bliss Carman and the Literary Currents and Influences of his Time* (1930), the literary influences upon Bliss Carman's poetry have been traced through a now-standardized lineup. Among the poets who apparently stand behind the work—including Tennyson, Browning, Rossetti, and Emerson—pride of place has invariably been given to the Romantics: Keats, Shelley, Wordsworth, and Coleridge. I would suggest that the Gothic dimensions of the Romantics, those characteristics more usually studied in the fiction of that era, have a not inconsiderable bearing on some of Carman's work. Mario Praz's *The Romantic Agony* (1933) has its droll revelations of several persistent Romantic figures: the linking of Beauty and Death, versions of Satan, the influence of "the divine marquis," de Sade, and the Fatal Woman. Sukumar Dutt's comprehensive study, *The Supernatural in English Romantic Poetry* (1938), still reads very well today. I mention these studies merely to suggest that a valid Gothic impulse may not be simply wished away from Carman's familiarity with the Romantics.

Then, of course, there is Edgar Allan Poe, whose presence in Carman has been affirmed by Cappon, who suggested that "There was a certain affinity between Carman's mood of transcendental reverie and the dream-like fantasy in Poe's poetry."[1] Poe's self-serving essay, "The Philosophy of Composition," advanced the importance of effect, and argued that a tone of sadness was the highest manifestation of Beauty—the death of a beautiful woman being his principal measure. Poe also wrote breast-clawing psychological parables along with wonderfully sepulchral physical horror—a demonstrably closer affinity with Carman's Gothic practice. Carman is but one of a multitude of Canadian writers who manifest the "northern shudder," or what Northrop Frye, in a review of A.J.M. Smith's *The Book of Canadian Poetry* (1943), felt was the outstanding achievement of the genre in Canada, "the evocation of stark terror."[2] (In *The Ledger* Robert Kroetsch suggests that "you MUST / marry the terror.")[3]

In his years at Harvard (1886–1888) Carman took three courses under Francis Child,[4] precisely when Child was producing *English and Scottish Popular Ballads* (1883–1898). If we require a confirmation of Carman's Gothic inclination, we need look little further than the ballad and its conventions; his own exercises in the genre, more literary than absolutely true to type, exist in many forms. The atmospheric extension into his other work is, again, not negligible. Furthermore, his friend and colleague Richard Hovey's attraction to matters medieval must figure somewhere in the equation. It is also important to remember that Carman had a cabin near Dr. and Mrs. King's home in the Catskills; it was called "Ghost House."[5] Finally, Carman's alleged melancholy may have been responsible for the usually sombre tones of his Gothic poems. Perhaps the sum of these indications is sufficient to grant Carman more than a passing familiarity with the mood and practice of Gothic measures. Margot Northey's definition of the mode, in *The Haunted Wilderness*, may suffice:

> "Gothic" refers here to a subjective view of the dark side of life, seen through the distorting mirror of the self, with its submerged levels of psychic and spiritual experiences. Non-realistic and essentially symbolic in its approach, the gothic opens up various possibilities of psychological, spiritual, or social interpretations. Its mood is pre-eminently one of terror or horror.[6]

It is interesting to note that Carman's dedicated acolyte, keeper of the flame, and virtually uncritical admirer, Rufus H. Hathaway, assisted in assembling such collections of Carman's work as *Ballads and Lyrics* and *Bliss Carman's Poems*. Three poems in particular, the more gruesome of Carman's supernatural productions—"The Night Washers," "The Hearse-Horse," and "The Red Wolf"—were omitted under Hathaway's protective attentions. Presumably these interfered with the implied portrait of the poet, and would compromise the popular view of the transcendental nature-worshipper and vagabond life-affirmer, thereby showing more of an earthy side of Carman. Nevertheless, several poems that will be considered in this paper as Gothic are effective, and relatively straightforward, as strictly carnal parables, far in excess of his more conventional spirit-thronged romances. (Carman's extraordinary achievement in his *Sappho* poems should have dispelled any such sentimental picture of the poet decades ago. The reconstructed fragments, which are often outstanding Imagist lyrics, contain some relatively unabashed eroticism.)

The Gothic would appear to be a natural but unhallowed adjunct to Carman's transcendental preoccupations. I am not attempting to link his practice with his supernaturalism or his sense of the numinous; I am not intent on suggesting connections with the Overword or with his frequent ambience of mystery. Here are a few malevolent entities, but no graveyard eruptions and loathsome putrescences. Carman's Gothic is not morbid, but mordant. His touches of the spectral can be rather sweet hauntings, and more didactic than terrific, ghastly-sombre, and horripilating. With Carman we are more often at the point where he soberly acknowledges, as in "Pulvis et Umbra," that "man walks the world with mourning / Down to death, and leaves no trace, / With the dust upon his forehead, / And the shadow in his face." The shade of A. E. Housman might well rejoice in such a tidy sentiment.

Carman began his occasional Gothic *danse macabre* in *Low Tide on Grand Pré* with the familiar "A Northern Vigil" and "The Eavesdropper." James Cappon grandly claimed of "A Northern Vigil" that "the sense of cosmic space and doom with their cold vastness gives a mystical depth to the emotions."[7] Donald Stephens considers that the poem echoes Poe's mystery;[8] more prosaically it is supposed to have been inspired by news of the death in childbirth of Carman's ex-fiancée, Julie Plant Cutler.[9] Tom Marshall, too, working on the notion of "psychological and cultural displacement" in Carman, believes that "the early Carman seems quite happy with Edgar Allan Poe's myth of the lost beloved, and perhaps he feels himself, as Poe apparently did, to be a culturally displaced person."[10] More recently Terry Whalen considers that "A Northern Vigil"

> . . . yearns toward a supernatural world in which a lost lover is hoped to have survived. That supernatural world is suggested in the poem in the ghostly mien of the actual winter night, its gloomy atmosphere. The vague effect of the images intimates the presence of a quite other world, which seems to peer through the cracks of the actual.[11]

There remains a road not taken. The poem is in nearly conventional ballad form—abab quatrains, with three-stress lines. Its wintry house by "the gray north sea" is persistently affected within and without by presences which project the lonely speaker's loss: "A voice is under the eaves, / A footfall on the floor." Outside snow-wraiths are active; the surrounding hills are eerie in this "ghostland"; inside, "shapes with the shadows throng / The firelit chamber floor." The lover misses the supple and tall Guendolen, who has a number of contradictory attributes: she is mistress, empress, and a child of whim; she has a wayward will and a mad wilful way, a proud imperious guise, serenity, and dignity. As he keeps watch under ''the low bleak sky'' with its ''ghostly moonlight,'' in this grim season when the lover paradoxically recognizes that ''there is set no bound / To love beneath the sun,'' he wishes for ''The soft mouth at my ear / With words too sweet to say.'' The scene is clearly primed for a ghostly visitation, and more.

Guendolen's ''guise,'' however, conceals a passionate nature beneath the ambiguity of her age and status. (The poem is strongly reminiscent of Browning's ''Porphyria's Lover,'' whose seemingly ingenuous speaker loved not too wisely, but well.) Associations with fire are persistent: the west is ''smouldering,'' a burning blue star is evident, the embers recall previous love-encounters which discreetly are memorialized in her ''dark tumultuous hair.'' As Guendolen's eagerly anticipated reappearance is only the wind, so the final stanza projects the night-long, orgasmic, unrequited burning:

> Lo, now far on the hills
> The crimson fumes uncurled,
> Where the caldron mantles and spills
> Another dawn on the world!

It is difficult to dismiss the suggestive psychological symbolism of ''A Northern Vigil'' and its strongly implied unsatisfied desire—the wild sweet will is specifically associated with night-time—even within the context of conventional Gothic creakings. Of psychological interest, the situation is part of a repeated old dream, a hopeless obsession, even a self-deluded sexual craving that does not sit well with cosmic space and cultural displacement.

I have written elsewhere about ''The Eavesdropper,'' a deliciously sinister and nicely controlled poem which I called a ''psychological parable.''[12] There are other opinions: Cappon finds that ''the atmosphere is vibrating with a cosmic mystery which stills all sensuous emotion'';[13] Stephens also finds that the poem's debt to Poe overcomes the prospect of ''strong sensual emotion.''[14] It too is in quatrains, rhyming abcb— Carman's favoured form—with four-stress lines, again dancing near standard ballad form. Here now is love in the flesh—the poem immediately follows ''A Northern Vigil'' in *Low Tide on Grand Pré*—but in a significantly ''paling autumn-tide.'' Personification foreshadows defeat to a very intense degree throughout; the lovers' cot is surrounded by ''the roaming forest wind'' as its ''lost children'' go ''straying homeward.'' However, the real lost children are the adult lingerers, whose joy is at least figuratively threatened.

Many of the poem's details have anticipatory negative connotations: the lines "memories of reluctant night / Lurked in the blue dusk of her hair" imply a curious reticence which later leads the girl to become silent, ponder "some maze of dream," and grow restless and vague. The long love's day features a "swarthy" afternoon, an echo of dusk, as "We watched the great deliberate sun / Walk through the crimsoned hazy world, / Counting his hilltops one by one." Large restless forces are at work here; these strays must also be brought to account. The eavesdropping horror will be the ultimate personification, a witness in this autumnal world where maze, darkening, and haze counterpoint and confound love's freedom. The atmosphere is one of loss; the implication is of sexual transgression.

At twilight the leaves' "dancing" is almost of necessity "gloomed" by a "Shadow," no longer that of the leaves, and given a menacing substance which the speaker rushes to see:

> I saw retreating on the hills,
>   Looming and sinister and black,
> The stealthy figure swift and huge
>   Of One who strode and looked not back.

The unnerving, even emasculating, suggestion is that the couple's lovemaking has been overseen and is now subject to indefinite and probably unpleasant actions. The capitalization of "One" and "Shadow" transforms "The Eavesdropper" into an allegory about, for instance, the compromises of freedom, guilt, or the loss of innocence—signalled beforehand by a singularly connotative environment. The speaker, it will also be noted, is the character with a rich visualization and an essentially playful, optimistic outlook; the girl's reactions tell us that she is the nervously guilty party. The poem's Gothic finale, the black Presence whose role of menace or punishment is only implied, not effected, is subtly led up to throughout. The movement is from innocence to experience; suggestive details are carefully deployed. "The Eavesdropper" goes a long way towards confirming that occasionally, under the appearance of artlessness and spontaneity in Carman's poems, there was actual sophistication.

"Behind the Arras" has its own celebrity; Whalen nominates it as "one of Carman's finest ghostly, weirdly supernatural poems."[15] Without attempting to "explain" the allegorical contraries of this poem about the house of life, or to determine laboriously if its psychological perspective is coherent, it must be acknowledged that Carman places a substantial spook at its heart. The "marvellous tapestry" with its variety of creatures is shaken by an "invisible will" which is identified as "the world-ghost, the time-spirit," but is also considered as a "banished soul"—which raises standard Gothic expectations of a tale to be told to a gibbering auditor, or of a torturous revenge to be taken. This spirit moves "With stealthy swift unmeaning to and fro, / Muttering low, / Ceaseless and daft and terrible and blind, / Like a lost mind," and indeed it often appears as a grim Idiot. These evolving and somewhat insidious characteristics are evoked, possibly, by some tapestried figures previously recorded, particularly those "degraded shapes" and "beings with hair, / And moving eyes in the face, / And white bone teeth and hideous grins"—the latter nothing if not semi-skeletal *mementi mori*.

The speaker is terrified to think that this spirit might appear at his shoulder, names it "No-Man's-Friend," and is increasingly repelled by its "gabbling parrot-talk." This Jungian shadow would drive him to match Hamlet's thrust at Polonius behind the arras, "Let out at one swift thrust / The cunning arch-delusion of the dust / I so mistrust," except that he worries that the face disclosed would be his own. Here are echoes of both Dorian Gray and the canon against self-slaughter. From this point this creature—prankful, moaning, sounding like a "demoniac loon"—develops increasingly positive qualities, the other aspect of the mystery at the heart of mankind. Here, too, is where the poem loses some affective force: its haunt, a reminder of idiocy, meaninglessness, and unreason, is terrifically more effective when performing like an irrational fear.

"The Red Wolf" appears only once after *Behind the Arras*, in Souster's and Lochhead's collection *Windflower* (1985). Only Desmond Pacey has prevented its almost total invisibility, noting that "The late Theodore Goodridge Roberts once said that if one wanted to find the real Carman, one should read 'The Red Wolf.' That haunted poem of despair seems to me, too, to be close to the core of Carman." Pacey also calls it "terrifying" and "carelessly written," but concludes that it is "a powerful evocation of the horrors of melancholia. . . ."[16] Not only is the poem undeniably almost inanely repetitious and attenuated, but also its hideous central character is wretchedly and purely nasty.

Written in abcb quatrains of irregular metre, "The Red Wolf" features a tall gaunt wolf which fails to haunt the poem; that honour goes to a "hateful yellow dwarf" who cries "Wolf!" continually at the speaker's door, and who is both "servitor and lord" to him. The dwarf is accorded a number of repellant phrases and characteristics: it is cringing, cunning, a "misbegotten spawn" who "skulks like a shadow at my door" with "uncanny glee." It has a "lewd ungodly laugh," leers when cursed, and is in sum "this Caliban I house." As the animal proper is allegorically identified as the Red Wolf of Despair, so the stunted familiar may reflect an aspect of the split personality. The speaker all too conveniently identifies this imp of the perverse as the "census-taker Time" or as "a host of mortal fears" come from "a vaster world beyond my door.'' In effect, the poem is a companion-piece to ''Behind the Arras''—the outside of the house of life.

The dwarfish agenbite of inwit, responsible for the erosion of all good in the speaker's existence, gets into his house and ultimately forces him to admit their horrid kinship. However, the recipient of these unwelcome attentions finally projects his own self-assertion in springtime, imagining that he will break the poisonous mutant in lines which would certainly offend the genteel R. H. Hathaway:

> . . . That day I will arise, put my heel
> upon his throat,
> And squirt his yellow blood upon the door;
> Then watch him dying there, like a spider
> in his lair. . . .

The wolf will flee; ''God's peace'' will return in this most optimistic of Carman's seasons. The dwarf, which is ''low and humped and foul, and shambles like an ape,'' fulfills several allegorical or symbolic functions under the rubric of ''despair'': it may be a morbid emblem of guilt, passivity, the shadow self, an Edward Hyde-like repressed primal personality, the spiritually grotesque underlying the superficiality of order, and even the familiar sadistic homunculus avenging itself on its normal sibling. Marry, then bury, the terror.

Ballads of Lost Haven contains the bulk of Carman's experiments with Gothic conventions. ''The Gravedigger,'' in strict ballad metre, is a good-humoured sea-shanty based on the metaphor of the sea as sexton, who buries all sorts and conditions of seafarers sent him by God. Carman's approach is vigorous, and his corpse-maker is unsentimental in attitude and presentation: ''For sure and swift, with a guiding lift, / He shovels the dead men down.'' This rollicking sexton, scornful of his orthodox equivalent, ''delves so fierce and grim'' but democratically. In complement to his gruesome side the gravedigger's bride is seen as virtually a siren. With sinister energy, some ships ''he'll save for a bleaching grave, / And shoulder them in to shore.'' Carman's analogy is imaginative: his gravedigger is old, crooked, burly, timeless, forceful, and inevitable. There is no horror here, just an honest workman seen in witty black comedy.

Cappon has said that ''The Yule Guest'' is ''an imitation of the old Ghost ballad and modernizes very successfully the bold and graphic simplicity of the old ballad style.''[17] It is in abcb quatrains, with three-stress lines. Its story, the night-time visit of a drowned lover, is in the folk-tale tradition, and the ''goblin firelight'' by which Yanna muses is virtually demanded by the occasion. This night, perhaps punningly, ''with grave regard she smiled,'' for she is ''remembering the morn she woke / And ceased to be a child." This is delightfully ambiguous: was this the actual loss of the loved one, or the loss of virginity? She opens her door to a crying "weird," the initially insubstantial Garvin: ". . . in the moonlight pouring / Through the half-open door / Stands the gray guest of yule and casts / No shadow on the floor." However, he is permitted attendance because she gave herself to him on a previous yule night, and the anniversary sees him now incarnate in corpsy flesh, with pale cheek and cold hands. A line of suggestive asterisks separates Yanna's wish that the dawn may never come and Garvin's tender soothing; departing conventionally before the morning light, and to the summons of his shadow shipmates, he kisses not her "burning mouth" but her forehead's golden lock—which turns grey, recalling a standard motif of supernatural encounters. The poem suggests a completely material and virile revenant; its elements of romance are merely foils to Carman's continued pursuit of an intercourse between the living and dead, and the implication of some words in "The Yule Guest" is more than inconsiderably Freudian.

The same sexual traffic focuses "The Marring of Malyn," with its six-stress couplets. The voyage home of the Snowflake, whose master, "a Norland laddie," is Malyn's beloved, is packed with storm and omen: "The lift is black above them, the sea is mirk below, / And down the world's wide border they perish as they go." The sea is personified as "the Skipper's daughters," who attempt to seduce the young man with song and dance, promising kisses in their "eternal silence below the twilight's rim." Escape is futile for the ship; "the swift relentless phantom is hungering on her trail," and the pilot Death puts out from shore. "The ghost of wreckage upon the iron sea" is the inevitable result, but Carman continues his tale of seduction: ". . . the red dawn discover[s] a rover spent for breath / Among the merrymakers who fondle him to death." The sexual implications are clear, and deliberately offset by the innocence of teenaged Malyn, who is no sensual threat or temptation. A hackneyed orphan of the storm, she loses her mind and wanders, a lovely distrait. The Skipper rejoices "because a blue-eyed sailor shall wed his kith and kin," the ultimate stage in this imaginative and slightly lubricious aspect of Carman's story about the bleak and forever capacious tombs of the sea.

"The Nancy's Pride," in ballad metre with Carman's characteristic abcb quatrains, has a disappearance on a maiden voyage—a term that assumes sometimes interesting proportions in some of his sea poems. In Flying Dutchman fashion the ship reappears as "a fearsome sight," with "mildewed spar and sail" and a crew on "the rotting shrouds, / With the Judgement in their face." The ship's name reveals the poem's unemphatic allegorical level; once the pride of the fleet, it is now a "wraith" with the conventional returning dead. Carman's figurative tendency is more fully realized in "The Shadow Boatswain": on a splendid new day the ominously named Doomkeel has a "shadow crew," the wind has "a boding sound," and the speaker, seemingly fresh and alive, "can feel the icy fingers / Creeping in upon my bones." The voyage to "the Isles" will "slip the wake of being"; in the "Crossing the Bar" manner, the poem nicely sets light and optimism against the peremptory summons of the Shadow Boatswain. Carman was no stranger to allegory; the mode most clearly illustrates his commitment to symbolic expression if not to unqualified symbolism.

"The Kelpie Riders," which unfortunately has a seemingly tireless gallop in its six-stress couplets, is based on the legend of the Scottish spirit-steed which would lure mortals into riding and then drown them. The poem was created from two lines which Charles G. D. Roberts was unable to develop, and uses the German Lorelei myth, as Carman's biographer claims.[18] The Kelpie men, a "ghostly bivouac," are buried alive on the grey, static, blasted Bareau marshes. On a "doomful" April night they responded to the siren call ashore of "goblin maidens," who looked "more than a mortal might behold," and, wearied by an all-night revel, they lay down out of their natural element. Buried "asleep, unslain" in the morning, they are free to ride only in snowtime. The narrator, formerly an acolyte, once heard "the ghost of a voice" summoning him to drink of the well by the Kelpies, and identifying him as one of them in the tradition of the innocent inheritor of a cursed legacy. "I looked for my face in the crystal spring, / But the face that flickered there was a thing / To make the nape of your neck grow chill." He is trapped by the vision of a raven-haired enchantress or succubus, and sets to running with weird calls continually in his ears. He finds that he is pursued by a rider "with his moaning jibe and shadowy leer," crying kinship and mocking the victim's wish to win the maid: " 'Wind for a mourner, snow for a shroud!' " The runner is on "the leash of a ghoul"; it leaps on his neck before he can attain safety. In the awakening morning he discovers his face is that of his cadaverous pursuer. A year later he returns to the well, having identified a girl in Rochelle market as another whose "weird uncanny drives her on." She too, a "harridan of woe," visits the well and bewails her infatuation with a former loved one; now as an old man he realizes that eventually "the goblin maids shall love their own." While "The Kelpie Riders" owes a considerable debt to "La Belle Dame Sans Merci," it is relatively slight; the potential two-sided personality is not explored, or cleanly epitomized, and sentimentality, ever Carman's dangerous liaison, finally overwhelms the terror.

There are two final matters of the charnel from *More Songs from Vagabondia*. Of "The Hearse-Horse" Carman wrote to Hovey in July 1896, "I think 'Hearse Horse' is a good thing of its kind, but whether that kind ought ever to be printed is questionable."[19] The poem is comic macabre, as horse addresses coffin, wondering what it has there that "neither swears nor groans," and that doesn't protest the undertaker's terms. The second stanza gives the essence:

> Said the hearse-horse to the coffin,
> "What the devil have you there,
> With that purple frozen stare?
> Where the devil has it been
> To get that shadow grin?"
> Said the coffin to the hearse-horse,
> "Skin!"

The casket as interlocutor has equally unadorned answers to the horse's other queries: "Bones!" and "Worms!"

    This cheerful graveyard piece is followed by "The Night-Washers," which Miller tells us was "built around 'The Seven Lovely Sins' as society's new *credo* with 'the Scavenger Saints' embracing the 'Seven Deadly Sins.' "[20] In April 1895 Carman wrote of the poem to Gertrude Burton,

> It is not much, like a Breton legend put into verse, as a study in the horrible—like those fairy tales we used to hear, when the story led you on from room to room until you reached a closet, when the door opened and "out jumped a green mouldy man"—a little like that song you sing very low and slow and then ending in a fearful scream.[21]

In four-stress triplets, "the brothers of ghouls" seek the identity of the one seeing them washing shrouds, "stained with yellow and stiff with red." "Rinsing the linen that reeks and bleeds," they address the overseer as "Sir Fop," and predict their eventual attentions to him: their river will "wash the ache from your scrofulous bones." They also call themselves "the gossips of fame"; the poem is in its way a crisp satire on the vanity of human wishes. The viewer is invited to join these creatures' gruesome labour with the Mephistophelian promise of ninety years of sinning; otherwise he will become an outcast. This poem is a grim moral tract; the Christian associations with washing are here given a rude and unsavoury twist. Carman's subject here is mortality and the finite, hints of which, it may be suggested, accompany far less blatantly his more comfortable poems of spirit, spirits, and transcendence of the mortal.

    In "In St. Germain Street," from *Echoes from Vagabondia*, Carman presents the "ghostly banners" of chilly "hosts of rain" at wharves and slips, where "there at day's end they embark / To invade the realms of dark" as the sun reappears on the street. These lines seem to me emblematic of Carman's light and shade, rather more of the latter, in his strictly Gothic verses. His own practices in the manner have a tendency towards stylistic entropy. His characteristic habit of simply going on too long, enraptured by his own rhyming and hues, is evident in many of his Gothic forays where suspense, ambiguity, and starkness are traditionally of the essence. Too often sentimentality is commingled with the ostensible terror or the mystery. On the other hand, at best the uncanny Gothic atmosphere is self-sufficient and taut—in which case Carman usually has another agenda; the skin may crawl before the mind absorbs, before we identify the archetype or conventional figure which he employs. These less characteristically rapturous works have a strong whiff of the psychological even when their stories conform to familiar devices and situations, and they possess implied themes that venture well beyond storytelling amplified with mysterious thrills. As such, these poems are not unworthy of consideration, and may remind us that the "familiar" Carman is not always completely comfortable.

NOTES

1. James Cappon, *Bliss Carman and the Literary Currents and Influences of his Time* (Toronto: Ryerson, 1930), p. 11.
2. Northrop Frye, review of A.J.M. Smith, ed., *The Book of Canadian Poetry*, in *The Bush Garden: Essays on the Canadian Imagination* (Toronto: Anansi, 1971), p. 138.
3. Robert Kroetsch, *The Ledger* (London: Applegarth Follies, 1975), n.p.
4. Desmond Pacey, *Ten Canadian Poets: A Group of Biographical and Critical Essays* (Toronto: Ryerson, 1955), p. 72.
5. H. Pearson Gundy, ed., *Letters of Bliss Carman* (Kingston and Montreal: McGill-Queen's University Press, 1981), p. 116.
6. Margot Northey, *The Haunted Wilderness: The Gothic and Grotesque in Canadian Fiction* (Toronto: University of Toronto Press, 1976), p. 6.
7. Cappon, p. 15.
8. Donald Stephens, *Bliss Carman* (New York: Twayne, 1966), p. 45.
9. Muriel Miller, *Bliss Carman: Quest and Revolt* (St. John's: Jesperson Press, 1985), p. 56.
10. Tom Marshall, *Harsh and Lovely Land: The Major Canadian Poets and the Making of a Canadian Tradition* (Vancouver: University of British Columbia Press, 1979), p. 15.
11. Terry Whalen, *Bliss Carman and His Works* (Downsview: ECW Press, 1983), p. 105.
12. Louis K. MacKendrick, "Bliss Carman," in Jeffrey M. Heath, ed., *Profiles in Canadian Literature 3* (Toronto: Dundurn Press, 1982), p. 51.
13. Cappon, p. 16.
14. Stephens, p. 46.
15. Whalen, p. 103.

16. Pacey, p. 110.
17. Cappon, p. 19.
18. Miller, p. 56.
19. Gundy, p. 108.
20. Miller, p. 154.
21. Gundy, p. 96.

"A Gift for Some Purpose": Bliss Carman's Lyrics and their Influence on Early Twentieth-Century Poetry in Canada

A. R. KIZUK

Althaea, since my father's ploughshare, drawn
Through fatal seedland of a female field,
Furrowed thy body, whence a wheaten ear
Strong from the sun and fragrant from the rains
I sprang and cleft the closure of thy womb,
Mother, I dying with unforgetful tongue
Hail thee as holy and worship thee as just
Who art unjust and unholy.
     ALGERNON CHARLES SWINBURNE, *Atalanta in Calydon (348)*

If strange things happen where she is,
So that men say that graves open
And the dead walk, or that futurity
Becomes a womb and the unborn are shed,
Such portents are not to be wondered at,
Being tourbillions in Time made
By the strong pulling of her bladed mind
Through that ever-reluctant element.
     ROBERT GRAVES, *"On Portents" (169)*

Where do the roots go?
  Look down under the leaves.
Who put the moss there?
  These stones have been here too long.
Who stunned the dirt into noise?
  Ask the mole, he knows.
I feel the slime of a wet nest.
  Beware Mother Mildew.
Nibble again, fish nerves.
     THEODORE ROETHKE, *"The Lost Son" (17)*

This is what it's like to send firebombs down from
air-conditioned cockpits.
This is what it's like to be told to fire into a reed
hut with an automatic weapon.

It's because we have new packaging for smoked oysters
that bomb holes appear in the rice paddies.
It's because we have so few women sobbing
in back rooms.

ROBERT BLY, *"The Teeth Mother Naked At Last" (23)*

In November 1923, Carman wrote to Frederika Milne, one of several infatuated young women to whom he wrote many love letters in the last decade of his life:

> Do you know, Wayside, I don't know how I could keep along with this daunting life, and all its complexities and trials, if there had not come such vast and amazing new supplies of courage and knowledge in the past year—all the mystic Truth I ran into in Vancouver and since—and then this summer's strange fresh vital happy days. It all seems to have been sent as a gift for some purpose. (Gundy 316)

Both Gundy, editor of a volume of Carman's letters, and Carman's main biographer, Muriel Miller, interpret this gift as the poet's discovery of Theosophy and the "Mystic Way." Miller suggests that his pet name for Mrs. Milne, "Wayside," was an "allusion drawn from their 'Mystic Way' faith"—a faith shared by Carman's new Vancouver friends. For Miller, the purpose of this new "Way" was to recuperate his transcendental yearnings (Miller 254–55). She believes that Carman's "theosophical probings" led him to "a complete change in attitude towards Death in general," whereby Carman no longer feared death and, as he explained to Lorne Pierce, the "distasteful loud pestiferous lower-self" (256–57). Gundy points out, however, that when Carman first fell in love with Kate Eastman in the Spring of 1922, he saw her as "not a wayside but a fork in the road" (304). He told the same lie to Mrs. Milne the following year, calling her "Most blessed of Waysides and only Way's End" (314). Gundy also notes Carman's scepticism and irony on the subject of the "Way." For Gundy, the gift for which Carman gives thanks in 1923 is "insecure and incomplete," yet, as for Miller, its purpose remains a recuperation of Carman's "own sincere faith in a future life" (316).

Between these anxious commentaries on the sincerity of his mystical longings, on the one hand, and the theme of death and the afterlife in Carman's thought, on the other, Carman's Waysides tend to fall by the wayside. The biography and letters suggest that he was the sort of bachelor who could not sustain romantic interest in one woman for long (cf. Whalen 79). Of course, his long relationship with Mrs. King is the exception, yet that affair may have lasted precisely because it became for Carman a ritualized form of the Freudian "Family Romance."[1] More than any other poet of his generation, Carman blazed a trail for younger poets to follow into the twentieth century. The gift "sent" to Carman in the early 1920s was not so much his new-found faith as it was an excited openness to his lyricism among younger writers and intellectuals of the time. In this paper, I argue that the essence of Carman's lyricism lies in a submission to the Mother in contravention of Oedipal law. Julia Kristeva describes this Mother figure as: "for women, a paradise lost but seemingly close at hand, for men, a hidden god but constantly present through occult fantasy. And even psychoanalysts believe in it" (240). Indeed, analyst Anton Ehrenzweig argues that a "creative surrender" to the Mother may lie at the heart of all artistic creativity (136–37). Such submission—not to Woman, or Waysides, but to the Mother—is common in the poetry of the period Logan and French called "the Restoration or Second Renaissance Period in Canadian Literature" (280). In this context, Carman's lyrical gift can be seen as having cleared a path for poetry in Canada to follow until stopped in its tracks by Canadian literary modernism.

My purpose in this paper is literary historical insofar as I attempt to establish a context for comparison and contrast of Carman and his younger contemporaries. When I speak of the "Family Romance," I mean to invoke Eli Mandel's description of it as "a kind of fairy tale" children use to sublimate Oedipal feelings. In Mandel's formulation, these feelings, for writers, become a "story of resentments," which "rewrite the past," thereby challenging "mortality and time . . . to set the poet/writer forth on his perilous journey on which all shall be won or lost" (ix–x). In my use of this symbolism, I do not attempt a psychoanalysis of Bliss Carman; my aim is simply to illuminate in part certain choices and arrangements of image and symbol prevalent in his art. I will suggest, however, that the seductive tenderness of his poetic world should be taken into account in any Mandelian or Bloomian view of Carman's influence in the early twentieth century.

Breaking In/The Mother: Carman's Poetic World

Carman's many thematically integrated books of verse inscribe a trajectory that begins in a unifying Romantic vision, attains its apogee in a threefold vision of human values, and terminates in a vision of desire as a mirror-image of itself.[2] In some of the most important criticism available on Carman, John R. Sorfleet, Tracy Ware, D.M.R. Bentley, and Malcolm Ross have separately probed the mystical underpinnings and integrity of Carman's poetic vision. In an influential article, Sorfleet demonstrates the philosophical coherence of Carman's earlier poetry, reflecting a moment of mystical illumination located in "the seminal experience incorporated in 'Low Tide on Grand Pré' " (Sorfleet, "Transcendentalist" 190). Ware examines this experience as being one of harmony between "epiphanic and linear" time that is integral to this poem, a unifying pattern in the *Low Tide on Grand Pré* volume as a whole, and "central to Carman's poetry" (Ware 40). Bentley explores the symbolics of Carman's mid-career unitrinian philosophy, arguing convincingly that *Sappho: One Hundred Lyrics* (1903) is not only as philosophically coherent as earlier mystical poems, but evinces, as well, a remarkable "narrative and organizational skill" as a long poem and as a mythography (Bentley, "Threefold" 30). Ross, in a lecture delivered in 1984, returns the argument to the earlier poems, dismissing later periods for a lack of "authentic mystical experience" (Ross 57). For Ross, the Delsartean or unitrinian "pseudo-theology" that he accepted from Mrs. King "cost Carman most of his magic and much of his music":

> After 1905 there is a serenity and an untroubled celebration of beauty. A kind of benevolent and amorphous deity seems to reign from within the rind of the visible world. This is not the stuff of great religious poetry in which the vast and gibbering dark is acknowledged and endured. (65)

Within a context of Carman's images and symbols, however, the deity of which Ross disapproves *is* the rind of the visible world; the gibbering dark has been plucked from that fruit. Carman's vision is ultimately that of a Ruskinian imagination re-creating itself in all its sensuality, and what Carman calls "the code" of the Mother is an important part of this vision. I hope to demonstrate this by probing the lock on this "code unwritten" with interpretive tools drawn from contemporary critical practice and psychoanalysis.

It is appropriate to begin with Terry Whalen's monograph, for it is representative of Carman's critical reception today. Also, many of his insights suggest the possibility of a psychological reading of Carman's mystical vision. Whalen identifies an aesthetic principle of Santayana as essential to Carman's poetry: the assimilation of phenomena, "words, images, emotions, or systems of ideas, to the deeper cravings of the mind" (Whalen 98). He points out, as well, that Carman's speakers often yearn "towards a supernatural world in which a lost lover is hoped to have survived," and this melancholy produces an atmosphere which "intimates the presence of a quite other world, which seems to peer through the cracks of the actual" (105). Thus, Carman's melancholy can be seen as a restless and wondering emotion that attaches itself to a highly symbolic poetic world. Within this "visual country of the mind" (81, citing Shepard 167), a desire is at work which is forever unsatisfied in that it craves what has been taken away. For psychoanalysts, this lost object of desire will be the phallus, which is to say that the phallus becomes, here, a symbol for the objective of desire. Whalen does not pursue this possibility. Interested in a psychology of place, he interprets Carman's simultaneous impulses to melancholy and joy as a profoundly empathic response to the natural environment—the tumbling climate of the Atlantic region, in this case. Ware's analysis of natural imagery in "Low Tide on Grand Pré" lends strong support to this thesis (Ware 45-46). "In an important way," concludes Whalen, Carman "*is* the landscape that he knows" (104). In a different way, however, Carman's symbolic landscapes are what the speakers of his lyrics ultimately *desire*.

At this point, I want to deepen the discussion by turning to a single motif, the opposition between indoors and outdoors in Carman's lyrics. Most of the preoccupations of Carman's poetry can be organized under the heading of this threshold motif. In stanzas, Carman builds pretty rooms—little rooms with a hall mirror, a vestibule, an open door, and a view. For Ross, the poem "A Northern Vigil" is exemplary of Carman's poetic sense of an uncluttered outdoors (54). Here, Ross sees Carman at his hauntingly melancholy best, as did Northrop Frye back in 1954 (Frye 35). For Whalen, the poem's "shaded picturing of the real" creates an other-worldly symbolism resonant with the particularity of place (104). The speaker of "A Northern Vigil" projects his grief into a wintry landscape, which encloses his house and cuts him off from the world of other men. In this gloomy isolation, he seems to hear a "footfall on the floor":

> Threshold, mirror and hall,
>   Vacant and strangely aware,
> Wait for their soul's recall
>   With the dumb expectant air.   (*LT* 78, [35])[3]

The speaker senses the presence in nature of the lost object of his desire, outside his door, and implores the dead beloved—"imperious" empress, mistress, and child—to

> Come, for the night is cold,
>   The ghostly moonlight fills

> Hollow and rift and fold
> Of the eerie Ardise hills!
>
> The windows of my room
> Are dark with bitter frost,
> The stillness aches with doom
> Of something loved and lost.   (80 [36])

Yet, for all the melancholy and autochthonic mythopoesis of this poem, its moving invocation of lost desire invokes no ghostly *lover*. The speaker remembers that her kiss was warm, but what he actually calls forth is some presence or dread that can keep the house-keepers in line:

> And though thy coming rouse
> The sleep-cry of no bird,
> The keepers of the house
> Shall tremble at thy word.   (82–83 [37])

Though praised for its sense of place and natural scene, "A Northern Vigil" is curiously indoorsy, even domestic.

   Many of Carman's lyrics evocative of the out-of-doors contain similar reminders that the speaker speaks from within a room, a cabin, a tent, a walled garden, and so forth. I am thinking of such relatively well-known poems as "Pulvis et Umbra," "The Vagabonds," "The Eavesdropper," "A More Ancient Mariner," "The Last Room," "April Weather," "Morning in the Hills," "On the Plaza," "The Gate of Peace," and so on. In "May in the Selkirks," Carman's last poem before his death in June 1929, a passage on the pleasant clamorousness of a British Columbia landscape pivots into a closing quatrain on sublime wonder by moving through these lines: "And the tall evergreens watching at the threshold— / Keeping the silence of the Lord of out-of-doors" (*PBC* 163). Even in an early outdoorsy poem like "The Pensioners," Carman's young men "must arise and walk therein"—not "on the hill," but *in* "her April train" (*LT* 32 [22]). Similarly, the open road of the *Vagabondia* poems is hardly a way through unenclosed space, but rather a series of Wayside Inns that for a night become Only Way's Ends (*SV* 13). Many of Carman's speakers in the open road poems are actually indoors or stand "in the Tavern door to drink" (*SV* 50). Carman's first poem in *Songs from Vagabondia* (a joint effort with Richard Hovey in 1894, as were the other books in this extremely popular series), for example, ends:

> Outside the winter; inside, the warmth
> And a sweet oblivion of turmoil. Why?

> All for a gentle girlish hand
> With its warm and lingering good-bye.   ("A Waif" 5)

In "The Mendicants," wilderness is God's "open house" (47 [49]). In "In the House of Idiedaily," Carman's last poem in the volume, indoors and outdoors signify each other: the "poppies" of an idyllic, vernal out-of-doors re-present the dinner wine of a busy, well-kept boarding-house, and vice versa—notwithstanding a fortunate "brown maiden" who "Bettered all the dusk she strayed in" (51–53).

In two ambitiously philosophical poems of the 1890s, we learn a little more about Carman's symbolic house-keeping. Sorfleet and Ross have fruitfully explored the mysticism of these poems; I trust that my observations will not depart from their more substantial readings (Freud's rhetoric and symbolics are, after all, not unlike an inverted "Patristic exegesis" [Todorov 254]). In "Beyond the Gamut," the speaker meditatively explores "a new room in the house of knowledge," though he knows his "thought cannot far without the symbol" (*BA* 66, 68 [51–52]). With this caveat, then, transcendence is figured as "life's larger room" and death as a wayside "tavern" (71, 74 [53, 55]). Life, however, becomes an undecidable neither/nor, entangled in a conjunction of good and evil, leading, I think deliberately, to an expression of the limits of the symbolism that constitutes Carman's poetic world:

> Life be neither hermitage nor revel;
> Lent or carnival alone were vain;
> Sin and sainthood—Help me, little brother,
> With your largo finder-thought again!   (74 [55])

In "Behind the Arras," the speaker again uses a house as a symbol for the object of contemplation: the soul's experience of life and death as a continuity beyond what mere human senses can perceive. Here, being, the "weaver" of life, experiences an "utter and imperious ache" that initiates life's rhythms, "agonies of bliss, my kin." By way of this rhythmic pleasure, being will "enter in" mankind's "prison house of sense" (11–12 [64]). In these idealist speculations, however, the speaker runs afoul of Oedipal law, for how could psychoanalysts not read a refusal of the primal scene in such lines as these:

> Then with a little broken laugh I say,
> Snatching away
> The curtain where he grinned,
> (My feverish sight thought) like a sin unsinned,
> "Only the wind!"   (9 [64])

Furthermore, the descent of being into life is here symbolized as the sexual penetration of an unsatisfied woman, "The virgin silence, till / She yields for rapture shuddering, yearning still." Even transcendence is figurally Oedipal: " 'The womb of silence to the crave of sound / Is heaven unfound' " (11 [64–65]). In Carman's struggle to acquire an intellectual tidiness in his middle years, his contained and containing poetics of a Ruskinian sensual perception ground themselves in a vision of art as a speaking womb: a womb of silence made capable of speech by the presence of the poet's vision within that region—the "crave of sound." Building on James Cappon's reading of the poem, Ross explains that the "dread questions" of death and the gibbering dark are here too impatiently "dissolved" (Ross 62–63), so that the poem lacks Carman's haunting melancholy, the guarantor of what Gundy and Miller anxiously perceive as Carman's sincerity. And so it does. It lacks a proper sense of Oedipal dread.

For Ross, "the poetry of mystery comes to a climax" in "Behind the Arras," "but now it enshrouds rather than illuminates" (61). Ross is following Sorfleet here, who sees Carman's tidy unitrinian theology, grounded in Santayana, as marking "the end of Carman's most productive years" (Sorfleet, "Transcendentalist" 208–209). Bentley, however, has shown *Sappho* (1903) to be a meditation on mortality and the afterlife that at least matches the early Carman in its fusions of joy and melancholy ("Threefold"). I would suggest further that Carman's vision never deviates from his recognition, in "Low Tide on Grand Pré," of the "epistemological problem of perception versus projection," the out-of-doors as a "subjective correlative of the mood created" (Ware 39–40). Carman's parenthetical catachresis, "My feverish sight thought," captures the problem splendidly. I agree with Whalen's argument that "Carman is always an elegiac poet" whose work "expresses a constant desire to reconcile himself to death. . . . In this way he is an especially interesting love poet, for his love poetry is expressive of his most deeply existential needs" (Whalen 119). Writing on *Hamlet*, Lacan has argued that "insofar as the subject must mourn the phallus," an unresolved Oedipal complex can initiate a kind of writing that is always elegiac ("Hamlet" 46). The late poem "After a Parting" mourns Hamlet's absence from a Denmark lacking "royal presence," whose women no longer look on men with "shining eyes" (*WG* 58–60). Yet how is it that the speaker of a poem like "Behind the Arras" can erase the affective signature of dread and melancholy from the imaginative containment of the poem's language? How can this vision, in contravention of Oedipal law, displace the Father without shame? For a displacement of the Father is intimated in the speaker's wish to transform the "dread veiled mysteriarch" into "a happy Ariel"—"Only the wind!" (*BA* 9 [63–64]).

Part of the answer may be heisted from the possibility that Carman regarded the title poem of *Behind the Arras* (1895) as an up-beat but serious companion-piece to "The Red Wolf." Both poems have the same subject. The "happy Ariel" of the former simply inverts the latter's "Caliban I house" (*BA* 39). This figure occupies the threshold of Carman's poetic world, like the "footfall on the floor" in "A Northern Vigil." It is both "kin / And kin to the wolf at the door!" in "The Red Wolf" (42), and "bliss, my kin" yet "Ceaseless and daft and terrible and blind, / Like a lost mind" in "Behind the Arras" (12, 8 [65, 63]). Odell Shepard, surely the most unanxious of Carman's critics, described "The Red Wolf" in 1923 as "one of the least pleasant and least forget-table things that have come from his pen—a poem which gives us a glimpse of the savageries lying asleep in man's brain and blood, of the dark red gulfs of animalism over which we sustain our lives" (142):

> I loathe him, yet he lives; as God lets Satan live,
> I suffer him to slumber at my door,
> Till that long-looked-for time, that splendid
>   sudden prime,
> When Spring shall go in scarlet by my door.
>
> That day I will arise, put my heel upon his throat,
> And squirt his yellow blood upon the door;
> Then watch him dying there, like a spider in his lair,
> With a "Wolf, wolf, wolf!" at my door.   (*BA* 42–43)

According to T. G. Roberts and Desmond Pacey, the poem represents "the real Carman" (Pacey, *Ten* 85), the melancholy, mourning Carman that Gundy and Miller anxiously recover from the life. This bit of light verse is hardly melancholic, however; but it is colourfully ironic. Why does the speaker place his foot on the dwarf's throat? Why does this cause the dwarf's blood to squirt? Why is the blood yellow? Why is he like a spider? Why are there "sweet ripe nuts" on the doorstep where he stands (38)? Surely "foot" is a displacement of "hand," the dwarf a figure for the phallus. Like Theodore Roethke (whose poem "The Lost Son" is an interesting tropic intertext for "Behind the Arras"), Carman allows a connection between death and early adolescent onanism in the composition of his poetic world (Malkoff 53).

The dwarf is the phallus. But whose? Is it a self-castration that the poem's "killing" memorializes? Not exactly, for the dwarf is also a mediating figure between childhood idleness and adult responsibility: "joy and youth and flame and love and bliss" (41) and the threat of penury and personal failure implied in the lyric's cliché-refrain.[4] This figure dwells at the threshold of an undecidable either/or that binds in disjunction "bliss" and the wolf, infant and beast, master and slave, "servitor and lord" (39, 42). In this aporia, or alogical hesitation between contraries, the Child and the Father cancel each other out, so that what remains after the child-speaker kills the dwarf is only a blank, an absence of the phallus, as presumably prepubescent "children return to my door" in "God's great peace" (43). Returning to the more serious, more joyous "Behind the Arras," we may note that the speaker would not attack this Caliban/Ariel figure in the threshold, this "banished soul" (7 [62]),

> But that I fear I should disclose a face
> Wearing the trace
> Of my own human guise,
> Piteous, unharmful, loving, sad, and wise
> With the speaking eyes.   (8 [63])

But he *would* rid the house "of his grim pranks," which occasion mourning and melancholy. In the effort to accomplish this, the speaker's "sight thought" hesitates before a "trace" of kinship, in which the phallus will always be only the site of a castration. Thus, Carman's symbolics recuperate shame and melancholy by way of a double sacrifice that nullifies antagonism between Father and son by denying the phallus to both of them. As Lacan says, fathers and sons are partners in the Oedipal scene. Procreation moves through the mother, and the best any man can do is but to "stand in for the cause of desire" (*Ecrits* 287).

It is in "Windflower," in *Low Tide on Grand Pré*, that Carman first claims that neither death nor love "nor any name / Known among men" can "blur the wild desire with shame" (27–28). This windflower-speaker follows "The feet of straying winds,"

> And then my heart beat once and broke
>   To hear the sweeping rain forebode
> Some ruin in the April world,
>   Between the woodside and the road.
>
> To-night can bring no healing now;
>   The calm of yesternight is gone;
> Surely the wind is but the wind,
>   And I a broken waif thereon.   (28)

Ross acknowledges the libidinous aspect of the poem as an uninhibited "aching desire," but insists that it symbolizes a "mortal quest for beauty and transcendence'' (55). He quotes D. G. Jones's point that Carman's lyricism captures "what it means to love a woman or the world" (Ross 56; Jones 96), but not Jones's apology for Carman's conception of nature as "not so much childish as childlike" (95). The poem's unashamed but broken speaker dwells at the threshold of Carman's symbolic world, like the dwarf in "The Red Wolf" and the mirror in "A Northern Vigil." And so, too, is that forbidden and foreboding, deliberately vague "ruin" in the poetic world. The windflower is actually part of a fairly elaborate phallic symbolism that weaves throughout Carman's extensive *oeuvre*, growing in thresholds (cf. *WG*, "In April" 63) and often autoerotic, as in the closing couplet of the late sonnet "New Moon: I"—"While the adoring soul in stillness waits, / Love like the frailest windflower revives" (*S* 3). "Windflower," however, makes it clear that there will be no healing, no object to desire in the April world, only the raw uncathected drive itself. Thus, Carman returns in his imagination to the origin and cause of desire through a willingness to share in the Father's loss.

At this point, I would like to submit that two modes of perception are essential to Carman's lyricism: an Oedipal but ultimately self-castrating displacement of the Father on the one side, and a Romantic expansion of perceived reality through sensual imagining on the other. These two modes interlock at the threshold of the perceiver and the perceived in Carman's poetic world. As he says in *The Kinship of Nature* (1903), "We are children living in fear of the fabulous giant, if we do not remember that fact is solidified fancy" (83).

Certainly, in "Bahaman," a sea-ballad written after a Bahamian holiday in 1898, Carman congratulates himself for painting "the vision not the view,—the touch that bids the sense good-bye," so that "the arc of truth be circled," collapsing time and space into a " 'Once upon a time' " (*PBC* 73–74; cf. *The Poetry of Life* 45). In this self-confidence, the speaker awakens "in a clean white room,"

> Warmed and freshened, lulled yet quickened in that
> Paradisal air,
> Motherly and uncapricious, healing every hurt or care,
> Wooing body, mind and spirit firmly back to strong
> and fair.
>
> (*PBC* 75)

The poem celebrates the achievement of an enclosing imagination that has successfully asserted itself as an epistemological enclave—"this cloister garden hidden from the passing view"—within natural reality.

Later Poems: In Stanzas Pretty Wombs

Writing to thank an acquaintance for a gift of books in 1932, George Santayana remarked, "But why send me Bliss Carman? Life is too short for that" (Santayana 274). After tapping his symbolism into order in his middle years, Carman continued to write a great deal, and his vision grew clearer still. For Sorfleet, 1910 marked a resurgence of "mystical vision" of "nature and divine immanence" as Carman came to employ less of the tidy house-keeping of Mrs. King's unitrinianism ("Introduction" 12). Hence "Mirage," a dramatic monologue written in 1910, may be seen as pivotal in the trajectory of Carman's later career. The poem's speaker records a mystical experience: "The House of space and time grew tense" with rapture, while "A mighty prescience seemed to brood . . . Yearning for form,"

> The vision I have tried to catch,—
> All earth's delight and meaning grown
> A lyric presence loved and known.   (*PBC* 119)

The mystical experience here is the vision of a Platonic companion for the speaker's soul, a beautiful, eternal woman whose three most striking features are her girlish sensuality, her "emperor's" head of curls, and the innocence of an "eager Mary" standing "In Love's adoring attitude," looking avidly "into the angel's eyes." This verse paragraph ends ambiguously with the line, "My vision looks forever so," and one must decide whether the speaker really means to say that his vision is an eternal likeness of Mary awaiting impregnation by the angel. This hesitation, passed on to the reader, seems a deliberate strategy. It prepares the reader to accept as unanswerable the three questions with which the poem ends. "In other years," men will ask, "Why all this vast of sea and space, / Just to enframe a woman's face?" Beneath the blithe certainty of this deferral there is another:

> How real was she? Ah, my friend,
> In art the fact and fancy blend
> Past telling. All the painter's task
> Is with the glory. Need we ask
> The tulips breaking through the mould?   (121)

Thirdly, the speaker evades the simple but crucial question, "Why?" An artist must "Spend without stint the joy and power" of the moment, "Yet leave the why untold." The final line of the poem, separated from the rest, states simply, "My sketch is all I have to say." Thus, the reader is driven back to the central image of "My vision" and its two halves: the girl-emperor-mother who gazes entirely seductively into the vision's other part, "the angel's eyes." This image of the imagination has been caught just at the moment before the two parts will join sexually in one, to produce an analogue in Carman's poetic world of the Saviour in historical time who is at once Father and Divine Child.

I believe that it is through such imagery as this that we can begin to understand the desire at the heart of Carman's lyrics. For here the Child bears the mark of an elided phallus within the threshold of the enclosure that will house the Mother and the Father in sexual union. What is the phallus in this scenario if not an image of the self, crucified, "out there," beyond the gateway to profane space and the disorder of history? Hence, the subject hesitates, and the condition of hesitation becomes permanent, constant as in love. Epistemologically as well, he is bound to the parenthesis of this hesitation to which he has surrendered. Then, in creativity, desire weaves a thatched aegis of symbol and euphony that not only effects a take-over of reality, in an economy of frustrations and satisfactions, but takes it out—dissolves the forms of reality, liquidates them, and boils them down to the pigments of a powerful and rich imaginative counterforce.

Not unlike Sorfleet and Ross on "Beyond the Gamut" and "Behind the Arras," Cappon (1930) regards "Mirage" as a crisis-poem in which Carman bids farewell to "cosmic idealism of nature" and "mystic exaltation" (219). Cappon, too, notices the hesitation in "Mirage," but interprets it myopically in terms of Carman's indecision regarding whether to write a love lyric or a monologue in Browning's manner. The poem is an able tribute to Browning, all the more interesting for being inimitable in its own right. It is significant, however, that Cappon and Sorfleet regard "Mirage" and other lyrics written at the same time so differently. This divergence can be explained by pointing out that Sorfleet's readings are based on intertextual resonances of the literature of mystical experience. The interest for Cappon, Ross, Gundy, and Miller, who generally disapprove of the later work, lies mainly in the lyrics' affective qualities. A proper sense of melancholy is perceived to be lacking; the beatitude is thought to be insincere. This negative and often anxious response simply avoids interpretive difficulties caused by the pleasure that infuses the later poetry. Hence Cappon attempts to excuse the cured melancholic of "Mirage" by calling it "an embarrassed attempt to reconcile two different ways of feeling life," "meditative musing" and "erotic experience" (220). He suggests falsely that Carman's depleted "mystical fancy" "often finds shelter" in medieval or saintly legends (in *Far Horizons* [1925], there are only about a half-dozen such pieces).

For Cappon, the poem "The Givers of Life" in *April Airs* (1916), however, redeems the poet's excesses to the extent that the poem's subject "bears the continuous strain of the ecstatic superlative with more grace than usual" (224). Though the poem soars "too near the exaggerations of Feminism," there is truth enough "to give it substance" (226). Cappon's own embarrassed confusion is apparent here. There are many far more substantial poems in the book than this, as Sorfleet's selections in *The Poems of Bliss Carman* clearly demonstrate. If it is the poem's subject that Cappon condones, moreover, he gets the subject sadly wrong. The poem is not "in praise of womanhood" any more than Irving Layton's "Death of Moishe Lazarovitch" is a poem on manhood. It is a paean to the Mother:

> Who looked on the world before them, and summoned
> and chose our sires,
> Subduing the wayward impulse to the will of
> their deep desires?
>
> Sovereigns of ultimate issues under the greater laws,
> Theirs was the mystic mission of the eternal cause.
>
> (*AA* 59)

In this poem, the Mother commands a "viewless" knowledge, "Sowing the seeds of wisdom, guarding the living springs" (58). Her truth, antecedent to man's knowledge, reproduces itself parthenogenetically. There are no Fathers in the world-view that the poem celebrates. Though she chooses "our sires," they are subjects of her will and "deep desires." The Mother lights "the lamp of manhood in the lonely boy," and when boys become men, they sacrifice their lives as galley-slaves for her "fruitful ease, / Though we break at the toiling benches or go down in the smoky seas" (59, 62). Carman twice speaks of the "code" of the Mother (59, 62). This Great Code of Carman's is an "unwritten" creed, and its key is conceivably the Mother's "teeming desire," a yearning that is "ever and ever the same," and which crowns her "lovers with gladness," her "sons with delight" (60). The apposition of sons and lovers in this context echoes the theme of D. H. Lawrence's famous novel. We know that in later years Carman read and approved of Lawrence (Gundy 365–66); and in his second to last poem, the "sons and lovers" of the motherland are still "heart fast forever with the Sweetheart of the Sea" (*PBC* 161). Furthermore, in this world, men who are faithful become lords in the best men's right.

The poem "Te Deum," like "The Givers of Life" a poem of thanksgiving written in 1916, clarifies what is the best a faithful man can hope to have in Carman's vision of the world. Were I a painter, the speaker cries,

> I should be lord of a world of rapture, master
>   of magic and gladness, too,—
> The touch of wonder transcending science, the
>   solace escaping from line and hue;
> I would reveal through tint and texture the
>   very soul of this earth of ours.   (*PBC* 126)

In "The Givers of Life," however, this power, right, and magic are gifts from the founder-women who wear a "crown of rapture" as "Martyrs of all men's folly, over-rulers of fate" (61). The Mother awaits her rapturous martyrdom, by which she will return men to an original condition, "as it was in the first of days" (61). Rapture and sacrifice are inseparable and essential to her sovereignty, which recognizes no Father. In "Behind the Arras," the child stood in the place of the Father, wearing the guise of an angel. Here, again, with alluring laughter, "Veiled in mysterious beauty," the Mother has "walked with angels at twilight and looked upon glory's face" (62). Earlier in the poem, Carman accredits the Mother with "the starry vision" and "inspiriting hope" promised by "Night, the brooding enchantress" (61). Sacrifice and rapture shall be the same for Mother and Child, even as the Father shall be banished from the scene. In this way, Carman's poetic career terminates in a vision of the imagination withdrawn into itself. The Oedipal triangle collapses into an Ophion and Egg binarism, "a little heaven of ardor" (61).

There are several other later poems of Carman's visionary desire that might be discussed. In *Far Horizons* (1925), "The Place of Wisdom" (14–16), "Twilight in Eden" (65–66 [145–47]) and "A Voice in the Garden" (67–69 [138–39]) are particularly interesting in terms of the Mother, the threshold, and the mystery of desire. Whalen points to "Revelation" (73–75 [157–58]) as demonstrating that, despite Carman's pontificating tone, "his sense of the mystery of life is still present" (115). Like *April Airs* (1916), *Wild Garden* and *Sanctuary*, both published in 1929, develop an allegory of desire and the turning of the seasons. A striking instance of the imagination imagining itself, in its "cabin doorway," as a poetic world enwombed or invaginated, appears in "A Mountain Gateway":

> I know a vale where I would go one day,
> When June comes back and all the world once more
> Is glad with summer. Deep in shade it lies

> A mighty cleft between the bosoming hills,
> A cool dim gateway to the mountains' heart.
>
> (*AA* 43 [131])

"Companioned" by "wood ghosts of twilight" that "absolve the day," the speaker is given an auditory vision of rapturous, undistraught "seraphs singing at the birth of time." In the later poems, the indoors expands to become the House of Nature or God's Tent, and in these poems poetic creativity becomes equivalent to God's. God is Himself never present, for He is at all times the "One who strode and looked not back" and a renunciation of the phallus ("The Eavesdropper," *LT* 88 [41]). The once widely popular poem "Vestigia" concerns the mark of His absence, literally "His footprint in the sod," left for the child to fill and feel "that kindling ecstasy" (*LP* 3 [145]). In "Shamballah," the indoors becomes a mystical city that sends forth poets to establish no temple save beauty, no creed save truth, no power and purpose save love, "For the saving of peoples untold" (*FH* 79 [152]). In earlier poems, the imagination at work envisioning the out-of-doors may be seen in retrospect as exercising a divine power, as in "Pulvis et Umbra," where from "my cabined room / The white soul of eager message" is released upon a stream of euphonious ballad quatrains (*LT* 68 [27]). This sanctified creativity derives from a desire that takes its gratification from submission to what Carman at his most dogmatic calls an "infinite directrix, / Focused to a finite sphere,— / Nurtured in an earthly April, / In what realm to reappear?" (*RR* 41 [108]).

I have been arguing that Carman's poetic career inscribes an arc that begins in mysticism and melancholy for a lost wholeness, curves through a philosophical economy, and terminates in a symbolics of desire turned in upon itself. I have concentrated on Carman's threshold imagery in an effort to illuminate the manner in which Carman's imagination attaches itself to a symbolic other world. Oedipal fears and wishes transform this order of images and symbols into eroticizing simulacra of the Mother's body—pretty wombs, as it were, with a hall mirror, a vestibule, a door, and a pleasant view. For Shepard, Carman's weakest verse suffered from solipsism and his best was "religious in its ultimate meanings" (141, 68). In this regard, I would want to say that neither the self nor God can endure Carman's displacement of both son and Father to an absence, a mere footprint at Eden's door. Self and God do indeed dissolve in these representations of desire. Yet I find I must agree in part with Shepard when he says that Carman was "no mere mural decorator . . . [for] he has himself built the walls which he paints." "We arrive then at something like unity" (61), Shepard says, as Carman makes "his poetry a clear mirror of his mind in a time when most poets have taken perverse delight in offering the world only shattered bits of brilliant but meaningless glass'' (67). He goes too far, but it is true that this sense of unity excerpted from history's disarray is what Carman had to offer the younger poets of his time.

Breaking Out: Carman as Other

It will not be possible for me to detail the specific qualities of the Bliss (who could resist?) that Carman's speakers (and readers) might experience in the mirror of his imagination. I should, however, discuss at least briefly the strange paradox of a desire that is ultimately a form of self-castration. As another visionary, arguably of Carman's ilk, Norman O. Brown, rhapsodizes graphically in *Love's Body*:

> Zeus had an erection, in the head; and bears a child. And he bears a child via castration; his head is split by the blow of an axe. The father produces children from his head. Paternal power is not natural virility or paternity but castration denied; a lie, a veil made of the pubic hair of mother. "The father-image is a thin mask covering the image of the pre-Oedipal mother." (77–78)

From another perspective, this pre-Oedipal Mother is part of what Lacan calls the mirror-stage of human development, in which an infant first becomes self-aware by reflecting upon another consciousness. For Lacan, the phallus is a symbol for what sons and mothers lack and hence desire. As a term within these interpretive codes, the Mother is a reflection of the site of symbol-making within the child's incipient awareness, and this site is destined to be marked by castration as a story explaining a theoretical gap between the earliest human experiences of want and the proposition that any object of desire must always already be absent. In adult life, this site comes under the control of culture and civilization, Lacan's Symbolic Order. Here, the Father rules, having recuperated the phallus by denying its loss, and functioning "fundamentally to unite (and not set in opposition) a desire and the law" (*Ecrits* 321). As Brown exclaims, "the witness that stands up in court is denying castration; the testimony is false testicles; and civilization is a lie" (78). There is never any escaping the threat of castration, and only two responses are commonly found: denial (by which, luckily enough, sons become fathering husbands, useful to procreation) and submission (by which sons recover a simulacrum of unity between self and other, useful to some forms of art).

Thus, in Carman's symbolic order (which sets imagination and reality in opposition), creative surrender to the Mother is also a submission to a condition of constant lack; and willingness to suffer the windflower's fate amounts to an acceptance of Oedipal crime and punishment. Gayatri Spivak sees in a similar pattern of resistance and ultimate acceptance the itinerary of the Great Tradition of English Romantic poetry. In her view, Wordsworth's "rejection of paternity" in the Annette Vallon case amounts to "a reinstatement of the subject as son (rather than father) within Oedipal law, and then, through the imagination, a claim to androgyny" (195)—poet as Mother and Father of the poem, "Imagination as the androgyny of Nature and Man—Woman shut out" (204). "As a feminist reader of men on women," Spivak sees no clear locus for woman in the Romantic Tradition. Much the same holds for the legacy of Carman's poetic vision in the early twentieth century.

This would seem to have been true at least of the poet's life. In 1927, Carman ended his affair with Kate Eastman by writing to her:

> I also was carried away. And my own sincere love and caring remain. I think, if you will, I will try to transfer you to the plane of my own family at 2590. For there, certainly, there can be no doubt of my sentiment and attachment. . . .
>
> So don't cry, Kate. And God love you for every blessed and lovely thing you have done for me. I am no one. Not even a name or a signature.
>
> Love to my family. [unsigned] (Gundy 348)

From a letter to Dr. Fewster of May 25, 1923, 2590 would appear to be the Fewsters' street address in Vancouver (309).[5] However, a few days before Carman wrote to Kate, he had written to another young woman who was in love with him, explaining that he had "never deliberately avoided domestic responsibilities," but "did instinctively" (347). He says also that he likes to sign his letters differently, depending on the recipient. "My Vancouver family, the Fewsters," as he says, always call him "Blissie." This letter contains news of Mrs. King's frail but recovering health and expresses Carman's wish that Mrs. King "could know you as I do. 2590 was a true haven to me, such as you can hardly guess."

Whatever the gift was that Carman felt he had received after recovering from tuberculosis in 1920, discovering or rediscovering the "Mystic Way," and finding himself in great popular demand during his reading tours in Canada and the United States, it was not constancy in love. He even appears to consider leaving the Family Romance that he had had for so many years with Dr. and Mrs. King for a younger family, Dr. and Mrs. Fewster. The beautiful, vivacious, intelligent, strong-willed young women who sought him out never stood a chance.

Carman either returned to Mrs. King and the sanctuary of her husband's home in New Haven, Connecticut, or assigned his unsanctified lovers to the spiritual "plane" of some familial bond. His only permanent relationships with women, as Gundy rightly emphasizes, were family and surrogate family relationships, "as tender as those between women" (303). In a 1923 letter to Peter McArthur, a lifelong friend, Carman explains gaily that for him marriage is quite powerless against the strength of his submission:

> Good heavens! My dear Peter: I am shocked as any good Victorian (even a he-Victorian) might be at your report of a report that Mr. Carman is to be married. Indeed you almost "gave me a turn" in the ancient ladylike phrase. There is no truth in it. I won't quote Mark [Twain] and say that the report is grossly exaggerated. But I *will* say it seems to me eminently unfair. It is well known that Mr. Carman has been under Jane government all his life, having had a grandmother, a sister, aunts indomitable, cousins innumerable. . . . However, then, would such a gentle and subservient spirit find courage to be so partial as your report implies?
> Nevair!
> Imposseeble, my dear Peter! (303–304)

A constancy within inconstancy, then, and the paradoxical pleasures of submission—these are essential to Carman's lyric gift, transcending the "distasteful loud pestiferous lower-self" and guaranteeing the seamless impenetrability of his vision. In the *oeuvre* as in early poems like "The Eavesdropper" or "Low Tide on Grand Pré," there is always in Carman's poetic world the foreknowledge that the lover will forsake the woman, that time has already sundered soul from soul and always will, and that the phallus belongs to the Wayside and not the Way.

Near the end of his career, Carman found himself explaining an amusing encounter with androgyny to Mrs. Milne, or "Wayside," the young mother and socialite divorcée with whom I began this paper. Carman writes of a small boy at one of his poetry readings:

> Oh yes, he had met Mr. Carman. "He was fine! O he was wonderful! He didn't talk like a man, he talked like a *mother!*"
> Can it really be our old friend John Pan of the Catskills who makes such an impression? I shall certainly have to be introduced to myself anew. (317)

That small boy's wide-eyed wonder is emblematic of Carman's Canadian reception in the first decades of the century. Space forbids a detailed accounting here, yet further research would discover vast treasures of Carman-like aporias, or sites of deconstructive investigation, and self-enclosing symbolic structures in the Romantic tradition—vast, vast treasures!—in the lyric revival of Wilson MacDonald, Marjorie Pickthall, Robert Norwood, Arthur Stringer, A. M. Stephen, F. O. Call, and others, not to mention the mythological treatments of birth and renewal in W.W.E. Ross's *Sonnets* (1932) and the first part of Leo Kennedy's *The Shrouding* (1933), or Al Purdy's early Vagabond poems in *The Enchanted Echo* (1944) and the many threshold poems in Livesay's *Signpost* (1932). I have elsewhere discussed the self-enclosing literariness of Pickthall's poetic world, as well as the uncathected desire that drives the symbolics of Norwood's devotional poetry.[6] Interestingly, the death of the Mother figures prominently in the consolidation of several early twentieth-century Canadian poets' art. Pickthall's *The Drift of Pinions* (1913), Norwood's *Mother and Son* (1925), Pratt's *The Iron Door: An Ode* (1927), and Arthur Bourinot's *Sonnets in Memory of My Mother* (1931) are all poetic memorializations of the Mother. Audrey Alexandra Brown, Bourinot, and Livesay are also interesting in that they each resist the Carmanian threshold as a kind of entrapment. Furthermore, close readings of MacDonald, Stephen, Stringer, and the early Purdy would indicate that vernacular poets in the first half of the century turned to Carman's "exhaustive, and exhausting, catalogue" of "Pan's spirit . . . all the voice of creation," as an authentic and model representation of an indigenous sense of place (Bentley, "Pan" 68).

As Carman said of David Thompson, so of himself, "His was the foot must find a road / For the world to enter by" (*FH* 8 [151]). We should be aware, however, that it *is* a poetic world that enters our own, like a bubble on a stream of history—and that within its tapestried walls a footprint is all that remains of the Father. In Mandel's sense of the Family Romance, however, the most obvious candidate for a Bloomian son to Carman's elided Father is Ernest Fewster, since he and Carman dedicated books of poems to each other, which were thematically and structurally akin (*Wild Garden* and Fewster's *White Desire* [1930]). Yet, as always with this not-so-simple poet, the nature of Carman's influence upon Fewster is highly problematic, for if Fewster is the weak son to Carman as renowned poet, still Carman is "Blissie" to Fewster as the Father of his "Vancouver family." As a literary influence, Carman presents no strong Father-figure, no dragon for the next generation to joust. Instead, he presents a tender abrogation of the phallus as a symbol of the power of the imagination to represent reality. One cannot therefore oppose Carman as an influence without being driven into an either/or position, in which the reader must choose to effect mastery over the text (Cameron 138–39, 150) or to submit utterly, in Muriel Miller's words, as an "unrelenting Romantic" (278). Perhaps one of the reasons the first decades of Canadian poetry are so often neglected in the literary history is that anxieties of influence are in this case so highly problematic. At least one strong modern poet, however, John Glassco in *The Deficit Made Flesh* (1958), particularly in the poems "The Burden of Junk" (36–38), "The White Mansion" (47–48), and "An Old Faun" (63–64), appears to have responded to this condition with the hesitation, joy, and doubt appropriate to it.

NOTES

1.   Pacey on Mrs. King: Carman saw in Mrs. King rather a mother than a mistress. His dependence upon her was merely a transfer of the dependence which as a youth he had placed in his mother and as a young man in Mrs. Hovey Senior, whom he always referred to as Mother Hovey (*Creative* 79). Mitchell Kennerley: Carman and Mrs. King "had intimate relations at 10 E. 16 which they always advised me of by leaving a bunch of violets—Mary Perry's favorite flower—on the pillow on my bed" (73).
2.   Frye provides the basis for a psychological interpretation of the poet's work, but goes no further than this provocative remark: Carman's Romantic "sense of unity . . . projected as some form of pantheism" and his "conscious mind . . . were disastrously at odds" (34).
3.   I use the following abbreviations in the text: *Low Tide on Grand Pré, LT; Songs from Vagabondia, SV; Behind the Arras, BA; The Rough Rider, RR; April Airs, AA; Later Poems, LP; Far Horizons, FH; Wild Garden, WG; Sanctuary, S.* When poems also appear in Sorfleet's *The Poems of Bliss Carman* (*PBC*), I give those page numbers in square brackets.
4.   The technique Carman uses here is precisely that used so often in country and western ballads, building a song from the repetition of a cliché. When reading Carman, it is well to remember that the lyrics are a brand of spoken popular music. Banfield describes popular song in 1900 as a "ballad mentality" that continued into the 1920s and 1930s, "and even later," displaying the "low common denominator . . . of the ballad's mindless facility" (4).
5.   In a letter dated May 7, 1989, Carole Gerson kindly confirms my guess. In the Vancouver City Directory for the 1920s, 2590 West 5th Avenue, a respectable but modest district, is the Fewsters' address.
6.   "The Case of the Forgotten Electra: Pickthall's Apostrophes, and Feminine Poetics in Early Twentieth-Century Canada," *Studies in Canadian Literature* 12, 1 (June 1987), 15–35; "Religion, Place, and Self in Early Twentieth-Century Canada: The Poetry of Robert Norwood," *Canadian Literature* 115 (Winter 1987), 66–77.

WORKS CITED

Banfield, Stephen. *Sensibility and English Song: Critical Studies of the Early Twentieth Century.* Cambridge and New York: Cambridge University Press, 1985.

Bentley, D.M.R. "Pan and the Confederation Poets." *Canadian Literature* 81 (1979): 59–71.

———. "Threefold in Wonder: Bliss Carman's *Sappho: One Hundred Lyrics.*" *Canadian Poetry* 17 (1985): 29–58.

Bly, Robert. *Sleepers Joining Hands.* New York: Harper and Row, 1985.

Brown, Norman O. *Love's Body.* New York: Random House, 1966.

Cameron, Barry. "Lacan: Implications of Psychoanalysis and Canadian Discourse." In John Moss, ed., *Future Indicative: Literary Theory and Canadian Literature.* Ottawa: University of Ottawa Press, 1987. 137–51.

Cappon, James. *Bliss Carman and the Literary Currents and Influences of his Time.* Toronto: Ryerson, 1930.

Carman, Bliss. *Songs from Vagabondia* (Co-author, Richard Hovey). Boston: Small, Maynard, 1894.

———. *Behind the Arras: A Book of the Unseen.* Boston and New York: Lamson, Wolffe, 1895.

———. *Low Tide on Grand Pré: A Book of Lyrics.* 3rd ed. Boston and New York: Lamson, Wolffe, 1895.

———. *The Kinship of Nature.* Toronto: Copp Clark, 1903.

———. *The Poetry of Life.* Toronto: Copp Clark, 1905.

———. *The Rough Rider and Other Poems.* New York: Kennerley, 1909.

———. *April Airs.* Boston: Small, Maynard, 1916.

———. *Later Poems.* Toronto: McClelland and Stewart, 1921.

———. *Far Horizons.* Toronto: McClelland and Stewart, 1925.

———. *Sanctuary.* Toronto: McClelland and Stewart, 1929.

———. *Wild Garden.* Toronto: McClelland and Stewart, 1929.

———. *Pipes of Pan.* Toronto: Ryerson, 1929.

Ehrenzweig, Anton. "The Creative Surrender." In Leonard Tennenhouse, ed., *The Practice of Psychoanalytic Criticism.* Detroit: Wayne State University Press, 1976. 136–51.

Frye, Northrop. *The Bush Garden: Essays on the Canadian Imagination.* Toronto: Anansi, 1971.

Glassco, John. *The Deficit Made Flesh.* Toronto: McClelland and Stewart, 1958.

Graves, Robert. *Collected Poems.* New York: Doubleday, 1958.

Gundy, H. Pearson, ed. *Letters of Bliss Carman.* Kingston and Montreal: McGill-Queen's University Press, 1981.

Jones, D. G. *Butterfly on Rock: A Study of Themes and Images in Canadian Literature.* Toronto: University of Toronto Press, 1970.

Kennerley, Mitchell. "Kennerley on Carman." *Canadian Poetry* 14 (Spring/Summer 1984): 69–74.

Kristeva, Julia. *Desire in Language: A Semiotic Approach to Literature and Art.* Ed. Leon S. Roudiez. Trans. Thomas Gora, Alice Jardine, and Leon S. Roudiez. New York: Columbia University Press, 1980.

Lacan, Jacques. *Ecrits: A Selection.* Trans. Alan Sheridan. New York and London: Norton, 1977.

———. "Desire and the Interpretation of Desire in *Hamlet.*" In Shoshana Felman, ed., *Literature and Psychoanalysis, The Question of Reading: Otherwise.* Baltimore: Johns Hopkins University Press, 1980.

Logan, John Daniel and Donald G. French. *Highways of Canadian Literature: A Synoptic Introduction to the Literary History of Canada (English) from 1790 to 1924.* Toronto: McClelland and Stewart, 1923.

Malkoff, Karl. *Theodore Roethke: An Introduction to the Poetry.* New York: Columbia University Press, 1966.

Mandel, Eli. *The Family Romance*. Winnipeg: Turnstone, 1986.

Miller, Muriel. *Bliss Carman: Quest and Revolt*. St. John's: Jesperson Press, 1985.

Pacey, Desmond. *Creative Writing in Canada: A Short History of English-Canadian Literature*. Toronto: Ryerson, 1952.

———. *Ten Canadian Poets: A Group of Critical Essays*. Toronto: Ryerson, 1958. 59–133.

Roethke, Theodore. *Selected Poems*. Ed. Beatrice Roethke. London: Faber and Faber, 1969.

Ross, Malcolm. "Bliss Carman and the Poetry of Mystery: A Defence of the Personal Fallacy." *The Impossible Sum of Our Traditions: Reflections on Canadian Literature*. Toronto: McClelland and Stewart, 1986. 43–66.

Santayana, George. *The Letters of George Santayana*. Ed. (with Introduction and Commentary) Daniel Cory. New York: Scribner's, 1955.

Shepard, Odell. *Bliss Carman*. Toronto: McClelland and Stewart, 1923.

Sorfleet, John R. "Transcendentalist, Mystic, Evolutionary Idealist: Bliss Carman, 1886–1894." In George Woodcock, ed., *Colony and Confederation: Early Canadian Poets and their Background*. Vancouver: University of British Columbia Press, 1974. 189–210.

———, ed. "Introduction." *The Poems of Bliss Carman*. Toronto: McClelland and Stewart, 1976. 5–12.

Spivak, Gayatri Chakravorty. "Sex and History in *The Prelude* (1805): Books IX to XII." In Richard Machin and Christopher Norris, eds., *Post-Structuralist Readings of English Poetry*. New York: Cambridge University Press, 1987. 193–226.

Swinburne, Algernon Charles. *The Complete Works of Algernon Charles Swinburne*. Tragedies, Vol. 1. Eds. Sir Edmund Gosse and Thomas James Wise. London and New York: William Heinemann and Gabriel Wells, 1926. 265–351.

Todorov, Tzvetan. *Theories of the Symbol*. Trans. Catherine Porter. Ithaca: Cornell University Press, 1977.

Ware, Tracy. "The Integrity of Carman's *Low Tide on Grand Pré*." *Canadian Poetry* 14 (1984): 38–52.

Whalen, Terry. "Bliss Carman (1861–1929)." In Robert Lecker, Jack David, and Ellen Quigley, eds., *Canadian Writers and their Works: Poetry Series*. Vol. 2. Downsview, Ont.: ECW Press, 1983. 77–132.

Bliss Carman's Pageants, Masques and Essays and the Genesis of Modern Dance[1]

LAUREL BOONE

Although they are neglected today, Bliss Carman's stage works were of crucial importance to him, and the work of which they are the visible remainder changed Carman's world and our own. I would like to focus attention on a Bliss Carman heretofore unrecognized in literary circles—the Carman who, as an American essayist and teacher, made an important contribution to modern dance as we know it.

The deepest roots of Carman's masques and pageants and the ideas in his essays may be found in Fredericton. One of the earliest influences on Carman—and one usually ignored—was the Church of England. He attended Christ Church Cathedral, and, as a tall youth of sixteen, he helped decorate the Cathedral with Christmas greens (Moffitt, Dec. 24, 1877). Then—as now—the Cathedral offended certain Frederictonians with its High Church propensities, and this pageantry was not lost on young Bliss. As an adult, Carman shed most of the doctrines of orthodox Christianity. One, however, the doctrine of the trinity, remained deeply embedded in his mind and heart.

George Parkin, the headmaster of the Fredericton Collegiate School, influenced Carman powerfully. Parkin introduced Carman to classical literature and to modern British and American literature; Carman may have read the works of Ralph Waldo Emerson under Parkin's tutelage; and, through Parkin, John Ruskin's works may also have played a part in Carman's education. Parkin studied educational theory, and he believed that full intellectual development could take place only along with moral and physical development. He, too, helped decorate the Cathedral that Christmas, and he spent long hours tramping through the woods around Fredericton and canoeing on the St. John River with Carman and his school-fellows.[2]

Carman's cousin and Collegiate School friend Charles G. D. Roberts also helped to shape Carman's youth.[3] It is clear from Roberts's letters to Carman and his accounts of their canoeing and camping expeditions that Roberts was the leader. In personality, the cousins were very different—Roberts was compactly built and athletic, quick of wit and tongue, assertive if not downright bossy, omni-competent (at least in his own eyes), and practical. When Roberts found that being a Poet—as distinguished from merely writing poetry—was a Good Thing, he decided that Carman should be one, too. Carman was willing.

After they grew up, Roberts and Carman remained close friends, but they were not kindred spirits. Carman found his alter ego in Richard Hovey,[4] whom he met when he went to Harvard in 1887. Both men had ostensible occupations, but both were really engaged in seeking they knew not what. In the philosophy lectures of Josiah Royce, Carman found a modern version of the Emersonian idealism that already appealed to him strongly. Hovey worked as an actor. But their chief inspiration came from conversations with Bernard and Senda Berenson, Tom Meteyard and Bertram Goodhue, Ralph Adams Cram, and other members of their club, a loose fellowship that gathered in Tom Meteyard's mother's kitchen to discuss the nature of art.

In 1889, Hovey met Mrs. Henrietta Russell, and this proved to be a turning point in Carman's life as well as in Hovey's. Mrs. Russell was America's foremost interpreter of the philosophy of François Delsarte. Delsarte was a French singer whose voice had been ruined by bad training. He studied human gesture in all kinds of circumstances —nursemaids tending their charges, miners' families waiting at the pithead after a disaster, men conducting business, lovers dallying—and he schematized what he saw. He believed that the body consists of three regions: the head, the torso, and the limbs. Gestures originating in each region, he thought, express rationality, spirituality, and physicality. Further, gestures are concentric (towards the body), expressing rationality; eccentric (away from the body), expressing physicality; or normal (with no inward or outward direction), expressing spirituality. Gestures also occur in opposition (showing physicality), parallel (showing rationality), or succession (showing spirituality). Of course, no body part is actually isolated, and no gesture actually occurs without others, and so the threes multiply by three again and again. Delsarte also formulated a "Law of Correspondence": "To each spiritual function responds a function of the body; to each grand function of the body corresponds a spiritual act." That is, no gesture is meaningless; although the gesturer may have no particular meaning in mind, the viewer cannot help but interpret the gesture in a specific way. On this theoretical foundation, Delsarte devised a method by which he trained orators and actors until about 1859. He died in 1871 (Shawn, *ELM*). Ten or twelve years later, Henrietta Knapp, as she then was, arrived in Paris to study with Delsarte's son. By this time, the Delsarte exercises in gesture had evolved—no one knows quite how—into a kind of gymnastic system for promoting physical, mental, and spiritual well-being. When her training was finished, Henrietta Knapp (now married to Delsartean actor Edmund Russell) burst upon the drawing-rooms of London, Newport, Boston, and New York to teach society women this system.

Henrietta Russell and Richard Hovey became lovers in 1891. Apart from Mrs. Russell, prosody had become Hovey's passion, and he formulated Delsarte's ideas into a kind of measuring scale for prosody. He added a Hegelian component to his work when he theorized that opposition expresses the particular, parallelism expresses the universal, and "succession reconciles the two into a spiritual synthesis" (Macdonald 76). Hovey applied these theories to a verse drama cycle about Launcelot and Guinevere. He decided to write nine plays in three groups. Each group would consist of a drama, telling the physical or historical part of the story; a tragedy, in which the emotional component would be enacted; and a masque, expressing the spiritual meaning of the two plays. The third of the three groups would synthesize all the emotional and social issues raised in the cycle.

At this time, Carman was on the editorial staff of the *Independent*. In July 1891, Hovey submitted his article "Delsarte and Poetry" to Carman, who accepted it, suggested that he expand his ideas into a fuller article or book,[5] and added, "I am a perfect ignoramus in this line, but I am ravenous for more knowledge" (Gundy, *Letters* 41). The next summer—1892—Hovey spent the ragweed season in Windsor, Nova Scotia, with Carman and Roberts, and he liked it so well that, the following year, he brought with him the now-divorced Mrs. Russell. Mrs. Russell set up housekeeping in a tent in the Roberts yard; Hovey and Carman shared another tent. Mrs. Russell gave Delsarte lecture demonstrations in Windsor, and photographs of Mrs. Roberts and the Roberts children's governess in their Delsarte costumes suggest at least domestic success. Carman wrote to his sister Murray from this "Vagabondia" camp, "I am studying Delsarte, and find whole new worlds of knowledge and hope in modern thought" (Gundy, *Letters* 59). After a few weeks, Mrs. Russell extended her tour to Halifax, and Carman told Murray, "Her lectures on Delsarte are very suggestive and thorough. I got a lot out of them. She is a very able woman . . . brilliant and intellectual" (Gundy, *Letters* 61).

In April 1894, Carman, acting as a literary advisor for Stone and Kimball, commissioned Hovey to translate four plays by the Belgian Symbolist Maurice Maeterlinck, plays that Carman believed would be of great literary and dramatic influence. He spent April, May, and June 1896 in Europe, partly in Paris consorting with the French Symbolists. When he returned to Boston, he began writing a weekly column for the *Evening Transcript*.

Even then, Carman was not sure of the direction he wanted his life to take. Back in Fredericton, he had made vague stabs at teaching, the law, surveying, even selling screen doors. Following his cousin's lead, he had become a poet, but he couldn't live on that. Nothing crystallized until, at Harvard, he found someone to talk to and a job he could do: editorial work. For the rest of his life, he used part-time or temporary editorial jobs with magazines and publishers to bolster his income. Writing a newspaper column did not seem to be his vocation either, but, by producing his thousand words a week for the *Boston Transcript*, he kept bread on his table for six years while preserving a good deal of freedom for poetry. He also became an instructor to the nation, or at least to that part of it that read the *Transcript* and the other papers that soon syndicated his column. Carman believed—with the poets of classical antiquity and the French Symbolists—that true poets are prophets, leading their readers to a higher plane of spiritual understanding. After a five-year education in Delsartean theory, after hammering out prosodic ideas with Hovey, and after experiencing Symbolism at its source, Carman undertook to tell *Transcript* readers what art really is, what a poet is, what poets are trying to do, how to tell whether any art is good, how inimical society is to artists, and (very mildly) how society should mend its ways.

In February 1897, Roberts took an editorial job in New York, and Carman moved down from Boston at least partly at his instigation. Also, the Hoveys (Richard and Henrietta were now married) had started an acting school in the Carnegie Studios, and they wanted Carman to help them. Carman's theatrical ambitions did not extend beyond private merrymaking, in which he shone as an impersonator and mimic, and so his assistance was minimal and short-lived. However, under the Hoveys' aegis he came to his second great turning point: he met Mary Perry King.[6]

Mary Perry—we all know what a malign influence she turned out to be. In fact, she was exactly what Carman wanted and needed. They were the same age: thirty-five. She had trained as a teacher, learned Bell's Visible Speech, studied acting at the Philadelphia Academy of Arts and the Opera Comique in Paris, and married Dr. Maurice King, changing her name from Rebel Thorn Perry to Mary Perry King. She became a student of Henrietta Russell Hovey, and she achieved some success as an actress. When she and Carman met casually in 1896, her life, too, was changing. She had decided that the stage was not really for her, and that her mission would be to train women and girls to reach their fullest potential by harmonizing their minds, spirits, and bodies through Delsartean exercise. Breath and voice control were central to her scheme, along with what had come to be called Harmonic Gymnastics.

In the spring of 1897, Carman made an extended visit to the home of Richard Hovey's parents in Washington, D.C. Mary Perry King turned up, and she and Carman wrote the prospectus for the school she wanted to establish. During the first half of 1897, they also became lovers. That July, Mary Perry, Dr. King, and Carman decided to establish a summer school at Twilight Park, a colony near Haines Falls in the Catskills. They rented a large cottage with a spacious ground floor, which they christened "Moonshine." While it was being renovated, they all stayed in an inconvenient cabin that Carman dubbed "Ghost House" when he lived there alone in subsequent seasons. For seven years, Mary Perry King, assisted by Carman, conducted a winter school in New York and a summer school at Moonshine. Carman described the New York school as "a gymnasium for women . . . where her work was carried on . . . under conditions of sanitation and beautiful housing which, it seemed to her, the training of personality deserves." Society ladies paid for King's instruction, but working women did not pay, since she wanted to help them escape their poverty and oppression by strengthening what we would call their self-image. Her gymnasium contained "the minimum amount of machinery," because she placed "most stress on free gymnastics, breathing, and voice work" ("Apostle" 583).

Carman stopped contributing his weekly column to the *Boston Transcript* in early 1903, when he took on the editorship of L. C. Page's magazine, the *Literary World*. He continued to write a similar essay each month as an editorial in the *Literary World*, and at the same time he organized the *Transcript* columns into three books: *The Kinship of Nature, The Friendship of Art*, and *The Poetry of Life*. In these books, Carman brings together his ideas about art: that all arts work together, all partaking, though in differing degrees, of the three basic human capabilities, "finding out the truth and distinguishing it from error . . . perceiving goodness and knowing it from evil, and . . . discriminating between what is ugly and what is fair" (*PL* 24). Yearning for unattainable perfection, the artist will "give vent to that longing in imperishable forms of art. And these creations in colors, in sounds, in magical words, remain to convict the actual world of its shortcomings and stimulate it to fairer endeavor" (*PL* 91). Defining the use of art, he asserts that "correlating the three vital forces is at once perhaps the most important and the least understood element in personal success" (*FA* 198). "I do not wish," he says, "to confine the word 'useful'. . . to material needs. . . . If we allow ourselves only what are called the necessities of life, we are only keeping alive one third of our being; the other two thirds of our manhood may be starving to death. The mind and the soul have their necessities, as well as the body'' (*PL* 20). Carman's editorial work provided him with ''the necessities of life''; Mary Perry King embodied those necessities of the mind and soul without which he felt he would starve. The two of them set out to convert society to their three-fold approach to health, beauty, and art. The world, Carman said, ''is always tending toward perfection, and it is man's business to help that tendency. He must make his life more and more beautiful, simply because by so doing he makes himself more healthy and happy. To this end, art supplies him with standards, and keeps him constantly in mind of what perfection is'' (*PL* 46).

Carman had found his vocation, but pursuing it was not easy. His alter ego, Richard Hovey, died suddenly in 1900, the Arthurian cycle and prosodic work unfinished. His oldest friend, Charles G. D. Roberts, was not at all in sympathy with either his theories or his love affair with Mary Perry King. Roberts was well known as a man who never said a bad word about anyone—except Mary Perry King. Jealousy over Carman's company was obviously one component of his hatred of her, and another was Carman's developing quasi-religious faith, which Roberts disdained and therefore blamed on King. But probably the most bitter component was that, after about 1900, Roberts had no influence whatsoever over Carman's writing. Socially, they remained the best of friends, but their attachment weakened as Carman stopped trying to make himself over in his cousin's image.

Catastrophe struck in 1904, when Mary Perry King suffered a mental and physical breakdown caused in part by the duplicity their love affair made necessary. That summer, while Dr. King was abroad, the lovers carried on so openly that he could no longer ignore the situation. He demanded that his wife give up Carman or he would divorce her. Suddenly, Dr. King, by then in Japan, took sick, and Mary Perry rushed to his side. He lived, but they did not return from their travels until 1906. By then, Carman had had to pay all the bills of the now-defunct school, and he was in deep financial trouble. To make matters even worse, Mary Perry had changed. Before her breakdown, she had been lively, comical, and of a more or less reasonable disposition; she now became fat, torpid, and very temperamental.

In spite of these changes, she and Carman worked together on a book of connected essays, *The Making of Personality*, and they laid plans for a new theatre school in California. Here they would train performers for classical works adapted by Carman and new works they would compose together to illustrate their philosophy. The school would begin a "new educational movement, in which the three rhythmic arts, poetry, music, and dancing, or interpretive motion, [would be] combined for artistic and cultural purposes" (*DOD* vi). Mary Perry King had decided that interpretive dance was an essential part of the training their school must offer. She knew Isadora Duncan and may have crossed paths with her as early as 1897–98 when the Duncans, like the Hoveys, lived and taught in the Carnegie Studios; King had studied oriental dance while she was in the Far East; and she could not have escaped at least hearing about Ruth St. Denis's *Radha*, the "Hindu" dance sensation of 1906.[7] To prepare herself for such an ambitious teaching role, King spent the fall of 1907 in Cambridge studying philosophy, psychology, music, swimming, and ballet. The plan to move to California fell through, but in the winter of 1907–1908, the Kings bought Sunshine House, in the commuter town of New Canaan, Connecticut. Dr. King's honour having somehow been satisfied, Carman moved from New York to the Ardsley Inn in New Canaan, and through 1908, 1909, and part of 1910, the Kings renovated Sunshine House to make it suitable for the school.

Meanwhile, Carman continued to make ends meet with a series of editorial odd jobs, because, while his books of poetry improved his reputation, they did nothing for his bank balance. Indeed, when financial disaster brought him into court in 1906, his publisher, the rapacious L. C. Page, testified that Carman had no royalties coming to him, that actually he was overdrawn, and that this condition had been chronic for years.[8] *The Making of Personality*, published in 1908, was a critical success, but it cost Carman dearly. He had agreed to give Page four prose books, of which *The Kinship of Nature, The Friendship of Art*, and *The Poetry of Life* were the first three. The fourth was to be a treatise on prosody, perhaps along the lines of Hovey's work, but Carman persuaded Page that a book on Personal Harmonizing would do as well. When he submitted the manuscript, Page turned it down. He would not allow Mary Perry King's name on the title page, and the book had too much of King's writing in it to reach the stylistic standard Page demanded.[9] Finally, Carman rewrote the book completely.

In the fall of 1910, the Unitrinian School of Personal Harmonizing enrolled its first class. Carman's speech at the graduation exercises, held at Moonshine in August 1911, shows that the purpose of the school had been adapted to necessity: he bade the graduates go forth, whether as personal harmony teachers, dance teachers, or school teachers, to spread the unitrinian ideal of perfection through personal harmonizing. He described King as the continuer of a process in educational theory that began with "Rousseau's plea for freedom, Pestalozzi's impassioned love of his fellow beings, Froebel's sagacious comprehension of nature's laws, [and] Delsarte's profound and clarifying discovery" (*Address* 17). He inspired the graduates with the thought that a single person can add little "to the world's splendid overflowing treasury," but that, because of the school, "our feet are on the foundations of the world, partial aims are merged in those which are universal, and we become co-workers with the Lord of Life. We are no longer merely students acquiring knowledge for our own gratification, no longer merely artists proud in the perishable achievements of our skill, but seers and prophets of a new day, taking part in the creation of that better world which is to be" (*Address* 3–4). As a graduation recital, the students were to perform the pageant *Daughters of Dawn*.

Carman had not written this performance piece out of the blue. By the early years of the century, the American taste for extravaganza had transmuted itself into an enthusiasm for mixed-art non-narrative performances. In the late 1890s, Isadora Duncan danced to poetry recited by her brother, sometimes accompanied by their mother at the piano and sometimes not (Kendall 30, 63). In 1909, Augustin Duncan had directed outdoor performances of a combined music, dance, and poetry piece, "The Canterbury Pilgrims," that became so popular that President Taft invited the troupe to present it at the White House (MFR D163, 523–28). A craze for masques and pageants swept the country, and Carman had a well-connected friend on the New York theatre scene: his cousin-in-law Mary Fanton Roberts. She and Charles G. D. Roberts had been lovers around the turn of the century, and in 1906 she had married Charles's brother William Carman Roberts. She edited the *Craftsman* magazine, for which Carman wrote, and she was New York's most prominent dance critic before such a job description existed. She befriended Isadora Duncan when her first American tour almost collapsed, she kept abreast of all the new dance and theatre ideas, and she kept in touch with Carman.[10]

Fifteen years earlier, Carman's Pewter Mugs Club had enjoyed performing, in costume, "the mystical rites of the Egyptian Osiris to the fragrant odour of burning incense and the droning accompaniment of intoning voices" (Miller 153). At the same time, Carman had experienced Hovey's grappling with the masque form. Three segments of Hovey's projected nine-play cycle were to have been masques, and before his death he had published two of them. In 1906, Carman wrote a preface explaining the function of these masques to introduce the play that he and Henrietta Hovey had organized out of the fragments Richard had left. Conceiving a plan to write masques himself, he hired "an out-of-work repertory company to put on a classical masque," but, because it failed to attract a large enough audience, it flopped (Miller 218).

Nevertheless, masques and pageants appealed to Carman because they combined the rhythmic arts—poetry, music, and dance—into one

symbolic or mythical presentation. He and Mary Perry King intended
to spread unitrinianism, not just by teaching its doctrines in their school,
but also by training students to express these ideals in stage performances.
Carman had written a five-part poetic homage to women called "The
Givers of Life," and in 1910 he and King expanded it into *Daughters
of Dawn*, subtitled "A Lyrical Pageant or Series of Historic Scenes For
Presentation With Music and Dancing." They planned to present it
at the school-closing in 1911, test it in New York under the sponsorship
of a patron, and then stage a professional production. It is not known
whether they followed this plan, but they and their students at least gave
a successful reading of it in May 1911 (Miller 218). Carman tried to
persuade his friend Mitchell Kennerley to publish *Daughters of Dawn*,
but Kennerley refused, ostensibly because of Mary Perry King's name
on the title page but probably for other reasons as well. Carman claims
in the preface that the book was "literally written in collaboration" with
King, and perhaps this explains why the poetry is not up to his best
standard. But his last book of poems, *The Rough Rider*, also published
by Kennerley, had sunk without a trace, and Kennerley may have feared
to take on another unitrinian work. Then too, the feminist content
of the pageant may have provoked Kennerley's refusal, for the nine
Daughters of Dawn are leaders of men, not mere handmaidens, and
the Modern Woman of the Epilogue is

> unlaced,
> Her foot is soft-shod;
> She is glad and free-paced
> As the creatures of God;
> Her way is the path to perfection her sisters of morning
>   have trod.   (116–17)

Subversive stuff, this.

Kennerley relented and published the book in 1913, by which
time a composer had written a musical score. Readers were advised that
"The dramatic rights for acting and reading of Daughters of Dawn,
together with its music, stage directions and costume specifications for
acting and for reading, illustrated by tableaux vivants, may be had of
the authors. There are also lantern-slide illustrations that may be used
together with music to accompany readings from the Pageant" ([ii]).
The *New York Times* called the book "less a poem than a sign of the
times" because the heroines are "forerunners . . . before the modern
woman." The *Boston Evening Transcript* recommended that the scenes
"be performed with music and pantomime, in costume, as wholly in
line with the glorious spirit of Eurhythmics and the ever-growing

influence of educational pageantry.'' This reception must have satisfied Kennerley, because he brought out *Earth Deities and Other Rhythmic Masques* the next year. If the frontispiece represents the actual costuming, the ''Earth Deities'' wore only a swathe of tulle, but, as with *Daughters of Dawn*, would-be performers could send for dramatic rights, music, pantomime and dance instructions. The *Nation* and the *Literary Digest* both praised the quality of Carman's poetry, especially in the title masque, the *Literary Digest* quoting two long sections, and the *American Library Association Booklist* recommended the book.

An interviewer in 1916 wrote that Carman ''esteems the 'Daughters of the Dawn' [sic] and 'Earth Deities' . . . two of his most excellent performances'' (Arnold 6). I don't know how many pageants and masques Carman and King wrote, separately or together, nor is it clear how often they were staged in theatres. In some form, *Daughters of Dawn* was performed at the National Arts Club in New York (*Transcript*), and a planned Los Angeles engagement had to be given up only because Henrietta Russell Hovey had gossiped too much about Carman's and King's romantic attachment (Gundy, *Letters* 188–89). David Bispham, an impresario, singer, and sometime lover of Isadora Duncan, saw a pageant called ''Moment Musical'' at Moonshine in 1914. In 1917, he produced three-week runs of Carman-King masques in Indianapolis and Chicago, and a Cleveland run had started when Bispham quit after Mary Perry King threw one tantrum too many. King rehearsed a pageant called ''A Play in a Chinese Garden'' for production in the summer of 1924, and she conducted rehearsals for a masque or pageant in 1926.[11]

After writing advertising copy for a few post-war months, which he thoroughly enjoyed (''Odds Bodkins''), and after almost dying of tuberculosis in 1919–20, Carman turned to the lecture circuit in the United States and Canada to make his living. Two events stand out in connection with his continuing effort to achieve his unitrinian goals. In 1922, the Canadian Club of Montreal entertained their sixty-one-year-old laureate by having a group of little girls sing ''The Dance of the Maple Leaves'' while dancing around him and crowning him with a crepe-paper wreath. Silly as this was, Carman appreciated it. He told the children that he was ''deeply interested in the relation between poetry and dancing,'' and that he ''believed in the poetry of motion. . . . [A]s poetry could be expressed in music, so it could be expressed in dancing. Poems had been written for singing and he had written poems intended to be portrayed in dancing'' (''Canadian Recognition'' 13). Three years later, in December 1925, Carman gave a series of lectures at the University of Toronto on poetry and its relationship with life, religion, art, and nature. There is little unitrinianism in the book in which Lorne

Pierce published these lectures, except what can be read between the lines. In one lecture, Carman says, "I undertook this series of talks because out of life I have evolved certain ideals about life, a certain philosophy . . . that has been of inordinate value to me, and which I should like to pass on" (*Talks* 58). Yet in the preface, written after he had read the book, he remarks, "I couldn't believe that anyone who could take part in writing *The Making of Personality* could produce anything as ill-considered as these talks. Yet they were not ill-considered, they were very carefully considered. The fund of careful thought behind them, out of which they sprang, was neither small nor shallow" (*Talks* 7). The lectures were transcribed from her own shorthand notes by Blanche Hume, Pierce's experienced and trustworthy secretary, and then edited by Pierce himself. I suspect that Pierce cut out what he considered unfit to pass on to posterity, just as he gutted some of the poems he put into his *Selected Poems*.[12]

Did Carman achieve his life's goals? Yes and no. No, he didn't make many permanent converts to unitrinianism, the school broke up, and no one reads his stage pieces. By the end of his life, practical types such as Pierce and Roberts had gained the ascendancy, and systems of thought that bundled together art, religion, and philosophy were completely out of fashion. Today, we almost laugh at unitrinianism and the notion that it could change the world.

But yes, actually, Carman, King, and their theories did change one segment of the world. In late 1913 or early 1914, a confused young San Franciscan named Ted Shawn read *The Making of Personality*.[13] He had planned to become a Methodist minister, but while in seminary he had taken sick. As he recuperated, he lost his vocation. He studied ballet to help him recover his co-ordination, and there he found a new calling: dance. But Shawn could not reconcile dancing with masculinity. Carman's and Hovey's three *Vagabondia* volumes had inspired a generation of young men with the idea that poetry was not effeminate, and now *The Making of Personality* sanctified Shawn's ambition to become a dancer. Shawn wrote to Carman, and Carman invited him to study at the Unitrinian School of Personal Harmonizing. He danced his way across the country with a Santa Fé Railroad troupe, left the show in New York, and spent a month training intensively, eight or nine hours a day, six days a week, with Mary Perry King.

But Shawn lost interest in King's regimen. She had no idea how to choreograph for a man and expected him to trip through girlish measures like her female students. Even worse, she wanted him to star in a vaudeville sketch. When he burst out that he had not come all the way to New Canaan to end up in vaudeville, she retorted, " 'And what else are you going to do? You're too big for a classic dancer. You started to dance ten or more years too late ever to acquire a ballet technique. You are mildly good-looking but you'll never stop traffic on Broadway. Just exactly what do you think you can do?' " He answered, " 'I shall become a great and internationally famous dancer with a style and technique of my own.' She . . . flopped back on her couch screeching with uncontrolled laughter" (Shawn, *1001* 22).

Shawn did exactly what he said he would do. In short order, he looked up Ruth St. Denis (who was already famous as an interpretive dancer), became her partner, and married her. In the summer of 1915, the couple founded their own dance school, Denishawn, in Los Angeles. Later, Shawn ridiculed the Unitrinian School of Personal Harmonizing, but Denishawn was in many ways a copy. Like Mary Perry King and Bliss Carman, Ted Shawn and Ruth St. Denis were deeply religious, and the faiths of all four included the compulsion to express godliness through motion. The daily routine at Denishawn followed Mary Perry King's pattern: stretching and relaxing exercises, barre and floor work, theory, and lunch, followed by swimming or private instruction and the learning of dances. The aim of both schools (apart from reforming society) was to train performers. Denishawn groomed students for an elevated version of show biz, and the Unitrinian School students became the stars of the Carman-King masques and pageants. Ted Shawn's commercial instincts and his methodical teaching, coupled with Ruth St. Denis's strange blend of mysticism and theatricality, made Denishawn successful, while the Unitrinian School dwindled and died. Shawn sneered that Mary Perry King never admitted to teaching Delsarte, but her own writings and Carman's belie this accusation. Shawn claimed that Henrietta Russell Hovey, whom he met three years before her death and who lectured at Denishawn, first explained King's exercises to him. Actually, Ruth St. Denis could have explained Delsarte to him, since she had been trained in the Delsartean method from her girlhood. But Shawn liked to congratulate himself on drilling Denishawn students in technique of his own invention. By giving the elderly Mrs. Hovey credit for the Delsarte foundation of that technique, he denied St. Denis that particular bit of glory, and he also avoided tarnishing his art by admitting that he learned it in a girls' personality school.

Shawn's mendacity doesn't alter the fact that modern dance was born at Denishawn. He and Ruth St. Denis taught movie stars Louise Glaum, Ruth Chatterton, Roszika Dolly, Ina Claire, Mary Hay, Mabel Normand, Blanche Sweet, and Lillian and Dorothy Gish, and Denishawn dancers made up the great set-pieces and pageants in "Intolerance" and many other D. W. Griffiths films.[14] Martha Graham, the first to teach modern dance in a university, trained at Denishawn. She rebelled against the prettiness of Denishawn dance, but the tenets of her new belief (and dance was a gospel to her, too) sound very familiar: she insisted that all motion must come from emotion; that "the full resources of body, intellect and emotion" must be brought to bear "on a moment of movement"; and that every movement has intellectual and emotional meaning (Mazo 154, 157). The dances she choreographed in the late 1920s "bore distinct relation to Delsarte abstractions," and her contraction and release technique, now central to modern dance, has its roots in the Delsarte system (Kendall 204; Sherman 87). As well as a whole generation of dancers, Graham also taught Bette Davis, Lorne Greene, Henry Fonda, Gregory Peck, and Richard Boone—who then instructed John Gielgud (McDonagh 198). Doris Humphrey's arcs of movement, her ideal of continuous motion, her music visualizations, and her meticulous teaching methods form a second pillar of modern dance. She, too, emerged from Denishawn. So did her partner, Charles Weidman, whose narrative choreography and irrepressible comic urge influenced Broadway dancing (Mazo 117–52). The main stream of American modern dance today is the artistic offspring of Martha Graham, Doris Humphrey, and Charles Weidman, and so of Denishawn.

This is not to deny the profound effects of other sources of modern dance. Isadora Duncan, a Delsarte practitioner from childhood, has no direct artistic descendants, but during her lifetime she exerted an enormous influence, not only on Carman, King, and others involved in dance, but on the world at large. Loie Fuller has no direct descendants either, but the influence of her Art Nouveau combination of coloured lights and swirling costumes has filtered down all the way to the Ice Capades. The women's dress reform movement also gave tremendous momentum to modern dance. Ruth St. Denis's mother was a doctor, a food faddist, and a fanatical dress reformer; little Ruthie wore overalls. Henrietta Russell Hovey urged society ladies and dance students alike to cast off their corsets and crippling shoes. Isadora Duncan proclaimed her belief in "the religion of the beauty of the human foot," and Paul Poiret designed sandals as well as tunics for her and her pupils.[15] Mary Perry King designed several styles of heelless, broad-toed shoes for street wear and dancing, the Janzen shoe company manufactured them, and Bliss Carman not only wore them but wrote a booklet about them. Until the Ballets Russes revolution at the beginning of this century, ballet dancers danced encased in whalebone, their arms and legs operating without reference to their rigid torsos, and their wooden-toed shoes giving their legs the plasticity of hinged stilts. The forerunners of modern dance bent their uncorseted bodies freely without isolating one part from another, and they wore as little as the law allowed so that their gestures could convey the intellectual, emotional, and spiritual meaning of their dances.

Even taking these other influences into account, the succession from François Delsarte through Henrietta Russell Hovey to Bliss Carman and Mary Perry King, and thence to Ted Shawn, Denishawn, and the dance of today is the only continuous line in the history of modern dance in North America. Furthermore, dancing is now a respectable career for men, and Ted Shawn, inspired by Carman's book *The Making of Personality*, made it so. In spite of the fact that Shawn derided him as "a nodding sunflower," it was Bliss Carman who showed him the path he could follow, and it is to Bliss Carman that we owe at least some of the thanks for modern dance as we know it.

NOTES

1. This article and the two papers on which it is based were prepared with the support of the Social Sciences and Humanities Research Council of Canada. Part of this article was read at the Bliss Carman Symposium under the title "Bliss Carman's Unconventional Works: Masques, Pageants, Essays," and part was read at the May 1989 meeting of the Association for Canadian Theatre History under the title "Personal Harmonizing: Bliss Carman and the Genesis of Modern Dance."
2. Stewart 19–41, 44–45, 52–62; Moffitt, Dec. 24, 1877.
3. Biographical information about Charles G. D. Roberts is taken from Adams and Boone.
4. Biographical information about Carman, Hovey, and Henrietta Knapp Russell Hovey is taken from Gundy, *Letters*; Miller; and Macdonald.
5. Hovey published seven essays in the *Independent*: "Delsarte and Poetry" 43 (Aug. 27, 1891): 1267; "The Technique of Poetry" 44 (Apr. 7 and 21, 1892): 473, 544; "On the Threshold" 44 (Nov. 3, 1892): 1546–47; "The Technique of Rhyme" 45 (Oct. 19, 1893): 1399; "The Elements of Poetic Technique" 46 (Sept. 27 and Oct. 4, 1894): 1241, 1275.
6. Biographical information about Mary Perry King is taken from Miller; Carman, "Apostle"; and Gundy.
7. Miller 225; Blair 28–30; Carman, "Apostle" 583; Kendall 51–54.
8. *New York Herald Tribune* (June 9, 1929): [n.p]. Clipping, MFR D164, 647.
9. King's articles "Personal Harmonizing" and "The Cinderella of the Arts" are so disorganized and overwritten that they exonerate Page from charges of anti-feminism or personal prejudice.
10. Kendall 29; Blair 182–83; MFR D164, 558–68.
11. Duncan 254; Miller 226, 234, 256, 259.
12. For instance, compare the versions of "Pulvis et Umbra" and "Easter Eve" in Pierce (36 and 107) and Sorfleet (23 and 108).
13. Biographical information about Ted Shawn is taken from Shawn, *1001*; Mazo; and Kendall. The latter two seem to have obtained most of their information from Shawn himself or from Ruth St. Denis, and neither dancer was careful with the truth. Discrepancies, particularly in self-revealing information such as dates and attributions, are common.
14. Shawn, *1001* 49, 53, 54, 69; Kendall 116, 131, 136, 138, 140, 142.
15. Mazo 36, 37; Roberts, "Isadora" 10.

WORKS CITED

Adams, John C. *Sir Charles God Damn*. Toronto: University of Toronto Press, 1986.
Arnold, Chloe. "A Stroll With Bliss Carman." *New York Morning Telegraph* (Oct. 22, 1916): 6.
Blair, Fredrika. *Isadora: Portrait of the Artist as a Woman*. New York: Morrow, 1986.
Boone, Laurel. *The Collected Letters of Charles G. D. Roberts*. Fredericton: Goose Lane, 1989.
"Canadian Recognition of Bliss Carman, if Late, is Now Widespread and Generous." *Maple Leaf* 1:1 (Mar. 1922): 13.
Carman, Bliss. *The Friendship of Art*. Boston: Page, 1904. [*FA*]
———. *The Kinship of Nature*. Boston: Page, 1905.
———. *The Poetry of Life*. Boston: Page, 1905. [*PL*]
———. *The Making of Personality*. Boston: Page, 1908.
———. *Address to the Graduating Class MCMXI of the Unitrinian School of Personal Harmonizing*. New York: Tabard, 1911.
———. "An Apostle of Personal Harmonizing." *Good Housekeeping* 52 (May 1911): 581–85.
———. *To Those Who Wear Shoes*. New York: Jantzen Shoe Co., 1913.
———. *Talks on Poetry and Life*. Transcribed by Blanche Hume and edited by Lorne Pierce. Toronto: Ryerson, 1925.
——— and Mary Perry King. *Daughters of Dawn*. New York: Mitchell Kennerley, 1913. [*DOD*]
——— and Mary Perry King. *Earth Deities and Other Rhythmic Masques*. New York: Mitchell Kennerley, 1914.
"Daughters of Dawn" [review]. *Boston Transcript* (Apr. 19, 1913): 8.
[*Daughters of Dawn*, review]. *New York Times* (May 11, 1913): 288.
Duncan, Isadora. *My Life*. New York: Boni and Liveright, 1927.
[*Earth Deities*, review]. *Literary Digest* 50 (Jan. 16, 1915): 113.
[*Earth Deities*, review]. *Nation* 101:2617 (Aug. 26, 1915): 270.
[*Earth Deities*, review]. *American Library Association Booklist* 12:3 (Dec. 1915): 122.
Gundy, H. Pearson. "Lorne Pierce, Bliss Carman and the Ladies." *Douglas Library Notes* 14:4 (Autumn 1965).
———, ed. *Letters of Bliss Carman*. Kingston and Montreal: McGill-Queen's University Press, 1981.
Kendall, Elizabeth. *Where She Danced*. New York: Knopf, 1979.
King, Mary Perry. "Personal Harmonizing." *Good Housekeeping* 53 (Sept. 1911): 345–53.
———. "The Cinderella of the Arts." *Independent* 92 (Nov. 10, 1917): 288–89.
Macdonald, Allan Houston. *Richard Hovey: Man and Craftsman*. Durham, N.C.: Duke University Press, 1957.
Mazo, Joseph H. *Prime Movers: The Makers of Modern Dance in America*. New York: Morrow, 1977.
McDonagh, Don. *Martha Graham*. New York: Praeger, 1973; rpt. New York: Popular Library, 1975.
Miller, Muriel. *Bliss Carman: Quest and Revolt*. St. John's: Jesperson, 1985.
Moffitt, Charles. Diaries, Vol. 30. University of New Brunswick Archives (original) and Provincial Archives of New Brunswick (microfilm).
"Odds Bodkins" [pseud.]. "The 8-pt. Page." *Advertising and Selling* (June 26, 1929): 42.
Pierce, Lorne, ed. *The Selected Poems of Bliss Carman*. Toronto: McClelland and Stewart, 1954.
Roberts, Mary Fanton. "Isadora—The Dancer." *Denishawn Magazine* (Summer 1925): 9–13.

————. Papers. Archives of American Art, Smithsonian Institution. Reels D160–D164. [MFR]

Shawn, Ted. *Every Little Movement: A Book About François Delsarte.* 1954; rpt. Brooklyn: Dance Horizons, 1963. [*ELM*]

Shawn, Ted, with Gray Poole. *One Thousand and One Night Stands.* New York: Doubleday, 1960. [*1001*]

Sherman, Jane. *Denishawn: The Enduring Influence.* Boston: Twayne, 1983.

Sorfleet, John R., ed. *The Poems of Bliss Carman.* Toronto: McClelland and Stewart, 1976.

Stewart, Margaret A. "Bliss Carman: Poet, Philosopher, Teacher." M.A. Diss., Dalhousie University, 1976.

In Summary

R. L. McDOUGALL
D.M.R. BENTLEY
DOUGLAS LOCHHEAD

R. L. McDougall

"**W**hatever happened to Bliss Carman?"
Raymond Souster puts this question at the top of his Foreword
to the selection of Carman's poetry which he and Douglas Lochhead
published in 1985, and he later attributes it to John Betjeman, as part
of a conversation Betjeman had with John Robert Colombo in the 1970s.
Maybe the editors, in a kind of sub-text, are saying that this new edition
of the poet's work is what is happening to Bliss Carman in 1985, and
it's not a bad answer. But in the Foreword they answer the question
in another way, specifically though briefly, in terms of the ups and downs
(mostly downs) of a literary reputation. Several papers in the present
volume (conspicuously Mary McGillivray's) have reflected or enlarged
upon this response.

Perhaps, however, we do not need to do much more than look
at the question itself, which is full of meanings quite as interesting as
the answers. Who (whether John Betjeman or someone else) asks such
a question, and why? Clearly, the phrase "whatever happened," with
a query after it, is charged with implications. Time has passed. The
impulse is one of caring. The questioner is perplexed, brows furrowed,
puzzled that someone who once commanded his interest, perhaps his
respect, even his loyalty, has disappeared from view. His feelings may
be seasoned with disappointment at expectations unfulfilled. His caring
is nostalgic. "Whatever happened to Bliss Carman?" he asks; and really
wants to know. We may answer, taking an easy line, "Tastes change,
and Carman came a cropper." But we may at the same time say to ourselves: true literary monuments do not disappear from view. Is it better,
then, not to be the subject of such a question at all?

I don't think so. Much will depend on how bent we are on establishing a pecking order for poets in the Canadian barnyard. The fact that Carman belongs chronologically with the "poets of the Confederation" has invited ranking within this group. E. K. Brown tackled the problem head on in 1943, in *On Canadian Poetry*, because he thought that the pecking order amongst these poets had got badly out of whack: "Carman and Roberts," he wrote to D. C. Scott, "will no longer do as landmarks. I think that A. L. and you and Ned Pratt *will* do, and that you three must be the main landmarks." Fair game; it was a useful intervention. And history will judge Brown, as it judges Carman.

It has never been the purpose of the Reappraisals series, however, as I understand it, to get very heavily into this business of ranking, and I am in agreement with that. I see its function, rather, as one of re-examining the past, or near past, in terms of present-day scholarship, by this means throwing whatever new light is available on the man or woman in question, the work and the times, which is really quite Tainesian (remember Hippolyte?) and old-fashioned, but I can't help it. It is at any rate enough for me that Carman was much loved and honoured, both as a man and a poet, in his day, and that he died in a blaze of recognition as a laurel-crowned poet of Canada in the 1920s. He was very much a presence then, in that complex decade of shifting values. If, therefore, I must give a quick answer to the question "Whatever happened to Bliss Carman?", I will answer that he is present in this volume, very much alive, having been worked over thoroughly, back and forth and round about, sixty years after his death. Not a bad happening. "Poor Archie," D. C. Scott used to say of his friend Lampman. "Poor Blissie," we might feel like adding, mindful of his posthumous fall from high repute, but we would do so with even less reason than Scott had in Lampman's case, since neither of these poets was or is poor in any way that counts.

Pecking order? Well, we all have personal pecking orders, valid within limits, and would not define ourselves as individuals if we didn't. I must tell you that, in preparation for this assignment, I read well over one hundred poems by Bliss Carman in two or three sessions not far apart. One should not do this to any poet, least of all Carman, as it turned out, and I do not recommend the procedure. But having done it this way, I must say my piece: two debit entries appear which might not otherwise have surfaced. One I pass off lightly. It is what I call the "metronomic effect," and it can induce trauma after long exposure:

> Chunt-ah Chunt-ah Chunt-ah Chunt-ah
> Chunt-ah Chunt-ah Chunt
> Chunt-ah Chunt-ah Chunt-ah Chunt-ah
> Chunt-ah Chunt-ah Chunt

It is a difficulty of course easily reduced by shortened exposure, and I think by a careful study of David Bentley's paper on the mind-cure aspect of Carman's poetry, which he dealt with so effectively.

More substantial is the "haze effect" in Carman, which, being interpreted, means the abstractness and lack of focus which is pervasive over the wide expanse of these poems. Many will be familiar with the process of "distancing" in Carman and find it charming; and so it often is in single poems. Cumulatively, however, it has its penalties. No doubt transcendentalism had a lot to do with the "haze," though I can think of "mystic" poets (Blake, for example) who opted successfully for clear focus and a sharp image. And a point I learned from reading Carman's letters is that the choice in his case was a deliberate one. "Don't you think," Carman wrote to Louise Guiney very early in his career, "that Theodore [Winthrop] and Thoreau write when they are too near their object? Their eyes are too sharp, they strip the mountains of their haze. They will not let anything have its charm of distance, they must forever be diving into a lake before they speak of it." I'm not sure about "diving into a lake," but if I shift the image I think of the victory of Hercules over Anteus as he lifted Anteus above the earth from which he drew his strength.

The man and the work, the era and the place. Bliss Carman is an attractive figure, and it is pleasant to be in his company. He was very honest, I think, with others and with himself. He was generous with his time and with what money he had. He took his work seriously and was not fooled by the accolades showered upon him. Above all, he was a sensitive human being who, as a practising poet, reflected in a variety of ways the changing currents of thought and taste which marked the transition of the old century to the new. To enter this world through him is a valuable experience. In another context (an earlier number in this series; I think it was the D. C. Scott volume of 1980), I quoted a passage from Edmund Husserl which I liked then and which I like now and will therefore repeat. "It is a possible and highly important task," Husserl wrote to Levy-Bruhl in 1935, ". . . to project ourselves into (*sich einzufühlen*) a human community in its living and traditional sociality, and to understand it insofar as, . . . on the basis of its total social life, that community possesses the world, which for it is not a 'representation of the world' but the real world." That's a phenomenologist's way of saying that it is a good and even a moral thing to get out of our own skins from time to time and get into other skins in another place and time. I have also quoted, in a piece on cultural history written many years ago, Merleau-Ponty: "we do not have a timeless truth but the recovery of one time by another time." I'll hang up my hat on that.

D.M.R. Bentley

Since at least the end of the eighteenth century, poets and thinkers in Canada have tended to align themselves with one or other of two geopolitical axes: the east-west axis of nationalism and imperialism and the north-south axis of free trade and continentalism or—for the nationalist and imperialist—betrayal. When he is in London, England, Lorne Murchison has his "supreme moment . . . on the top of an omnibus lumbering west out of Trafalgar Square" and, of course, Sir John A. Macdonald in Pratt's poem affirms the east-west connection over the "north-south drift." As the papers in this book repeatedly confirm, Carman was a poet of the north-south axis, a man in tension between Canada and the United States. Duncan would have depicted him in his moment of epiphany manhattaning his way south out of Fredericton, New Brunswick.

Is it merely chance or a sign of these free-trade times that so many of these essays—four or five out of ten by my count—have unflinchingly grasped the poison ivy of what James Doyle calls "Bliss Carman and the United States"? Perhaps—to back-track a stage or two further—a Reappraisals volume on the "amiably pro-American" Bliss Carman was not possible until after November 22, 1988; certainly, ten years elapsed between the Lampman, Crawford, and Scott volumes of the late 1970s and early 1980s and the present one, and even Roberts—another expatriate—was honoured with a Reappraisals volume six years earlier than his cousin. In its very nature, the study of Canadian literature is a nationalistic (or, at least, patriotic) enterprise whose root assumptions are threatened by writers like Roberts and Carman who spent much of their time outside the country, devoting their energies to depicting American subjects, editing American magazines, addressing an American audience. As they read the present volume, nationalists will have to content themselves with the observation that, though the glass is about half empty of papers focusing on Carman and Canada, it is also about half full with treatments of the poet's physical and literary presence in this country, such as Al Kizuk's fresh look at Carman's impact on later Canadian poets. Louis K. MacKendrick's discovery of the presence in such poems as "A Northern Vigil" and "In St. Germain Street" of the "evocation of stark terror" that Frye sees as characteristic of Canadian poetry may also appeal to the nationalists, as may the testimony of Elizabeth Brewster and Al Purdy to the attraction and influence exerted by Carman on them. Only *may* in both cases because Frye is, of course, altogether too cosmopolitan and liberal for many nationalists, and the influence of a sell-out on two of the finest Canadian poets of the post-

Second World War period must be, at best, a mixed blessing. Never-theless, all cannot be lost from a nationalistic perspective when Carman's ghost or spirit—however Paterian or bland—can manifest itself in a volume of essays published in the national capital by a major Canadian university press over fifty years after his death. Synchronicity may be the last refuge of the patriot.

But there are surely reasons for the vicissitudes of Carman's reputation other than his expatriotism and the chinooks of Canadian nationalism that have warmed this country's feelings for its writers every forty years or so (Carman may have missed the hot air of the late 1960s and 1970s but he was much more fortunate in the 1920s). If not Carman's popular appeal, his uncanny persistence or—to use Mary McGillivray's word—"lingering" in Canada's collective consciousness, then certainly his critical reputation, his presence or absence in university classrooms and in graduate courses, has been profoundly affected by developments in the large movement of which he was a part: Modernism, the artistic and intellectual response to "modern life" (to use, again, Arnold's phrase and Carman's). In *All That Is Solid Melts Into Air*, Marshall Berman divides the "history of modernity" into "three phases": "the start of the sixteenth century to the end of the eighteenth"; the French Revolution to approximately the First World War; and the remainder of the twentieth century, a period dominated, at least until the end of the Second World War, by the High Modernists. Berman's account of the "landscape" of nineteenth-century modernity conjures up the world that all of the Confederation poets confronted in their different ways: "a landscape of steam engines, automatic factories, railroads, vast new industrial zones; of teeming cities that have grown overnight, often with dreadful conse-quences; of daily newspapers, telegraphs, telephones and other mass media. . . ." He continues, but I think the point has been made. "The great modernists of the nineteenth century all attack[ed] this environ-ment passionately," Berman observes, "yet all [found] themselves remarkably at home in it. . . ." Minor modernists did so too, and with more or less the same ambivalence: "The City of the End of Things" indicts, but it appeared in the *Atlantic Monthly*, the large-circulation Ameri-can magazine that Carman regarded as the "favourite periodical" of the Muse. Though most of the Confederation poets disliked large cities and bloated capitalists in theory, they were not altogether unhappy in practice about enjoying the advantages of the former and the company of the latter. An occasional nibble at the embroidered slippers of the establishment was permissible, but better not bite the hand that, directly or indirectly, feeds you.

"What has become of nineteenth-century modernism in the twen-tieth century?" asks Berman, and the answer, in Carman's case, is not pretty. Elsewhere (in the Preface to *Canadian Poetry* 14), I have attempted to place briefly on view the influence of Carman on some of his "great" Modern and neo-Romantic contemporaries and successors. Here I would like to argue, not for the first time, that the willed blindness of the third phase of modernity to the second—the self-enabling myth of discontinuity with their immediate past that was fostered by the High Modernists and accepted by their New Critical servants—was the major cause of the demise of Carman's critical reputation in Canada, for in this country that reputation survived the First World War and even the Depression to await the onslaughts in the 1940s, 1950s, and later of E. K. Brown, Desmond Pacey, Donald Stephens, and a number of others. To Brown in *On Canadian Poetry*, Carman is "cloying," "shrill," and too predictably melancholic. To Pacey in "Bliss Carman: A Reappraisal," he is not only "vague," "careless," "vulgar," "silly," "witless," "shallow," "perfervid," "embarrassing," and "effeminate," but "ignorant of the real issues of social and political life." To Stephens, at a particularly Ivor Wintery moment in *Bliss Carman*, a poem such as "Spring Song" is "atrocious," "infantile," "repulsive," and "very bad"—a piece by and about some "sap." Needless to say, there is an amusing side and some truth to these vituperations—Carman nods more often than Homer, Milton, or even Lampman—but there is a serious and telling side to them as well. The products of historical and aesthetic bias, they resemble the mating loon of Frye's "Conclusion" to the *Literary History of Canada* in occluding what they should be illuminating—in this instance, a poet whose engagement with modernity, with the effects of "*embourgeoisement*" (to use T. J. Jackson Lears' word), was arguably as intense and sustained as that of any of the makers of twentieth-century modern poetry in Canada, with the probable exception of Irving Layton (who, incidentally, began his attacks on "overmentalization" in territory long before explored by Carman: a diagnosis in *First Statement* and elsewhere of the "crippling malaise of the period" and its attendant symptoms of "confusion," "maladjustment," "hysteri[a]," and "neurastheni[a]").

Judging by the evidence of the present volume, admiring Carman's poetry is now not quite as suspect and unfashionable, not quite as liable for dismissal as mental masturbation over a long-dead literary corpse, as it was in the late 1940s when Malcolm Ross described it as a "secret sin." But, as we approach a *fin de siècle* and the end of a millennium, can anything be discerned about us that might resuscitate Carman's corpse and critical reputation? Is there a possibility that the hour-glass which took from 1914–1918 (when it was first turned over) to only a few years ago to run out could be turned over again? To the extent that (and here is the paradox of this book of essays) the very trends that are conducive to the study of Carman are those that are running against national identities and national literatures, the prognosis appears bleak. Canadian regionalism may reclaim a part of Carman; perhaps New England regionalism will reclaim another. Possibly multinational civilization will take him up, like racquet-ball or the Ladysmith Black Mambazo Band, as the flavour of a month, a week, an hour, or a few Warholian seconds. Yet there are a couple of interrelated developments, a couple of shifts in sensibility with the potential to be much, much more than trends, which just might cast Carman in a more sympathetic light than he has been in since the last War. One of these developments, and a sign, perhaps, of greater changes in the process of coming, is the growing resistance to those strains of Modernism (or post-modernism) which, like their critical corollaries, deconstruction and post-structuralism, have shown themselves in their obsession with language and their rejection of context (biography, history, and so on) to be, at best, curiously indifferent to the dangers to life on this planet by the multinational phase of modernity and, at worst, tacitly supportive of the incursions of technology and consumerism into every region, zone, and layer of terrestrial life. When fully formed, this reaction is not likely to take the form of a return to any pre-First World War golden age, for the very reason that such a return would now be recognized merely as a nostalgia for an early stage of the metastasis; rather, it will turn—for it must—to the second of the interrelated developments to which I referred a moment ago: the ecological movement. It *must* do this because ecology—a more complex and less sentimental ecology than most of us are used to—is the one arena in which technology can co-operate with nature to save, not only the life of this planet, but also—as important, whether we like it or not (and even as late-comers to modernity we do both)—western civilization and modern life.

A full turn to an ecological world view will bring with it, as all such turns and revisionings always do, a rethinking of every aspect of human life, including ethics and aesthetics. Referentiality and realism will return in art and criticism just as they have already in law and philosophy under the banners of applied ethics and legal and moral realism. Poetry may become imitative and formal again, though not in the sense of imitating the forms of the past—the sonnets, and odes, and serial poems of a tradition obsessed with compartments—but in the sense of emulating the shapes that Benoit Mandelbrot and others are discovering in and beneath the apparent flux and chaos of the utterly interconnected worlds of nature and man. To anyone raised on the austere geometrics of Modernism, such terms as "the Butterfly Effect," "devil's polymer," "fractal clusters," the "Noah" and "Joseph" effects, "Smale's horseshoe," "cauliflower shapes," "strange attractors," and "sea-horsetails" (see James Gleick, *Chaos: Making a New Science*) may be pranked with absurdity, but they also surely suggest something more: poetry—a poetry in which art and science are as thoroughly intertwined as man and nature.

In an essay that appeals immensely to deconstructive and post-structuralist critics for its assertion of the "metaphorical" nature of everything, Nietzsche suggests that the concept and term "leaf" only becomes possible when the differences between individual leaves are discarded or forgotten: "We obtain the concept, as we do the form, by overlooking what is individual and actual; whereas nature is acquainted with no forms and no concepts, and likewise with no species, but only with an X that remains inaccessible and undefinable for us" ("On Truth and Lies in a Nonmoral Sense," trans. Daniel Breazeale). Less quick to forget that the human brain is itself a part of nature, that—as Gregory Bateson has indicated in *Steps to an Ecology of Mind* and elsewhere—man can only extract meaning from nature because he is equipped *by nature* to do so, Carman is also less certain than Nietzsche that nature is mindless and inaccessible. Looking out of his window (an artificial but necessary barrier or "threshold"), Carman observes in *The Kinship of Nature* that "a cherry-tree . . . waving in the sunlight . . . bears some thousands of leaves, no two of which are precisely alike." Each leaf in this ordered and deterministic chaos has its "individual idiosyncrasy," yet all "conform to the type and character" that cherry-tree leaves have "gradually developed for themselves." "It would seem, then," he suggests with his characteristic gentleness, "that Nature is strictly a formalist in dealing with her tribes, that she permits them just so much liberty of action and freedom of thought as shall conserve the interest of the individual, and not enough to imperil the integrity of the sect." Carman goes on to reverence the "boundless liberality" of Nature over her "sober catholicity" (pp. 203–209), but he has already made in his very *modus operandi* the points that I wish in conclusion to take from him: the point that there is no ultimate distinction between man and nature and the point that there can be no survival of the individual, the species—humanity—without the survival of the whole. No man is an island, and neither is an island.

In this collection of essays, Doug Jones, Elizabeth Brewster, and others give us a modest and humble Carman who left not a mark but a trace, who identified himself with the moth, the windflower, the rain, and the foam. In a world already marked almost beyond repair, Carman's sense of man's kinship with the leaf, the butterfly, and the scarlet maple, his "tenderness for the natural world" and his sense of being "a living piece in a great organism," may yet prove to be his greatest virtue and his most appealing quality.

Douglas Lochhead

"I do not long for fame"

Following the invitation to contribute a summary statement to this volume, I began to prepare myself for a major encounter with Bliss Carman and his poetry in the following ways:

(a)   because it provided a good excuse for book-buying I began immediately to sound out the second-hand market and to collect for myself as many Bliss Carman titles as I could find—all editions, impressions— ephemera and in book form. In a short time I collected most of what is listed in R. E. Watters' *Checklist of Canadian Literature in English*. It seemed sensible for one who is quite maniacal about books, and the market waters were productive considering the unpredictable interest in Carman. Some book dealers were quite surprised that Carman was of interest these days;

(b)   I read a number of works of criticism of Carman's poetry which ranged from the somewhat sophomore–savage to the more than somewhat reverential;

(c)   and I read the poetry and a little prose from selections and collections.

Why, you may well ask, did you not read the poetry first, and then, only then, acquaint yourself with the criticism and biography? Well, you see, I knew that I would encounter "readings" of Carman by three distinguished Canadian poets—Al Purdy, Elizabeth Brewster and D. G. Jones. Also, some years ago, I did read some of the poetry as a student in public and high schools in Ontario. Then, in the 1980s, I made a more thorough examination of Carman's work in the preparation of a selection of his poetry, which I edited with Raymond Souster. This volume, by the way, was never intended to be a scholarly undertaking. Ray and I had a simple objective: to make Carman's poetry available to as wide a public as possible. Glenn Clever published *Windflower and Other Poems* in Ottawa at his Tecumseh Press.

So this was some of my homework. Summing up a lively book of essays on Carman is no task to be taken lightly.

I would offer some general impressions of what has been voiced in this volume:

190

(a)   the tone of the writers, notably the new critics, the younger ones, has been more receptive, more tolerant, better balanced and informed than that heard as late as a decade ago;

(b)   there has been expressed by many a need to place Carman in context, to reconstruct the literary scene in Canada and the United States as our poet fluttered and almost barged or mowed his way through it;

(c)   there have been beautifully articulated accounts of Carman's highs and lows—from his early years in the United States to his poetry in, say, *By the Aurelian Wall*;

(d)   and, most important, very firm evidence has been placed before our court, that Carman is indeed good and worth pursuing. I did not say that he was great. He would not have wanted that. Here is one of his poems that expresses his modesty; it appeared in some of his early twentieth-century volumes (I am not certain of its bibliographical progression). I acquired it in a copy set to music by Robert Coningsby Clarke and published in 1915 in London. It is not in Blanck's bibliography.

"I do not long for Fame" (Song)

I do not long for fame
Nor triumph nor trumpets of praise;
I only wish my name
To endure in the coming days,

When men say, musing at times,
With smiling speech and slow,
"He was a maker of rhymes
Yvonne loved long ago!"
(*Songs of the Sea Children*, CXIV, 1904)

(e)   a few further observations, or hopes, can be expressed as one reads Carman and essays about him. It quickly becomes obvious that he was very much a vagabond, a wanderer, a saddle-bag poet. I would express the hope that a literary person with a geographical bent may someday trace for us in map form a record of Carman's many moves, all his comings and goings. It would be a tangled and telling web indeed. Also his liaisons of one kind or another cry out for some graphic interpretation just to keep one alert as to Carman's many roles, who the poet was with and when and where.

It has been said that Wordsworth was possibly the most successful and professional literary bum of all time, what with sister Dorothy looking after him. Carman had many Dorothys during his writing life. It is important to remember the many people who loved and helped him.

The Carman Bibliography—Some Comments

It is appropriate to conclude these comments with some notice of the most important and difficult problem which confronts Carman scholars. Much valuable bibliographical material is to be found in Volume 2 of Jacob Blanck's *Bibliography of American Literature* (Yale University Press, 1957, pp. 42–76). This pioneering work was based largely upon the holdings of a limited number of major libraries in the United States, such as Harvard, Yale, New York Public Library and Library of Congress. Blanck also received considerable help from the Carman authority H. P. Gundy, former Chief Librarian of Queen's University, Kingston, Ontario.

A phrase which appears often in Blanck's bibliography is "not seen." Much, as Blanck himself acknowledges, remains to complete the Carman publishing record. It is probably the most daunting bibliographical challenge in Canadian literature. It is also one of the most fascinating. A proper analytical bibliography of Carman would take most of a lifetime.

Because of his many affiliations with newspapers, magazines and publishing companies, Carman was in a position to have his work printed as single poems, as groups and as books. Poems appeared in limited editions, as occasionals for private audiences only, in just about every ephemeral form.

The first paragraph of Blanck's bibliography outlines some of the difficulties facing any collector or bibliographer:

> Carman's first separate appearances were privately circulated broadsheets; many were of uncertain date. Some bear place names (New York, Washington, Cambridge, etc.). These must not be interpreted as place of printing since almost invariably they indicate the place of writing or of Carman's residence. As an example: *The Little Church of the Leaves* broadsheet carries the statement *Wolfville, Nova Scotia*; however, the broadsheet was printed from the types of *The Independent* (New York), Dec. 19, 1895. (Vol. 2, p. 42)

It is my view that the greatest need in Carman research is the compilation of a major bibliographical study of the poet's work from manuscripts and notebooks to the elusive broadsheets and other ephemera to the completed books. Only such a study will set the record straight as far as the chronology of Bliss Carman's writing career is concerned. With such a work available, a definitive collected edition of his poetry could be undertaken.

A Primary and Secondary Bibliography of Bliss Carman's Work

JOHN R. SORFLEET

Two concerns must be confronted by any bibliography. One is a matter of substance: Which works should be included? The other is a matter of organization: How should the works that *are* included be presented?

In regard to primary materials, this bibliography has tried to resolve some of the confusion that exists among critics and readers as to exactly which parts of the Carman canon can be termed books and pamphlets. The confusion exists because Carman printed—primarily for friends though sometimes for sale—some very short runs of some very short pamphlets which contained only a single poem or, at most, a few short poems (and to this he added various single-page typescripts and broadsheets). These evanescent materials have proved a problem, as readers of Carman soon learn: it seems that no two lists of Carman's publications are the same—most include only the longer books, while a few add (without consistent rationale) one or more of the shorter works without differentiating them from the longer ones. Since almost all of the poems were later reprinted in one of Carman's longer collections, the casual reader is not tremendously disadvantaged, but serious readers desire clarification. Consequently, the present bibliography attempts to resolve the difficulty by listing both authorized books and pamphlets, and by indicating the difference between the two to the reader through the provision of additional details for the shorter items. Thus, for all multipage "books" under thirty pages in length, the number of pages involved is given and, where possible, the number of copies printed is stated. Further, the volumes edited by Carman have been listed separately from the ones he wrote; this forestalls another possible area of confusion.

Finally, in regard to organization, the items have been chronologically arranged: this helps differentiate single-poem pamphlets (e.g., *Green Book of the Bards* and *Sappho: Lyrics*) from later books bearing similar titles. An additional benefit from chronological arrangement is that it enables readers to see the pattern of book publication which many critics (erroneously) have used as a key to analyzing the development of Carman's work and thought (regarding the limitations of this pattern, see my article earlier in this collection).

In regard to secondary materials, this bibliography—though selective (the listing of all mentions of Carman in newspapers and magazines and books about other writers would add half again to the length of this volume and would not be very helpful in spite of the extra pages, for the flakes of gold would be lost in a sea of sand)—is more extensive, more complete, and more current than any previously published. As well, it is available in a size and publication which will be most useful to current Carman readers. (However, a more extensive bibliography has been commissioned for ECW Press's *Annotated Bibliography of Canada's Major Authors* series.) Further, because these secondary materials are chronologically organized, the reader is enabled to see the degree of critical interest in Carman and the developing nature of critical thought about his work in each decade up to the present. Indeed, one inescapable conclusion is that the last two decades have produced the most serious critical response to Carman since he began publishing, and the papers of the present volume underline that conclusion.

I. Primary Sources in Chronological Sequence

A. Books and Pamphlets

Carman, Bliss. *Death in April.* Part One of *Corydon*, a projected trilogy in commemoration of Matthew Arnold. Fredericton: Private (Press of L. C. MacNutt), 1888. (13 pp.)
——. *Low Tide on Grand Pré: A Book of Lyrics.* First ed. New York: Charles L. Webster, 1893; Second ed. Cambridge & Chicago: Stone and Kimball, 1894. (The text of the first edition is reproduced in the second except for the alteration of a line in "The Eavesdropper" and the addition of three poems: "Marian Drury," "Golden Rowan," and "A Sea Drift.")
——. *Saint Kavin: A Ballad.* Cambridge, Mass.: John Wilson (University Press), 1894. (9 pp., 50 copies)
——, and Richard Hovey. *Songs from Vagabondia.* Boston: Copeland and Day, 1894.
——. *A Seamark: A Threnody for Robert Louis Stevenson.* Boston: Copeland

and Day, 1895. (10 pp.)

———. *At Michaelmas: A Lyric*. Wolfville, N.S.: Private ("The Acadian" Press), 1895. (10 pp., 100 copies)

———. *Behind the Arras: A Book of the Unseen*. Boston: Lamson, Wolffe and Company, 1895.

———, and Richard Hovey. *More Songs from Vagabondia*. Boston: Lamson, Wolffe and Company, 1896.

———. *Ballads of Lost Haven: A Book of the Sea*. Boston: Lamson, Wolffe and Company, 1897.

———. *The Girl in the Poster*. For a Design by Miss Ethel Reed. Springfield, Mass.: Will Bradley (Wayside Press), 1897. (9 pp., 100 copies)

———. *By the Aurelian Wall and Other Elegies*. Boston: Lamson, Wolffe and Company, 1898.

———. *The Green Book of the Bards*. Cambridge, Mass.: Will Bradley (University Press), 1898. (12 pp., 100 copies)

———. *A Winter Holiday*. Boston: Small, Maynard and Company, 1899.

———. *The Vengeance of Noel Brassard: A Tale of the Acadian Expulsion*. Cambridge, Mass.: Will Bradley (University Press), 1899 (misprinted MDCCCCXIX). (23 pp., 100 copies)

———, and Richard Hovey. *Last Songs from Vagabondia*. Boston: Small, Maynard and Company, 1900.

———. *Christmas Eve at St. Kavin's*. New York: Ingalls Kimball, 1901. (15 pp., 222 copies)

———. *Ballads and Lyrics*. London: A. H. Bullen, 1902.

———. *Ode on the Coronation of King Edward*. Boston: L. C. Page & Company, 1902.

———. *Sappho: Lyrics*. With Excerpts from a Literal Rendering by H. T. Wharton. [New York: Private, 1902]. (8 pp., 60 copies)

———. *From the Book of Myths*. Boston: L. C. Page & Company, 1902, rev. 1904.

———. *From the Green Book of the Bards*. Boston: L. C. Page & Company, 1903.

———. *The Kinship of Nature*. Boston: L. C. Page & Company, 1903.

———. *Songs of the Sea Children*. Boston: L. C. Page & Company, 1903.

———. *Sappho: One Hundred Lyrics*. With an Introduction by Charles G. D. Roberts. London: Chatto & Windus, 1903.

———. *The Word at St. Kavin's*. Nelson, N.H.: The Monadnock Press, 1903. (28 pp., 300 copies)

———. *A Vision of Sappho*. [New York: Private, 1903]. (7 pp., 60 copies)

———. *Songs from a Northern Garden*. Boston: L. C. Page & Company, 1904.

———. *The Friendship of Art*. Boston: L. C. Page & Company, 1904.

————. *Poems*. 2 Vols. New York: Scott-Thaw Co.; London: John Murray, 1904; L. C. Page & Company, 1905 (Page adds "A Vision of Sappho" and a portrait of Carman).

————. *From the Book of Valentines*. Boston: L. C. Page & Company, 1905.

————. *The Poetry of Life*. Boston: L. C. Page & Company, 1905.

————. *Pipes of Pan*. Definitive Edition, Containing "From the Book of Myths," "From the Green Book of the Bards," "Songs of the Sea Children," "Songs from a Northern Garden," "From the Book of Valentines." Boston: L. C. Page & Company, 1906.

————. *The Princess of the Tower; The Wise Men from the East; To the Winged Victory*. New York: The Village Press, 1906. (18 pp., 62 copies)

————. *The Gate of Peace*. New York: The Village Press, 1907. (14 pp. Eighty-eight of the 112 copies were destroyed in a fire; a new edition of 60 copies was printed in New Canaan in April 1909.)

————. *The Making of Personality*. Boston: L. C. Page & Company, 1908.

————. *The Rough Rider, and Other Poems*. New York: Mitchell Kennerley, 1909.

————. *An Apostle of Personal Harmonizing*. n.p., n.d. Reprinted from *Good Housekeeping*, May 1911. (8 pp.)

————. *Address to the Graduating Class MCMXI of the Unitrinian School of Personal Harmonizing founded by Mary Perry King at Moonshine, Twilight Park, in the Catskills*. New York: Private (Tabard Press), 1911. (28 pp., 250 copies)

————. *A Painter's Holiday and Other Poems*. New York: F. Sherman, 1911.

————. *Echoes from Vagabondia*. Boston: Small, Maynard and Company, 1912.

————, and Mary Perry King. *Daughters of Dawn: A Lyrical Pageant or Series of Historic Scenes for Presentation with Music and Dancing*. New York: Mitchell Kennerley, 1913.

————, and Mary Perry King. *Earth Deities and Other Rhythmic Masques*. New York: Mitchell Kennerley, 1914.

————. *April Airs: A Book of New England Lyrics*. Boston: Small, Maynard and Company, 1916.

————. *Four Sonnets*. Boston: Small, Maynard and Company, 1916. (4 pp., 438 copies)

————. *James Whitcomb Riley*. An Essay by Bliss Carman, and Some Letters to him from James Whitcomb Riley [August 30, 1898–October 12, 1915]. New York: Private (George D. Smith), [1917].

————, and Mary Perry King. *The Man of the Marne and Other Poems*. New Canaan, Conn.: The Ponus Press, 1918. (26 pp.)

————. *"An Open Letter" from Bliss Carman*. Boston: Small, Maynard and Company, 1920. (17 pp.)

————. *Later Poems*. With an Appreciation by R. H. Hathaway. Toronto: McClelland & Stewart, 1921.

————. *Ballads and Lyrics.* Toronto: McClelland & Stewart, 1923. (This is a different selection from the one published under the same title in 1902.)

————. *Far Horizons.* Toronto: McClelland & Stewart, 1925.

————. *Talks on Poetry and Life.* Being a Series of Five Lectures Delivered before the University of Toronto, December, MCMXXV. Transcribed and Edited by Blanche Hume. Toronto: The Ryerson Press, 1926.

————. *Wild Garden.* New York: Dodd, Mead & Company, 1929.

————. *Sanctuary: Sunshine House Sonnets.* With Prefatory Memoir by Padraic Colum. Toronto: McClelland & Stewart, 1929.

————. *The Music of Earth.* With Foreword and Notes by Lorne Pierce. Toronto: The Ryerson Press, 1931.

————. *Bliss Carman's Poems.* Arranged by R. H. Hathaway. New York: Dodd, Mead & Company, 1931.

————. *The Selected Poems of Bliss Carman.* Edited with an Introduction by Lorne Pierce. Toronto: McClelland & Stewart, 1954. (A number of the poems are significantly and silently abridged by Pierce; these abridgements were carried over into *Poets of the Confederation*, edited by Malcolm Ross and published by McClelland & Stewart in 1960.)

————. *The Poems of Bliss Carman.* Selected, with an Introduction, List of Important Biographical Dates, and Notes on the Poems, by John Robert Sorfleet. Toronto: McClelland and Stewart, 1976.

————. *Windflower: Poems of Bliss Carman.* Edited, with a Foreword and Preface, by Raymond Souster and Douglas Lochhead. Ottawa: Tecumseh Press, 1985.

B. Volumes Edited

Carman, Bliss, ed. *The World's Best Poetry.* 10 vols. Philadelphia: John D. Morris and Company, 1904.

————, ed. *The Oxford Book of American Verse.* [New York]: Oxford University Press, 1927.

————, and Lorne Pierce, eds. *Our Canadian Literature.* Representative Verse, English and French. Toronto: The Ryerson Press, 1935.

II. Selected Secondary Sources in Chronological Sequence

Stewart, G., Jr. "A New Canadian Poet." *The Week*, 5 (Oct. 1888), 734–735.

MacFarlane, W. G. "New Brunswick Authorship—Part II." *The Dominion Illustrated*, 7 (1891), 424–425.

Lloyd, J.A.T. "Onomatopoeia and Mr. Bliss Carman." *The Week*, 9 (Oct. 1892), 709.

Anonymous. "Recent Poetry." *The Week*, 11 (Dec. 1893), 86.

White, Gleeson. "Carman Saeculare." *The Bookman*, 5 (Feb. 1894), 155–156.

Roberts, Charles G. D. "Mr. Bliss Carman's Poems." *Chap-Book*, 1 (June 15, 1894), 53–57.

Sladen, Douglas. "A July Holiday with Bliss Carman." *The Week*, 11 (Sept. 7, 1894), 973–974.

Marquis, T. G. "Crude Criticism." *The Week*, 13 (March 6, 1896), 350–351.

Brown, Harry W. "Bliss Carman's Latest Book of Poems." *The Canadian Magazine*, 6 (March 1896), 477–481.

Waldron, Gordon. "Canadian Poetry—A Criticism." *The Canadian Magazine*, 8 (Dec. 1896), 101–108.

De Mille, A. B. "Canadian Poetry: A Word in Vindication." *The Canadian Magazine*, 8 (March 1897), 433–438.

[Whiteside, Ernestine R.] "Canadian Poetry and Poets, II." *McMaster University Monthly*, 8 (Nov. 1898), 68–74.

White, Greenough. "A Pair of Canadian Poets." *The Sewanee Review*, 7 (Jan. 1899), 48–52.

Pollock, F. L. "Canadian Writers in New York." *Act Victoriana*, 22 (April 1899), 434–439.

Mowbray, J. P. "The New Pagan Lilt." *The Critic*, 41 (Oct. 1902), 308–313.

Archer, William. "Bliss Carman." *Poets of the Younger Generation*. London: Bodley Head, 1902.

Marshall, J. [*Pipes of Pan*]. *Queen's Quarterly*, 11 (Oct. 1903), 203–208.

Stringer, Arthur. "Canadians in New York; America's Foremost Lyrist [sic]: Bliss Carman." *The National Monthly of Canada*, 4 (Jan. 1904), 3–5.

Rittenhouse, Jessie B. "Bliss Carman." *The Younger American Poets*. Boston: Little, Brown, 1904.

de la Mare, Walter. "The Poetry of Life." *The Bookman*, 30 (May 1906), 72.

McArthur, Peter. "On Having Known a Poet." *The Atlantic Monthly*, 97 (May 1906), 711–714.

MacFarland Kenneth. "The Poetry of Bliss Carman." *The Literary Miscellany*, 2 (Summer 1909), 35–39.

Lee, H.D.C. *Bliss Carman: A Study in Canadian Poetry*. Buxton: Herald Printing Co. Ltd., 1912.

Muddiman, Bernard. "A Vignette in Canadian Literature." *The Canadian Magazine*, 40 (March 1913), 451–458.

Munday, Don. "The Faith of Bliss Carman." *Westminster Hall Magazine and Farthest West Review*, 6:2 (Sept. 1914), 9–12.

Sherman, F. F. *A Checklist of First Editions of Bliss Carman*. New York: The Author, 1915.

Braithwaite, W. S. "The Imaginative Vision of Bliss Carman." *Boston Evening Transcript*, May 10, 1916.

Edgar, Pelham. "Canadian Poetry." *The Bookman*, 49 (July 1919), 623–628.

MacDonald, Elizabeth Roberts. "The Genius Loci in Canadian Verse." *The Canadian Magazine*, 53 (July 1919), 236–240.

French, Donald G. "When The Critic Smiles." *The Canadian Magazine*, 53 (Oct. 1919), 509–516.

Hathaway, Rufus H. "Bliss Carman's Rare Editions." *The Canadian Bookman*, 1 (Oct. 1919), 16–17.

———. "Bliss Carman: Poet of the Sea." *The Sailor*, 2 (July 1920), 19–20.

———. "Bliss Carman: An Appreciation." *The Canadian Magazine*, 56 (April 1921), 521–536 (reprinted in Carman's *Later Poems*).

Douglas, R. W. "Canada's Poet Laureate—Bliss Carman." *British Columbia Monthly*, 19 (July 1922), 5–6, 12; 19 (Aug. 1922), 3–4, 14–16.

Hind, C. Lewis. "Bliss Carman." *More Authors and I*. New York: Dodd, Mead & Company, 1922.

Shepard, Odell. *Bliss Carman*. Toronto: McClelland & Stewart, 1923.

Roberts, Lloyd. "Uncle Bliss." *The Book of Roberts*. Toronto: The Ryerson Press, 1923.

Hathaway, Rufus H. "Bliss Carman's First Editions." *The Canadian Bookman*, 6 (Jan. 1924), 8–9.

R., N. "Bliss Carman and the Tribute of Youth." *British Columbia Monthly*, 24 (May 1925), 5.

Hathaway, Rufus H. "The Poetry of Bliss Carman." *The Sewanee Review*, 33 (Oct. 1925), 467–483; reprinted as a fifteen-page pamphlet by the University Press of Sewanee, Tenn.

Van Patten, Nathan. "Bliss Carman and the Bibliophile." *Queen's Quarterly*, 33 (Nov. 1925), 202–205.

Woodrow, Constance D. "An Extraordinary Interview." *The Canadian Bookman*, 8 (Jan. 1926), 13.

Hathaway, Rufus H. "The Eighteen Nineties of Canadian Poetry." *Ontario Library Review*, 10 (Feb. 1926), 51–55.

———. "Who's Who in Canadian Literature: Bliss Carman." *The Canadian Bookman*, 8 (Oct. 1926), 299–302.

Wade, H. G. "The Bard of Mount and Moor." *The Canadian Bookman*, 9 (Feb. 1927), 39–40.

Stevenson, O. J. "The Dawning's Troubador." *A People's Best*. Toronto: Musson, 1927.

Hawthorne, Julian. *Bliss Carman, 1861–1929*. Palo Alto, Calif.: The Author, 1929 (reprinted from the *San Francisco Chronicle*, June 16, 1929).

Anonymous. "Bliss Carman." *Literary Digest*, 102 (July 6, 1929), 21.

———. "Poet Laureate of Canada Passes Away." *Overland Monthly*, n.s. 87 (July 1929), 219.

Hathaway, R. H. "Vale! Bliss Carman." *The Canadian Bookman*, 11 (July 1929), 155–159.

Woodrow, Constance D. "New Brunswick Honours Bliss Carman." *The Canadian Bookman*, 11 (Sept. 1929), 209.

Cappon, James. "Bliss Carman's Beginnings." *Queen's Quarterly*, 36 (Oct. 1929), 637–665.

Colum, Padraic. "Bliss Carman's *Sanctuary*." *The Commonweal*, 11 (Dec. 1929), 225.

Roberts, Charles G. D. "Bliss Carman." *Dalhousie Review*, 9 (Jan. 1930), 409–417.

———. "More Reminiscences of Bliss Carman." *Dalhousie Review*, 10 (April 1930), 1–9.

———. "Carman and His Own Country." *Acadie*, 1:1 (April 15, 1930), 2–4.

Hathaway, R. H. "Carman's Books: A Bibliographical Essay." *Acadie*, 1:1 (April 15, 1930), 4–6.

Leisner, August Roberts. "Carman's 'Spring Song.'" *Acadie*, 1:1 (April 15, 1930), 6–7.

Rhodenizer, V. B. "Carman's Last Visit to Wolfville." *Acadie*, 1:1 (April 15, 1930), 9–10.

Clarke, George Frederick. "April on the Saint John." *Acadie*, 1:1 (April 15, 1930), 11–12.

Anonymous. "When Bliss Carman Wrote 'Advertising.'" *Western Home Monthly*, 31 (April 1930), 30, 61.

Pound, A. M. "My First and Last Days with Bliss Carman." *Acadie*, 1:2 (May 1, 1930), 19–20.

Leisner, A. R. "Bliss Carman's 'Low Tide on Grand Pré.'" *Acadie*, 1:2 (May 1, 1930), 20.

L[eisner], A. R. "Carman's 'The Mendicants.'" *Acadie*, 1:3 (May 15, 1930), 5–6.

L[eisner], A. R. "Bliss Carman's 'The Girl in the Poster.'" *Acadie*, 1:4 (June 1, 1930), 11.

Lawrence, Margaret. "In Memory of Bliss Carman." *Canadian Home Journal*, 27 (June 1930), 14.

L[eisner], A. R. "Bliss Carman's 'The Marching Morrows.'" *Acadie*, 1:5 (July 1930), 8.

Fewester, Ernest. "Bliss Carman at Vancouver." *Acadie*, 1:5 (July 1930), 25–27 (note that Fewester is a mis-spelling of Fewster).

L[eisner], A. R. "Bliss Carman's 'A Captain of the Press Gang.' " *Acadie*, 1:7 (Sept. 1930), 8.

Cappon, James. *Bliss Carman and the Literary Currents and Influences of His Time*. Toronto: The Ryerson Press, 1930.

Hathaway, R. H. "Carman's Memorial Unveiling." *The Canadian Bookman*, 12 (Dec. 1930), 262–263.

Wade, H. G. "Bliss Carman's Shrine." *Western Home Monthly*, 32 (Feb. 1931), 28.

King, Morris L., and Lorne Pierce. *Bliss Carman's Scrap-Book: A Table of Contents*. Toronto: The Ryerson Press, 1931.

Garvin, J. W. "Bliss Carman." *The Canadian Bookman*, 14 (March 1932), 34–35.

Ross, Malcolm. "A Symbolic Approach to Carman." *The Canadian Bookman*, 14 (Dec. 1932), 140–144.

MacKay, L. A. "Bliss Carman." *The Canadian Forum*, 13 (Feb. 1933), 182–183.

Roberts, T. G. "The Writing of the Red Wolf." *The Canadian Bookman*, 15 (Aug. 1933), 103–104.

Pierce, Lorne. "Bliss Carman." *Three Fredericton Poets: Writers of the University of New Brunswick and the New Dominion*. Toronto: The Ryerson Press, 1933.

Pierce, Lorne. "Bliss Carman." *A Standard Dictionary of Canadian Biography: The Canadian Who Was Who*, ed. C.G.D. Roberts and Arthur L. Tunnell. Toronto: Trans-Canada Press, 1934.

Miller, Muriel. *Bliss Carman, A Portrait*. Toronto: The Ryerson Press, 1935.

Roberts, Lloyd. "Bliss Carman: A Memory." *The Canadian Bookman*, 21 (April–May 1939), 42–46.

Roberts, Charles G. D. "Some Reminiscences of Bliss Carman in New York." *The Canadian Poetry Magazine*, 5 (Dec. 1940), 5–10.

Stringer, Arthur. "Wild Poets I've Known: Bliss Carman." *Saturday Night*, 56 (March 1, 1941), 29, 36.

Edgar, Pelham. "Bliss Carman." *Educational Record*, 57 (May 1941), 140–143 (reprinted in *Leading Canadian Poets*, ed. W. P. Percival. Toronto: The Ryerson Press, 1948).

Morse, William Inglis. *Bliss Carman: Bibliography, Letters, Fugitive Verses, and Other Data*. Windham, Conn.: Hawthorn House, 1941.

Livesay, F.H.R. "Bliss Carman at Nassau." *Saturday Night*, 59 (Nov. 20, 1943), 27.

Queen's University Library. *A Catalogue of Canadian Manuscripts Collected by Lorne Pierce and Presented to Queen's University*. Toronto: The Ryerson Press, 1946.

Bond, William H. "Manuscripts of Bliss Carman in the Harvard College Library." *The Canadian Collection at Harvard University*. Vol. 5. Cambridge, Mass.: Harvard University Press, 1947.

Ross, Malcolm M. "Carman by the Sea." *Dalhousie Review*, 27 (Oct. 1947), 294–298.

Massey, Vincent. "Roberts, Carman, Sherman: Canadian Poets." *The Canadian Author & Bookman*, 23 (Fall 1947), 29–32.

Maxwell, L.M.B. *The River St. John and Its Poets*. Sackville, N.B.: Tribune Press, 1947.

Bailey, Alfred G. "Creative Moments in the Culture of the Maritime Provinces." *Dalhousie Review*, 29 (Oct. 1949), 231–244.

Pacey, Desmond. "Bliss Carman: A Reappraisal." *Northern Review*, 3 (Feb.–Mar. 1950), 2–10.

Gray, C. "The Mystery of Bliss Carman's Ashes." *Maclean's Magazine*, 64 (Aug. 1, 1951), 40.

Pacey, Desmond. "Bliss Carman." *Ten Canadian Poets*. Toronto: The Ryerson Press, 1958.

Rashley, Richard E. "The Sixties Group, The Second Step." *Poetry in Canada: The First Three Steps*. Toronto: The Ryerson Press, 1958.

Pacey, Desmond. "A Garland for Bliss Carman." *The Atlantic Advocate*, 51 (April 1961), 18–24.

Gundy, H. Pearson. "The Bliss Carman Centenary." *Douglas Library Notes*, 10 (Summer 1961), 1–16.

Stephens, Donald. "A Maritime Myth." *Canadian Literature*, 9 (Summer 1961), 38–48.

Gundy, H. Pearson. "Lorne Pierce, Bliss Carman, and the Ladies." *Douglas Library Notes*, 14 (Autumn 1965), 2–24.

Stephens, Donald. *Bliss Carman*. New York: Twayne Publishers, 1966.

Gundy, H. P. "Bliss Carman and Edwin Arlington Robinson." *Douglas Library Notes*, 15 (Winter 1967), 2–7.

Milham, Mary-Ella. "Arcady on the Atlantic." *Humanities Association Bulletin*, 19:2 (1968), 42–51.

Gundy, H. P. "Bliss Carman and the Pewter Mugs." *Douglas Library Notes*, 17:1 (Autumn 1968), 7–14.

Rogers, A. Robert. "American Recognition of Bliss Carman and Sir Charles G. D. Roberts." *Humanities Association Bulletin*, 22:2 (1971), 19–25.

Sorfleet, John Robert. "The NCL Series: An Appraisal Past and Present." *Journal of Canadian Fiction*, I:2 (Spring 1972), 92–96.

Gundy, H. Pearson. "Bliss Carman's Comic Muse." *Douglas Library Notes*, 20:3–4 (Winter 1972), 8–18.

Sorfleet, John Robert. "Transcendentalist, Mystic, Evolutionary Idealist: Bliss Carman, 1886–1894." *Colony and Confederation: Early Canadian*

Poets and Their Background, ed. George Woodcock. Vancouver: University of British Columbia Press, 1974.

Gundy, H. Pearson. "Flourishes and Cadences: Letters of Bliss Carman and Louise Imogen Guiney." *Dalhousie Review*, 51:2 (1975), 205–226.

Mantz, Douglas. "Regionalism? What Regionalism?" *Laurentian University Review*, 8:1 (1975), 84–91.

Sorfleet, John Robert. "Introduction." *The Poems of Bliss Carman*. Toronto: McClelland and Stewart, 1976.

Ross, Malcolm. "A Strange Aesthetic Ferment." *Canadian Literature*, 68–69 (Spring–Summer 1976), 13–25.

Gibbs, Robert. "Voice and Persona in Carman and Roberts." *The Marco Polo Papers: One*, ed. Kenneth MacKinnon. Halifax: Atlantic Canada Institute, 1977.

Marshall, Tom. "Mountaineers and Swimmers." *Canadian Literature*, 72 (Spring 1977), 21–28.

Nause, John. "Low Tide on the [sic] Grand Pré: An Explication." *CV II*, 3:2 (Summer 1977), 30–32.

Eggleston, Wilfred. "Bliss Carman in the Twenties." *Journal of Canadian Poetry*, 1:2 (Autumn 1978), 59–68.

Bentley, D.M.R. "Pan and the Confederation Poets." *Canadian Literature*, 81 (Summer 1979), 59–71.

Gundy, H. Pearson, ed. *Letters of Bliss Carman*. Kingston & Montreal: McGill-Queen's University Press, 1981.

Precosky, Don. "Bliss Carman—A Second Look." *Journal of Canadian Poetry*, 3:2 (Winter 1981), 22–30.

Bhojwani, Maia. "A Northern Pantheism: Notes on the Confederation Poets and Contemporary Mythographers." *Canadian Poetry: Studies, Documents, Reviews*, 9 (Fall–Winter 1981), 34–49.

MacKendrick, Louis K. "Bliss Carman." *Profiles in Canadian Literature*, #3, ed. J. M. Heath. Toronto: Dundurn Press 1982.

Bentley, D.M.R. "Carman's Unelusive Glories." *Canadian Poetry: Studies, Documents, Reviews*, 10 (Spring–Summer 1982), 112–119.

Whalen, Terry. *Bliss Carman*. Canadian Writers and Their Works, Poetry Series. Downsview, Ont.: ECW Press, 1983.

Bentley, D.M.R. "Preface: Minor Poets of a Superior Order." *Canadian Poetry: Studies, Documents, Reviews*, 14 (Spring–Summer 1984), v–vii.

Ware, Tracy. "The Integrity of Carman's *Low Tide on Grand Pré*." *Canadian Poetry: Studies, Documents, Reviews*, 14 (Spring–Summer 1984), 38–52.

Gundy, H. Pearson. "Kennerley on Carman." *Canadian Poetry: Studies, Documents, Reviews*, 14 (Spring–Summer 1984), 69–74.

Bentley, D.M.R. "Threefold in Wonder: Bliss Carman's *Sappho: One Hundred Lyrics*." *Canadian Poetry: Studies, Documents, Reviews*, 17 (Fall–Winter 1985), 29–58.

Miller, Muriel. *Bliss Carman: Quest and Revolt*. St. John's, Nfld.: Jesperson Press, 1985.

Ross, Malcolm. "Bliss Carman and the Poetry of Mystery: A Defense of the Personal Fallacy." *The Bicentennial Lectures on New Brunswick Literature*. Sackville, N.B.: Centre for Canadian Studies, Mount Allison University, 1985.

Doyle, James. "Canadian Writers & American Little Magazines in the 1890's." *Canadian Literature*, 110 (Fall 1986), 177–183.

Hatch, Ronald. "Confederation Poets." *Canadian Literature*, 115 (Winter 1987), 223–225.

Glickman, Susan. "Carman's 'Shelley' and Roberts' 'Ave.' " *Canadian Poetry: Studies, Documents, Reviews*, 24 (Spring–Summer 1989), 20–28.

CONTRIBUTORS

D.M.R. BENTLEY

Department of English
University of Western Ontario

LAUREL BOONE

Critic and Editor
Fredericton, New Brunswick

ELIZABETH BREWSTER

Department of English
University of Saskatchewan

JAMES DOYLE

Department of English
Wilfrid Laurier University

D. G. JONES

Faculté des lettres et sciences
humaines
Université de Sherbrooke

A. R. KIZUK

Department of English
Bishop's University

DOUGLAS LOCHHEAD

Department of English
Mount Allison University

GERALD LYNCH

Department of English
University of Ottawa

LOUIS K. MACKENDRICK

Department of English
University of Windsor

R. L. MCDOUGALL

Department of English
Carleton University

MARY B. MCGILLIVRAY

Department of English
St. Francis Xavier University

AL PURDY

Poet
Sidney, British Columbia

JOHN R. SORFLEET

Department of English
Concordia University

TRACY WARE

Department of English
Bishop's University

TERRY WHALEN

Department of English
St. Mary's University

REAPPRAISALS: Canadian Writers

This series is the outcome of symposia on Canadian writers presented by the Department of English, University of Ottawa. The object is to make permanently available the criticism and evaluation of writers as presented by scholars and literary figures at the symposia. Where considered significant by the editor, additional critical articles and bibliographical material are included.

Lorraine McMullen
General Editor

Other titles in the series:

THE GROVE SYMPOSIUM, edited and with an introduction by John Nause

The A. M. KLEIN SYMPOSIUM, edited and with an introduction by Seymour Mayne

THE LAMPMAN SYMPOSIUM, edited and with an introduction by Lorraine McMullen

THE E. J. PRATT SYMPOSIUM, edited and with an introduction by Glenn Clever

THE ISABELLA VALANCY CRAWFORD SYMPOSIUM, edited and with an introduction by Frank M. Tierney

THE DUNCAN CAMPBELL SCOTT SYMPOSIUM, edited and with an introduction by K. P. Stich

THE ETHEL WILSON SYMPOSIUM, edited and with an introduction by Lorraine McMullen

THE CALLAGHAN SYMPOSIUM, edited and with an introduction by David Staines

TRANSLATION IN CANADIAN LITERATURE, edited and with an introduction by Camille La Bossière

THE CHARLES G. D. ROBERTS SYMPOSIUM, edited and with an introduction by Glenn Clever

THE THOMAS CHANDLER HALIBURTON SYMPOSIUM, edited and with an introduction by Frank M. Tierney

STEPHEN LEACOCK: A REAPPRAISAL, edited and with an introduction by David Staines

FUTURE INDICATIVE: LITERARY THEORY AND CANADIAN LITERATURE, edited and with an introduction by John Moss

REFLECTIONS: AUTOBIOGRAPHY AND CANADIAN LITERATURE, edited and with an introduction by K. P. Stich

REDISCOVERING OUR FOREMOTHERS: NINETEENTH-CENTURY CANADIAN WOMEN WRITERS, edited and with an introduction by Lorraine McMullen